THOMAS JEFFERSON

WORD FOR WORD

MAUREEN HARRISON
STEVE GILBERT
EDITORS

EXCELLENT BOOKS
LA JOLLA, CALIFORNIA

EXCELLENT BOOKS
Post Office Box 927105
La Jolla, CA 92192-7105

Publisher's Cataloging in Publication Data

Thomas Jefferson: Word for Word/
 Maureen Harrison, Steve Gilbert, editors.
 p. cm. - (Word for Word Series)
Bibliography: p.
Includes Index.
1. Jefferson, Thomas, 1743-1826. 2. United States - Presidents.
I. Title. II. Harrison, Maureen. III. Gilbert, Steve.
IV. Series: Word for Word.
E302.J45 1993   LC 93-072421
973.4'6-dc20
ISBN 1-880780-02-X

INTRODUCTION

Thomas Jefferson: Word for Word, published in the two hundred fiftieth anniversary year of Jefferson's birth, is designed to easily acquaint readers, young and old alike, with the best of the writings of Jefferson. We have selected from a lifetime of Thomas Jefferson's diverse public and private writings those documents which we think will give the reader real insight into the essential Jefferson. Some are famous, some obscure, all are interesting, thought-provoking, and entertaining. This anthology, drawn from Thomas Jefferson's lifetime of political, philosophical, theological, and personal writings, uses as its basis Jefferson's original texts. What difference does going directly to the source documents make? How familiar is any reader with Jefferson's unedited draft of The Declaration of Independence:

> *We hold these truths to be sacred and undeniable;*
> *that all men are created equal and independent;*
> *that from that equal creation they derive rights*
> *inherent and inalienable, among which are the*
> *preservation of life, and liberty, and the pursuit*
> *of happiness.*

The writings of Thomas Jefferson are alive.

Few in Beijing's Tienanmen Square find inspiration in the authoritarian writings of Mao Zedong. Fewer still in Moscow's Red Square are inspired by the totalitarian writings of Karl Marx. But two hundred fifty years after his birth it is the democratic writings of Thomas Jefferson which inspire people striving for political freedom.

Presented word for word, just as they appeared in Thomas Jefferson's original handwritten manuscripts, are:

JEFFERSONIANA
The collected aphorisms of Jefferson

A SUMMARY VIEW OF THE RIGHTS
OF BRITISH AMERICA
The political pamphlet that made Jefferson famous

JEFFERSON'S DRAFT OF THE
DECLARATION OF INDEPENDENCE
Jefferson's immortal unedited statement of democracy

THE VIRGINIA STATUTE OF RELIGIOUS FREEDOM
*Jefferson's absolute guarantee of the freedom to worship,
written twelve years before the First Amendment*

THE PRESIDENTIAL PAPERS OF
THOMAS JEFFERSON
Two Inaugural and Eight State of the Union Addresses

THE AUTOBIOGRAPHY OF THOMAS JEFFERSON
*An eyewitness account of the American and French
Revolutions as viewed from Philadelphia and Paris*

THE JEFFERSON BIBLE
The Gospels according to Jefferson

THE OPINIONS OF THOMAS JEFFERSON
*Views on life, liberty and the pursuit of happiness drawn
from a lifetime of letters*

We believe that these writings are wholly representative
of Thomas Jefferson's lifetime. That we have chosen not
to include Jefferson's *Anas,* and only excerpts from his
Notes On The State of Virginia, is certainly no reflection
on their (or any other omitted works') literary value or
historical relevance.

All serious researchers into the writing of Thomas Jefferson owe, as we do, a debt of gratitude to those who have preceded us. Jefferson wrote: "I cannot live with books." We could not have written this book without reference to these important collected works:

H.A. Washington's *Writings of Thomas Jefferson*
W.C. Ford's *Thomas Jefferson's Correspondence*
P.L. Ford's *Writings of Thomas Jefferson*
J.P. Foley's *Jefferson Cyclopedia*
A.A. Liscomb's *The Writings of Thomas Jefferson*
J.P. Boyd's *The Papers of Thomas Jefferson*

We gratefully acknowledge for their help and assistance the librarians at the Library of Congress, The National Archives, and the University of Virginia. Special thanks is also owed to the librarians of Columbia University and the New York Public Library.

It is not within the scope of this anthology of Jefferson's writings to discuss his public accomplishments or private flaws. The Pulitzer Prize winning biography by Dumas Malone, *Jefferson and His Time*, is highly recommended to those looking for the man behind the words.

In April 1962 President John F. Kennedy made these remarks before a group of 49 Nobel Prize winners: "I want to welcome you to the White House. I think this is the most extraordinary collection of talent, of human knowledge, that has ever been gathered together at the White House, with the possible exception of when Thomas Jefferson dined alone."

No words of ours can express our deep admiration for the personal genius of Thomas Jefferson. We hope that our true rendition of his words will serve as adequate thanks.

M.H. & S.G.

This work is dedicated to our good and true friend
Diana

Is this the Fourth?

Reported to be Thomas Jefferson's last words spoken on his deathbed, July 4, 1826, the 50th anniversary of the Declaration of Independence.

TABLE OF CONTENTS

JEFFERSONIANA

JEFFERSONIANA

Ignorance of the law is no excuse.

Peace and friendship with all mankind is the wisest policy.

It is necessary to give as well as take in a government like ours.

Men are disposed to live honestly if the means of doing so are open to them.

I am not one of those who fear the people.

The equal rights of man and the happiness of every individual are the only legitimate objects of government.

The purse of the people is the real seat of sensibility.

The boisterous sea of liberty is never without a wave.

It is incumbent on every generation to pay its own debt as it goes.

I have never believed there was one code of morality for a public and another for a private man.

The will of the majority honestly expressed should give law.

A little rebellion now and then is a good thing.

Honesty is the first chapter of the book of wisdom.

I tremble for my country when I reflect that God is just.

A nation as a society forms a moral person, and every member of it is personally responsible for his society.

Our liberty depends on the freedom of the press. and that cannot be limited without being lost.

The appointment of a woman to office is an innovation for which the public is not prepared, nor am I.

The God who gave us life, gave us liberty at the same time.

Ignorance is preferable to error; and he is less remote from the truth who believes nothing, than he who believes what is a wrong.

The republican is the only form of government which is not eternally at open or secret war with the rights of mankind.

We are not to expect to be translated from despotism to liberty in a featherbed.

It behooves every man who values liberty of conscience for himself, to resist invasions of it in the cases of others; or their case, by change of circumstances, may become his own.

Delay is preferable to error.

I have sworn upon the altar of God, eternal hostility against every form of tyranny over the mind of man.

The earth belongs to the living, not to the dead.

We are not afraid to follow the truth wherever it may lead, nor to tolerate any error so long as reason is left free to combat it.

When angry, count ten before you speak, if very angry, a hundred.

The tree of liberty must be refreshed from time to time with the blood of patriots and tyrants. It is its natural manure.

When a man assumes a public trust, he should consider himself public property.

Conscience is the only clue that will eternally guide a man clear of all doubts and inconsistencies.

Under difficulties I have ever found one and only one rule, to do what is right, and generally we shall disentangle ourselves almost without perceiving how it happened.

To contribute by neighborly intercourse and attention to make others happy is the shortest and surest way of being happy ourselves.

I have ever deemed it more honorable and profitable, too, to set a good example than to follow a bad one.

I never consider a difference of opinion in politics, in religion, in philosophy, as cause for withdrawing from a friend.

Foreign relations are the province of the Federal Government; domestic regulations and institutions belong in every State to itself.

Of all the duties imposed on the executive head of a government, appointment to office is the most difficult and most irksome.

In a government bottomed on the will of all, the life and liberty of every individual citizen becomes interesting to all.

The government which can wield the arm of the people must be the strongest possible.

History in general only informs us what bad government is.

The duty of an upright administration is to pursue its course steadily, to know nothing of family dissensions and to cherish the good principles of both parties.

Where an office is local we never go out of the limits for the officers.

It will be forever seen that of bodies of men even elected by the people, there will always be a greater proportion aristocratic than among their constituents.

The happiness of society depends so much on preventing party spirit from infecting the common intercourse of life that nothing should be spared to harmonize and amalgamate the parties in social circles.

The Presidency is the only office in the world about which I am unable to decide in my own mind whether I had rather have it or not have it.

I am no believer in the amalgamation of parties, nor do I consider it as either desirable or useful to the public.

It accords with our principles to acknowledge any government to be rightful which is formed by the will of the nation substantially declared.

The spirit of this country is totally adverse to a large military.

Wars and contentions indeed fill the pages of history with more matter. But more blest is that nation whose silent course of happiness furnishes nothing for history to say.

For a people who are free and who mean to remain so, a well-organized and armed militia is their best security.

If there be one principle more deeply rooted than any other in the mind of every American, it is that we should have nothing to do with conquest.

Our citizens may be deceived for a while and have been deceived; but as long as the press can be protected we trust them for light.

Letters are not the first but the last steps in the progression from barbarism to civilization.

I place economy among the first and most important of Republican virtues, and public debt as the greatest of the dangers to be feared.

There is a debt of service due from every man to his country, proportioned to the bounties which nature and fortune have measured on him.

In most countries a fixed quantity of wheat is perhaps the best permanent standard of value.

The English would not lose the sale of a bale of furs for the freedom of the whole world.

I have made it a rule never to engage in a lottery or any other adventure of mere chance.

I have ever found in my progress through life, that acting for the public if we always do what is right, the approbation denied in the beginning will surely follow in the end.

The newspapers are the first of all human contrivances for generating war.

What all agree in is probably right; what no two agree in is most probably wrong.

If we are to dream, the flatteries of hope are as cheap and pleasanter than the gloom of despair.

Had the doctrines of Jesus been preached always as pure as they came from his lips, the whole civilized world would now have been Christian.

Whatever be the degree of talent it is no measure of right; because Sir Isaac Newton was superior to others in understanding, he was not therefore lord of the person or property of others.

Money and not morality is the principle of commerce and commercial nations.

My idea is that we should encourage home manufactures to the extent of our own consumption of every thing of which we raise the raw material.

Never fear the want of business. A man who qualifies himself well for his calling never fails of employment in it.

A tour of duty, in whatever line he can be most useful to his country, is due from every individual.

I have never conceived that having been in public life requires me to belie my sentiments or even to conceal them.

I have but one system of ethics for men and for nations - to be grateful, to be faithful to all engagements, and, under all circumstances, to be open and generous.

Matrimony illy agrees with study, especially in the first stages of both.

To most minds exile is next to death; to many beyond it.

The only reward I ever wished on my retirement was to carry with me nothing like the disapprobation of the public.

If some termination of the service of the chief magistrate be not fixed by the Constitution, his office will become for life.

The main objects of all science are the freedom and happiness of man.

To be really useful we must keep pace with the state of society and not dishearten if by attempts at what its population, means, or occupations will fail in attempting.

The information of the people at large can alone make them the safe, as they are the sole, depository of our religious and political freedom.

There are two subjects which I shall claim a right to further as long as I have breath, the public education and the subdivision of the countries into wards. I consider the continuance of Republican government as absolutely hanging on these two hooks.

A Republican government is slow to move, yet when once in motion its momentum becomes irresistible.

We may still believe with security that the great body of American people must for ages yet be substantially Republican.

Opinion and the just maintenance of it shall never be a crime in my view; nor bring injury on the individual.

I think all the world would gain by setting commerce at perfect freedom.

I had ever fondly cherished the interests of the West, relying on it as a barrier against the degeneracy of public opinion from our original and free principles.

Neither natural right nor reason subjects the body of a man to restraint for debt.

I know of no safe depository of the ultimate powers of society but the people themselves.

My principle is to do whatever is right and leave the consequences to Him who has the disposal of them.

Nothing betrays imbecility so much as being insensible of it.

I find friendship to be like wine, raw when new, ripened with age, the true old man's milk and restorative cordial.

I never yet saw a native American begging in the streets or highways.

I hope and firmly believe that the whole world will sooner or later feel benefit from the issue of our assertions of the rights of man.

I find that he is happiest of whom the world says least, good or bad.

Our first and fundamental maxim should be never to entangle ourselves in the toils of Europe.

No government can be maintained without the principle of fear as well as of duty. Good men will obey the last, but bad ones the former only.

Having seen the people of all other nations bow down to the earth under the wars and prodigalities of their rulers,

I have cherished the opposites, peace, economy, and riddance of the public debt.

I have no fear but that the result of our experiment will be that men may be trusted to govern themselves without a master.

To inform the minds of the people and to follow their will is the chief duty of those placed at their head.

I have such reliance on the good sense of the body of the people and the honesty of their leaders that I am not afraid of their letting things to wrong to any length in any cause.

We wish not to meddle with the internal affairs of any country. Peace with all nations and the right which that peace gives us with respect to all nations, are our object.
I have no inclination to govern men.

It ought to be supplicated from heaven by the prayers of the whole world that at length there may be on earth peace and good will toward men.

I cannot live without books.

A SUMMARY VIEW OF THE
RIGHTS OF BRITISH AMERICA

A SUMMARY VIEW
OF THE RIGHTS
OF BRITISH AMERICA
1774

Resolved, That it be an instruction to the said deputies, when assembled in General Congress, with the deputies from the other states of British America, to propose to the said Congress, that an humble and dutiful address be presented to his Majesty, begging leave to lay before him, as Chief Magistrate of the British empire, the united complaints of his Majesty's subjects in America; complaints which are excited by many unwarrantable encroachments and usurpations, attempted to be made by the legislature of one part of the empire, upon the rights which God, and the laws, have given equally and independently to all. To represent to his Majesty that these, his States, have often individually made humble application to his imperial Throne, to obtain, through its intervention, some redress of their injured rights; to none of which, was ever even an answer condescended. Humbly to hope that this, their joint address, penned in the language of truth, and divested of those expressions of servility, which would persuade his Majesty that we are asking favors, and not rights, shall obtain from his Majesty a more respectful acceptance; and this his Majesty will think we have reason to expect, when he reflects that he is no more than the chief officer of the people, appointed by the laws, and circumscribed with definite powers, to assist in working the great machine of government, erected for their use, and, consequently, subject to their superintendence; and, in order that these, our rights, as well as the invasions of them, may be laid more fully before his Majesty, to take a view of them, from the origin and first settlement of these countries.

To remind him that our ancestors, before their emigration in America, were the free inhabitants of the British dominions in Europe, and possessed a right, which nature has given to all men, of departing from the country in which chance, not choice, has placed them, of going in quest of new habitations, and of their establishing new societies, under such laws and regulations as, to them, shall seem most likely to promote public happiness. That their Saxon ancestors had, under this universal law, in like manner, left their native wilds and woods in the North of Europe, had possessed themselves of the Island of Britain, then less charged with inhabitants, and had established there that system of laws which has so long been the glory and protection of that country. Nor was ever any claim of superiority or dependence asserted over them, by that mother country from which they had migrated: and were such a claim made, it is believed his Majesty's subjects in Great Britain have too firm a feeling of the rights derived to them from their ancestors, to bow down the sovereignty of their state before such visionary pretensions. And it is thought that no circumstance has occurred to distinguish, materially, the British from the Saxon emigration. America was conquered, and her settlements made and firmly established, at the expense of individuals, and not of the British public. Their own blood was spilt in acquiring lands for their settlement, their own fortunes expended in making that settlement effectual. For themselves they fought, for themselves they conquered, and for themselves alone they have right to hold. No shilling was ever issued from the public treasures of his Majesty, or his ancestors, for their assistance, till of very late times, after the colonies had become established on a firm and permanent footing. That then, indeed, having become valuable to Great Britain for her commercial purposes, his Parliament was

pleased to lend them assistance against an enemy who
would fain have drawn to herself the benefits of their
commerce, to the great aggrandisement of herself, and
danger of Great Britain. Such assistance, and in such
circumstances, they had often before given to Portugal
and other allied states, with whom they carry on a
commercial intercourse. Yet these states never supposed,
that by calling in her aid, they thereby submitted
themselves to her sovereignty. Had such terms been
proposed, they would have rejected them with disdain, and
trusted for better, to the moderation of their enemies, or
to a vigorous exertion of their own force. We do not,
however, mean to underrate those aids, which, to us, were
doubtless valuable, on whatever principles granted: but we
would shew that they cannot give a title to that authority
which the British Parliament would arrogate over us; and
that may amply be repaid by our giving to the inhabitants
of great Britain such exclusive privileges in trade as may
be advantageous to them, and, at the same time, not too
restrictive to ourselves. That settlement having been thus
effected in the wilds of America, the emigrants thought
proper to adopt that system of laws, under which they had
hitherto lived in the mother country, and to continue their
union with her, by submitting themselves to the same
common sovereign, who was thereby made the central
link, connecting the several parts of the empire thus
newly multiplied.

But that not long were they permitted, however far they
thought themselves removed from the hand of oppression,
to hold undisturbed the rights thus acquired at the hazard
of their lives and loss of their fortunes. A family of
Princes was then on the British throne, whose treasonable
crimes against their people, brought on them, afterwards,
the exertion of those sacred and sovereign rights of

punishment, reserved in the hands of the people for cases of extreme necessity, and judged by the constitution unsafe to be delegated to any other judicature. While every day brought forth some new and unjustifiable exertion of power over their subjects on that side of the water, it was not to be expected that those here, much less able at that time to oppose the designs of despotism, should be exempted from injury. Accordingly, this country which had been acquired by the lives, labors, and fortunes of individual adventurers, was by these Princes, several times, parted out and distributed among the favorites and followers of their fortunes; and, by an assumed right of the Crown alone, were erected into distinct and independent governments; a measure, which it is believed, his Majesty's prudence and understanding would prevent him from imitating at this day; as no exercise of such power, of dividing and dismembering a country, has ever occurred in his Majesty's realm of England, though now of very ancient standing; nor could it be justified or acquiesced under there, or in any part of his Majesty's empire.

That the exercise of a free trade with all parts of the world, possessed by the American colonists, as of natural right, and which no law of their own had taken away or abridged, was next the object of unjust encroachment. Some of the colonies having thought proper to continue the administration of their government in the name and under the authority of his Majesty, King Charles the first, whom, notwithstanding his late deposition by the Commonwealth of England, they continued in the sovereignty of their State, the Parliament, for the Commonwealth, took the same in high offence, and assumed upon themselves the power of prohibiting their trade with all other parts of the world, except the Island

of Great Britain. This arbitrary act, however, they soon
recalled, and by solemn treaty entered into on the 12th
day of March, 1651, between the said Commonwealth, by
the Commissioners, and the colony of Virginia by their
House of Burgesses, it was expressly stipulated by the
eighth article of the said treaty, that they should have free
trade as the people of England do enjoy to all places and
with all nations, according to the laws of that
Commonwealth.' But that, upon the restoration of his
Majesty, King Charles the second, their rights of free
commerce fell once more a victim to arbitrary power; and
by several acts of his reign, as well as of some of his
successors, the trade of the colonies was laid under such
restrictions, as show what hopes they might form from
the justice of a British Parliament, were its uncontrolled
power admitted over these States. History has informed
us, that bodies of men as well as of individuals, are
susceptible of the spirit of tyranny. A view of these acts
of Parliament for regulation, as it has been effectedly
called, of the American trade, if all other evidences were
removed out of the case, would undeniably evince the
truth of this observation. Besides the duties they impose
on our articles of export and import, they prohibit our
going to any markets Northward of Cape Finisterra, in the
kingdom of Spain, for the sale of commodities which
Great Britain will not take from us, and for the purchase
of others, with which she cannot supply us; and that, for
no other than the arbitrary purpose of purchasing for
themselves, by a sacrifice of our rights and interests,
certain privileges in their commerce with an allied state,
who, in confidence, that their exclusive trade with
America will be continued, while the principles and power
of the British Parliament be the same, have indulged
themselves in every exorbitance which their avarice could
dictate or our necessity extort: have raised their

commodities called for in America, to the double and treble of what they sold for, before such exclusive privileges were given them, and of what better commodities of the same kind would cost us elsewhere; and, at the same time, give us much less for what we carry thither, than might be had at more convenient ports. That these acts prohibit us from carrying, in quest of other purchasers, the surplus of our tobaccos, remaining after the consumption of Great Britain is supplied: so that we must leave them with the British merchant, for whatever he will please to allow us, to be by him re-shipped to foreign markets, where he will reap the benefits of making sale of them for full value. That, to heighten still the idea of Parliamentary justice, and to show with what moderation they are like to exercise power, where themselves are to feel no part of its weight, we take leave to mention to his Majesty, certain other acts of the British Parliament, by which they would prohibit us from manufacturing, for our own use, the articles we raise on our own lands, with our own labor. By an act passed in the fifth year of the reign of his late Majesty, King George the second, an American subject is forbidden to make a hat for himself, of the fur which he has taken, perhaps, on his own soil; an instance of despotism, to which no parallel can be produced in the most arbitrary ages of British history. By one other act, passed in the twenty-third year of the same reign, the iron which we make, we are forbidden to manufacture; and, heavy as that article is, and necessary in every branch of husbandry, besides commission and insurance, we are to pay freight for it to Great Britain, and freight for it back again, for the purpose of supporting, not men, but machines, in the island of Great Britain. In the same spirit of equal and impartial legislation, is to be viewed the act of Parliament, passed in the fifth year of the same reign, by which American lands are made subject to the demands of British creditors, while their own lands were still continued unanswerable for their debts; from which, one of these conclusions must necessarily follow, either that justice is not the same thing in America as in Britain, or else, that the British Parliament pay less regard to it here than there. But, that we do not point out to his Majesty the injustice of these acts, with intent to rest on that principle the cause of their nullity; but to show that experience confirms the propriety of those political principles, which exempt us from the jurisdiction of the British Parliament. The true ground on which we declare these acts void, is, that the British Parliament has no right to exercise authority over us.

That these exercises of usurped power have not been confined to instances alone, in which themselves were interested; but they have also intermeddled with the regulation of the internal affairs of the colonies. The act of the 9th of Anne for establishing a post office in America, seems to have had little connection with British convenience, except that of accommodating his Majesty's ministers and favorites with the sale of a lucrative and easy office.

That thus have we hastened through the reigns which preceded his Majesty's, during which the violation of our rights were less alarming, because repeated at more distant intervals, than that rapid and bold succession of injuries, which is likely to distinguish the present from all other periods of American story. Scarcely have our minds been able to emerge from the astonishment into which one stroke of Parliamentary thunder has involved us, before another more heavy and more alarming is fallen on us. Single acts of tyranny may be ascribed to the accidental opinion of a day; but a series of oppressions, begun at a distinguished period, and pursued unalterably through every change of minsters, too plainly prove a deliberate, systematical plan of reducing us to slavery.

That the act, passed in the 4th year of his Majesty's reign, entitled "An act for granting certain duties in the British colonies and plantations in America, etc."

One other act, passed in the 5th year of his reign, entitled "An act for granting and applying certain stamp duties and other duties in the British colonies and plantations in America, etc."

One other act, passed in the 6th year of his reign, entitled "An act for the better securing the dependency of his Majesty's dominions in America upon the crown and parliament of Great Britain;" and one other act, passed in the 7th year of his reign, entitled "An act for granting duties on paper, tea, etc." form that connected chain of parliamentary usurpation, which has already been the subject of frequent applications to his majesty, and the houses of lords and commons of Great Britain; and no answers having yet been condescended to any of these, we shall not trouble his majesty with a repetition of the matters they contained.

But that one other act, passed in the same 7th year of the reign, having been a peculiar attempt, must every require peculiar mention; it is entitled "An act for suspending the legislature of New York."

One free and independent legislature, hereby takes upon itself to suspend the powers of another, free and independent as itself. Thus exhibiting a phenomenon unknown in nature, the creator, and creature of its own power. Not only the principles of common sense, but the common feelings of human nature must be surrendered up, before his Majesty's subjects here, can be persuaded to believe, that they hold their political existence at the will of a British Parliament. Shall these governments be dissolved, their property annihilated, and their people reduced to a state of nature, at the imperious breath of a body of men whom they never saw, in whom they never confided, and over whom they have no powers of punishment or removal, let their crimes against the American public be ever so great? Can any one reason be assigned, why one hundred and sixty thousand electors in the island of Great Britain, should give law to four millions in the States of America, every individual of whom is equal to every individual of them in virtue, in understanding, and in bodily strength? Were this to be admitted, instead of being a free people, as we have hitherto supposed, and mean to continue ourselves, we should suddenly be found the slaves, not of one, but of one hundred and sixty thousand tyrants; distinguished, too, from all others, by this singular circumstance, that they are removed from the reach of fear, the only restraining motive which may hold the hand of a tyrant.

That, by 'an act to discontinue in such manner, and for such time as are therein mentioned, the landing and discharging, lading or shipping of goods, wares and merchandize, at the town and within the harbor of Boston, in the province of Massachusetts bay, in North America,' which was passed at the last session of the British Parliament, a large and populous town, whose trade was their sole subsistence, was deprived of that trade, and involved in utter ruin. Let us for a while, suppose the question of right suspended, in order to examine this act on principles of justice. An act of Parliament had been passed, imposing duties on teas, to be paid in America, against which act the Americans had protested, as inauthoritative. The East India Company, who till that time, had never sent a pound of tea to America on their own account, step forth on that occasion, the asserters of Parliamentary right, and send hither many ship loads of that obnoxious commodity. The masters of their several vessels, however, on their arrival in America, wisely attended to admonition, and returned with their cargoes. In the province of New-England alone, the remonstrances of the people were disregarded, and a compliance, after being many days waited for, was flatly refused. Whether in this, the master of the vessel was governed by his obstinacy, or his instructions, let those who know, say. There are extraordinary situations which require extraordinary interposition. An exasperated people, who feel that they possess power, are not easily restrained within limits strictly regular. A number of them assembled in the town of Boston, threw the tea into the ocean, and dispersed without doing any other act of violence. If in this they did wrong, they were known, and were amenable to the laws of the land; against which, it could not be objected, that they had ever, in any instance, been obstructed or diverted from the regular course, in favor of popular offenders. They should, therefore, not have been distrusted on this occasion. But that ill-fated colony had formerly been bold in their enmities against the House of Stuart, and were now devoted to ruin, by that unseen hand which governs the momentous affairs of this great empire. On the partial representations of a few worthless ministerial dependents, whose constant office it has been to keep that government embroiled, and who, by their treacheries, hope to obtain the dignity of British knighthood, without calling for a party accused, without asking a proof, without attempting a distinction between the guilty and the innocent, the whole of that ancient and wealthy town, is in a moment reduced from opulence to beggary. Men who had spent their lives in extending the British commerce, who had invested, in that place, the wealth their honest endeavors had merited, found themselves and their families, thrown at once on the world, for subsistence by its charities. Not the hundredth part of the inhabitants of that town, had been concerned in the act complained of; many of them were in Great Britain, and in other parts beyond the sea; yet all were involved in one indiscriminate ruin, by a new executive power, unheard of till then, that of a British Parliament. A property of the value of many millions of money, was sacrificed to revenge, not repay, the loss of a few thousands. This is administering justice with a heavy hand indeed! And when is this tempest to be arrested in its course? Two wharves are to be opened again when his Majesty shall think proper: the residue, which lined the extensive shores of the bay of Boston, are forever interdicted the exercise of commerce. This little exception seems to have been thrown in for no other purpose, than that of setting a precedent for investing his Majesty with legislative powers. If the pulse of his people shall beat calmly under this experiment, another and another will be tried, till the measure of despotism be filled up. It would be an insult on common sense, to pretend that this exception was made, in order to restore its commerce to that great town. The trade, which cannot be received at two wharves alone, must of necessity be transferred to some other place; to which it will soon be followed by that of the two wharves. Considered in this light, it would be an insolent and cruel mockery at the annihilation of the town of Boston. By the act for the suppression of riots and tumults in the town of Boston, passed also in the last session of Parliament, a murder committed there, is, if the Governor leases, to be tried in the court of King's bench, in the island of Great Britain, by a jury of Middlesex. The witnesses, too, on receipt of such a sum as the Governor shall think it reasonable for them to expend, are to enter into recognizance to appear at the trial. This is, in other words, taxing them to the amount of their recognizance; and that amount may be whatever a Governor pleases. For who does his Majesty think can be prevailed on to cross the Atlantic for the sole purpose of bearing evidence to a fact? His expenses are to be borne, indeed, as they shall be estimated by a Governor; but who are to feed the wife and children whom he leaves behind, and who have had no other subsistence but his daily labor? Those epidemical disorders, too, so terrible in a foreign climate, is the cure of them to be estimated among the articles of expense, and their danger to be warded off by the Almighty power of a Parliament? And the wretched criminal, if he happen to have offended on the American side, stripped of his privilege of trial by peers of his vicinage, removed from the place where alone full evidence could be obtained, without money, without counsel, without friends, without exculpatory proof, is tried before Judges predetermined to condemn. The cowards who would suffer a countryman to be torn from the bowels of their society, in order to be thus offered a sacrifice to Parliamentary tyranny, would merit that everlasting infamy now fixed on the authors of the act! A clause, for a similar purpose, had been introduced into an act passed in the twelfth year of his Majesty's reign, entitled, 'an act for the better securing and preserving his Majesty's Dock-yards, Magazines, Ships, Ammunition and Stores;' against which, as meriting the same censures, the several colonies have already protested.

That these are the acts of power, assumed by a body of men foreign to our constitutions, and unacknowledged by our laws; against which we do, on behalf of the inhabitants of British America, enter this, our solemn and determined protest. And we do earnestly intreat his Majesty, as yet the only mediatory power between the several States of the British empire, to recommend to his Parliament of Great Britain, the total revocation of these acts, which, however nugatory they may be, may yet prove the cause of further discontents and jealousies among us.

That we next proceed to consider the conduct of his Majesty, as holding the Executive powers of the laws of these States, and mark out his deviations from the line of duty. By the Constitution of Great Britain, as well as of the several American States, his Majesty possesses the power of refusing to pass into a law, any bill which has already passed the other two branches of the legislature. His Majesty, however, and his ancestors, conscious of the impropriety of opposing their single opinion to the united wisdom of two Houses of Parliament, while their proceedings were unbiased by interested principles, for several ages past, have modestly declined the exercise of this power, in that part of his empire called Great Britain. But, by change of circumstances, other principles than those of justice simply, have obtained an influence on their determinations. The addition of new States to the British empire has produced an addition of new, and, sometimes, opposite interests. It is now, therefore, the great office of his Majesty to resume the exercise of his negative power, and to prevent the passage of laws by any one legislature of the empire, which might bear injuriously on the rights and interests of another. Yet this will not excuse the wanton exercise of this power, which we have seen his Majesty practice on the laws of the

American legislature. For the most trifling reasons, and, sometimes for no conceivable reason at all, his Majesty has rejected laws of the most salutary tendency. The abolition of domestic slavery is the great object of desire in those colonies, where it was, unhappily, introduced in their infant state. But previous to the enfranchisement of the slaves we have, it is necessary to exclude all further importations from Africa. Yet our repeated attempts to effect this, by prohibitions, and by imposing duties which might amount to a prohibition, having been hitherto defeated by his Majesty's negative: thus preferring the immediate advantages of a few British corsairs, to the lasting interests of the American States, and to the rights of human nature, deeply wounded by this infamous practice. Nay, the single interposition of an interested individual against a law was scarcely ever known to fail of success, though, in the opposite scale, were placed the interests of a whole country. That this is so shameful an abuse of power, trusted with his Majesty for other purposes, as if, not reformed, would call for some legal restrictions.

With equal inattention to the necessities of his people here, has his Majesty permitted our laws to lie neglected, in England, for years, neither confirming them by his assent, nor annulling them by his negative: so, that such of them as have no suspending clause, we hold on the most precarious of all tenures, his Majesty's will; and such of them as suspend themselves till his Majesty's assent be obtained, we have feared might be called into existence at some future and distant period, when time and change of circumstances shall have rendered them destructive to his people here. And, to render this grievance still more oppressive, his Majesty, by his instructions, has laid his Governors under such restrictions, that they can pass no law, of any moment, unless it have such suspending clause: so that, however, immediate may be the call for legislative interposition, the law cannot be executed, till it has twice crossed the Atlantic, by which time the evil may have spent its whole force.

But in what terms reconcilable to Majesty, and at the same time to truth, shall we speak of a late instruction to his Majesty's Governor of the colony of Virginia, by which he is forbidden to assent to any law for the division of a county, unless the new county will consent to have no representative in Assembly? That colony has as yet affixed no boundary to the Westward. Their Western counties, therefore, are of an indefinite extent. Some of them are actually seated many hundred miles from their Eastern limits. Is it possible, then, that his Majesty can have bestowed a single thought on the situation of those people, who, in order to obtain justice for injuries, however great or small, must, by the laws of that colony, attend their county court at such a distance, with all their witnesses, monthly, till their litigation be determined? Or does his Majesty seriously wish, and publish it to the world, that his subjects should give up the glorious right of representation, with all the benefits derived from that, and submit themselves the absolute slaves of his sovereign will? Or is it rather meant to confine the legislative body to their present numbers, that they may be the cheaper bargain, whenever they shall become worth a purchase?

One of the articles of impeachment against Tresilian, and the other Judges of Westminster Hall, in the reign of Richard the Second, for which they suffered death, as traitors to their country, was, that they had advised the King, that he might dissolve his Parliament at any time; and succeeding kings have adopted the opinion of these unjust Judges. Since the establishment, however, of the British constitution, at the glorious Revolution, on its free and ancient principles, neither his Majesty, nor his ancestors, have exercised such a power of dissolution in the island of Great Britain (On further inquiry, I find two instances of dissolutions before the Parliament would, of itself, have been at an end: viz., the Parliament called to meet August 24, 1698, was dissolved by King William, December 19, 1700, and a new one called, to meet February 6, 1701, which was also dissolved, November 11, 1701, and a new one met December 30, 1701.); and when his Majesty was petitioned, by the united voice of his people there, to dissolve the present Parliament, who had become obnoxious to them, his Minsters were heard to declare, in open Parliament, that his Majesty possessed no such power by the constitution. But how different their language, and his practice, here! To declare, as their duty required, the known rights of their country, to oppose the usurpation of every foreign judicature, to disregard the imperious mandates of a Minister or Governor, have been the avowed causes of dissolving Houses of Representatives in America. But if such powers be really vested in his Majesty, can he suppose they are there placed to awe the members from such purposes as these? When the representative body have lost the confidence of their constituents, when they have notoriously made sale of their most valuable rights, when they have assumed to themselves powers which the people never put into their hands, then, indeed, their continuing in office becomes dangerous to the State, and calls for an exercise of the power of dissolution. Such being the cause for which the representative body should, and should not, be dissolved, will it not appear strange, to an unbiased observer, that that of Great Britain was not dissolved, while those of the colonies have repeatedly incurred that sentence?

But your Majesty, or your Governors, have carried this power beyond every limit known or provided for by the laws. After dissolving one House of Representatives, they have refused to call another, so that, for a great length of time, the legislature provided by the laws, has been out of existence. From the nature of things, every society must, at all times, possess within itself the sovereign powers of legislation. The feelings of human nature revolt against the supposition of a State so situated, as that it may not, in any emergency, provide against dangers which, perhaps, threaten immediate ruin. While those bodies are in existence to whom the people have delegated the powers of legislation, they alone possess, and may exercise, those powers. But when they are dissolved, by the lopping off one or more of their branches, the power reverts to the people, who may use it to unlimited extent, either assembling together in person, sending deputies, or in any other way they may think proper. We forbear to trace consequences further; the dangers are conspicuous with which this practice is replete.

That we shall, at tis time also, take notice of an error in the nature of our land holdings, which crept in at a very early period of our settlement. The introduction of the Feudal tenures into the kingdom of England, though ancient, is well enough understood to set this matter in a proper light. In the earlier ages of the Saxon settlement, feudal holdings were certainly altogether unknown, and very few, if any, had been introduced at the time of the Norman conquest. Our Saxon ancestors held their lands, as they did their personal property, in absolute dominion, disincumbered with any superior, answering nearly to the nature of those possessions which the Feudalist term Allodial. William the Norman, first introduced that system generally. The lands which had belonged to those who fell in the battle of Hastings, and in the subsequent insurrections of his reign, formed a considerable proportion of the lands of the whole kingdom. These he granted out, subject to feudal duties, as did he also those of a great number of his new subjects, who, by persuasions or threats, were induced to surrender them for that purpose. But still, much was left in the hands of his Saxon subjects, held of no superior, and not subject to feudal conditions. These, therefore, by express laws, enacted to render uniform the system of military defence, were made liable to the same military duties as if they had been feuds; and the Norman lawyers soon found means to saddle them, also, with the other feudal burthens. But still they had not been surrendered to the King, they were not derived from his grant, and therefore they were not holden of him. A general principle was introduced, that "all lands in England were held either mediately or immediately of the Crown;" but this was borrowed from those holdings which were truly feudal, and only applied to others for the purposes of illustration. Feudal holdings were, therefore, but exceptions out of the Saxon laws of possession, under which all lands were held in absolute right. These, therefore, still form the basis or groundwork of the Common law, to prevail wheresoever the exceptions have not taken place. America was not conquered by William the Norman, nor its lands surrendered to him or any of his successors. Possessions there are, undoubtedly, of the Allodial nature. Our ancestors, however, who migrated hither, were laborers, not lawyers. The fictitious principle, that all lands belong originally to the King, they were early persuaded to believe real, and accordingly took grants of their own lands from the Crown. And while the Crown continued to grant for small sums and on reasonable rents, there was no inducement to arrest the error, and lay it open to

public view. But his Majesty has lately taken on him to
advance the terms of purchase and of holding, to the
double of what they were; by which means, the
acquisition of lands being rendered difficult, the
population of our country is likely to be checked. It is
time, therefore, for us to lay this matter before his
Majesty, and to declare, that he has no right to grant lands
of himself. From the nature and purpose of civil
institutions, all the lands within the limits, which any
particular party has circumscribed around itself, are
assumed by that society, and subject to their allotment;
this may be done by themselves assembled collectively, or
by their legislature, to whom they may have delegated
sovereign authority; and, if they are allotted in neither of
these ways, each individual of the society, may
appropriate to himself such lands as he finds vacant, and
occupancy will give him title.

That, in order to enforce the arbitrary measures before
complained of, his Majesty has, from time to time, sent
among us large bodies of armed forces, not made up of
the people here, nor raised by the authority of our laws.
Did his Majesty possess such a right as this, it might
swallow up all our other rights, whenever he should think
proper. But his Majesty has no right to land a single
armed man on our shores; and those whom he sends here
are liable to our laws, for the suppression and punishment
of riots, routs, and unlawful assemblies, or are hostile
bodies invading us in defiance of law. When, in the
course of the late war, it became expedient that a body of
Hanoverian troops should be brought over for the defence
of Great Britain, his Majesty's grandfather, our late
sovereign, did not pretend to introduce them under any
authority he possessed. Such a measure would have given
just alarm to his subjects of Great Britain, whose liberties

would not be safe if armed men of another country, and of another spirit, might be brought into the realm at any time, without the consent of their legislature. He, therefore, applied to Parliament, who passed an act for that purpose, limiting the number to be brought in, and the time they were to continue. In like manner is his Majesty restrained in every part of the empire. He possesses indeed the executive power of the laws in every State; but they are the laws of the particular State, which he is to administer within that State, and not those of any one within the limits of another. Every State must judge for itself, the number of armed men which they may safely trust among them, of whom they are to consist, and under what restrictions they are to be laid. To render these proceedings still more criminal against our laws, instead of subjecting the military to the civil power, his majesty has expressly made the civil subordinate to the military. But can his Majesty thus put down all law under his feet? Can he erect a power superior to that which erected himself? He has done it indeed by force; but let him remember that force cannot give right.

That these are our grievances, which we have thus laid before his Majesty, with that freedom of language and sentiment which becomes a free people claiming their rights as derived from the laws of nature, and not as the gift of their Chief Magistrate. Let those flatter, who fear: it is not an American art. To give praise where it is not due might be well from the venal, but would ill beseem those who are asserting the rights of human nature. They know, and will, therefore, say, that Kings are the servants, not the proprietors of the people. Open your breast, Sire, to liberal and expanded thought. Let not the name of George the Third, be a blot on the page of history. You are surrounded by British counsellors, but remember that they are parties. You have no ministers for American affairs, because you have none taken from among us, nor amenable to the laws on which they are to give you advice. It behooves you, therefore, to think and to act for yourself and your people. The great principles of right and wrong are legible to every reader; to pursue them, requires not the aid of many counsellors. The whole art of government consists in the art of being honest. Only aim to do your duty, and mankind will give you credit where you fail. No longer persevere in sacrificing the rights of one part of the empire to the inordinate desires of another; but deal out to all, equal and impartial right. Let no act be passed by any one legislature, which may infringe on the rights and liberties of another. This is the important post in which fortune has placed you, holding the balance of a great, if a well-poised empire. This, Sire, is the advice of your great American council, on the observance of which may perhaps depend your felicity and future fame, and the preservation of that harmony which alone can continue, both to Great Britain and America, the reciprocal advantages of their connection. It is neither our wish nor our interest to separate from her. We are willing, on our part, to sacrifice everything which reason can ask, to the restoration of that tranquillity for which all must wish. On their part, let them be ready to establish union on a generous plan. Let them name their terms, but let them be just. accept of every commercial preference it is in our power to give, for such things as we can raise for their use, or they make for ours. But let them not think to exclude us from going to other markets to dispose of those commodities which they can not use, nor to supply those wants which they cannot supply. Still less, let it be proposed, that our properties, within our own territories, shall be taxed or regulated by any power on earth, but our own. The God who gave us life, gave us liberty at the same time: the hand of force may destroy, but cannot disjoin them. This, Sire, is our last, our determined resolution. And that you will be pleased to interpose, with that efficacy which your earnest endeavors may insure, to procure redress of these our great grievances, to quiet the minds of your subjects in British America against any apprehensions of future encroachment, to establish fraternal love and harmony through the whole empire, and that that may continue to the latest ages of time, is the fervent prayer of all British America.

THE DECLARATION OF INDEPENDENCE

JEFFERSON'S DRAFT
39

THE FINAL DECLARATION
47

THOMAS JEFFERSON'S DRAFT OF THE DECLARATION OF INDEPENDENCE JUNE 11-28, 1776

A Declaration by the Representatives of the United States of America, in General Congress assembled.

When, in the course of human events, it becomes necessary for a people to advance from that subordination in which they have hitherto remained and to assume among the powers of the earth the equal and independent station to which the laws of nature and of nature's God entitle them, a decent respect to the opinions of mankind requires that they should declare the causes which impel them to the change.

We hold these truths to be sacred and undeniable; that all men are created equal and independent; that from that equal creation they derive rights inherent and inalienable, among which are the preservation of life, and liberty, and the pursuit of happiness; that to secure these ends, governments are instituted among men, deriving their just powers from the consent of the governed; that whenever any form of government shall become destructive of these ends, it is the right of the people to alter or abolish it, and to institute new government, laying its foundation on such principles, and organizing its powers in such form, as to them shall seem most likely to effect their safety and happiness. Prudence, indeed, will dictate that governments long established should not be changed for light and transient causes: and accordingly all experience hath shewn that mankind are more disposed to suffer while evils are sufferable, than to right themselves by abolishing the forms to which they are accustomed. But when a long train of abuses and usurpations, begun at a distinguished period, and pursuing invariably the same object, evinces a design to subject them to arbitrary power, it is their right, it is their duty, to throw off such government and to provide new guards for their future security. Such has been the patient sufferance of these colonies; and such is now the necessity which constrains them to expunge their former systems of government. The history of his present majesty is a history of unremitting injuries and usurpations, among which no one fact stands single or solitary to contradict the uniform tenor of the rest, all if which have in direct object the establishment of an absolute tyranny over these States. To prove this, let facts be submitted to a candid world, for the truth of which we pledge a faith yet unsullied by falsehood.

He has refused his assent to laws the most wholesome and necessary for the public good.

He has forbidden his governors to pass laws of immediate and pressing importance, unless suspended in their operation till his assent should be obtained; and when so suspended, he has neglected utterly to attend to them.

He has refused to pass other laws for the accommodation of large districts of people unless those people would relinquish the right of representation, in the Legislature a right inestimable to them and formidable to tyrants only:

He has dissolved representative houses repeatedly and continually, for opposing with manly firmness his invasions on the rights of the people:

He has refused for a long space of time to cause others to be elected, whereby the legislative powers, incapable of annihilation, have returned to the people at large for their exercise, the State remaining in the meantime exposed to all the dangers of invasion from without, and convulsions within:

He has endeavored to prevent the population of these States; for that purpose obstructing the laws for naturalization of foreigners: refusing to pass others to encourage their migrations hither; and raising the conditions of new appropriations of lands.

He has suffered the administration of justice totally to cease in some of these colonies, refusing his assent to laws for establishing judiciary powers:

He has made our judges dependent on his will alone, for the tenure of their offices, and amount of their salaries:

He has erected a multitude of new offices by a self-assumed power, and sent hither swarms of officers to harass our people and eat out their substance:

He has kept among us in times of peace standing armies and ships of war:

He has effected to render the military, independent of and superior to, the civil power.

He has combined with others to subject us to a jurisdiction foreign to our constitutions and unacknowledged by our laws, giving his assent to their pretended acts of legislation, for quartering large bodies of armed troops among us; for protecting them by a mock trial from punishment for any murders which they should commit on the inhabitants of these States; for cutting off our trade with all parts of the world; for imposing taxes on us without our consent; for depriving us of the benefits of trial by jury; for transporting us beyond seas to be tried for pretended offenses; for taking away our charters, and altering fundamentally the forms of our governments; for suspending our legislatures and declaring themselves invested with power to legislate for us in all cases whatsoever:

He has abdicated government here, withdrawing his governors, and declaring us out of his allegiance and protection:

He has plundered our seas, ravaged our coasts, burnt our towns and destroyed the lives of our people:

He is at this time transporting large armies of foreign mercenaries to compleat the works of death, desolation and tyranny, already begun with circumstances of cruelty and perfidy unworthy the head of a civilized nation:

He has endeavored to bring on the inhabitants of our frontiers the merciless Indian savages, whose known rule of warfare is an undistinguished destruction of all ages, sexes, and conditions of existence:

He has incited treasonable insurrections of our fellow-citizens, with the allurements of forfeiture and confiscation of our property:

He has waged cruel war against human nature itself, violating its most sacred rights of life and liberty in the persons of a distant people who never offended him, captivating and carrying them into slavery in another hemisphere, or to incur miserable death in their transportation thither. This piratical warfare, the opprobrium of *infidel* powers, is the warfare of the *Christian* King of Great Britain. Determined to keep open a market where men should be bought and sold, he has prostituted his negative for suppressing every legislative attempt to prohibit or to restrain this execrable commerce: And that this assemblage of horrors might want no fact of distinguished die, he is now exciting those very people to rise in arms among us, and to purchase that liberty of which *he* had deprived them, by murdering the people upon whom *he* also obtruded them: thus paying off former crimes committed against the *liberties* of one people, with crimes which he urges them to commit against the *lives* of another.

In every stage of these oppressions we have petitioned for redress in the most humble terms; our repeated petitions have been answered by repeated injury.

A Prince whose character is thus marked by every act which may define a tyrant, is unfit to be the ruler of a people who mean to be free. Future ages will scarce believe that the hardiness of one man adventured within the short compass of twelve years only, on so many acts of tyranny without a mask, over a people fostered and fixed in principles of liberty.

Nor have we been wanting in attentions to our British brethren. We have warned them from time to time of attempts by their legislature to extend a jurisdiction over these our States. We have reminded them of the circumstances of our migration and settlement here, no one of which could warrant so strange a pretension: that these were effected at the expense of our own blood and treasure, unassisted by the wealth or the strength of Great

Britain: that in constituting indeed our several forms of government, we had adopted one common king, thereby laying a foundation for perpetual league and amity with them: but that submission to their parliament was no part of our Constitution, nor ever in idea, if history may be credited: and we appealed to their native justice and magnanimity, as well as to the ties of our common kindred to disavow these usurpations which were likely to interrupt our correspondence and connections. They too have been deaf to the voice of justice and of consanguinity, and when occasions have been given them, by the regular course of their laws, of removing from their councils the disturbers of our harmony, they have by their free election re-established them in power. At this very time too they are permitting their chief magistrate to send over not only soldiers of our common blood, but Scotch and foreign mercenaries to invade and deluge us in blood. These facts have given the last stab to agonizing affection, and manly spirit bids us to renounce forever these unfeeling brethren. We must endeavor to forget our former love for them, and to hold them as we hold the rest of mankind, enemies in war, in peace friends. We might have been a free and great people together; but a communication of grandeur and of freedom it seems is below their dignity. Be it so, since they will have it: The road to glory and happiness is open to us too; We will climb it apart from them, and acquiesce in the necessity which denounces our eternal separation.

We therefore the representatives of the United States of America in General Congress assembled do, in the name and by authority of the good people of these States, reject and renounce all allegiance and subjugation to the Kings of Great Britain and all others who may hereafter claim by, through, or under them; we utterly dissolve and break off all political connection which may have heretofore subsisted between us and the people or Parliament of Great Britain; and finally we do assert and declare these Colonies to be free and independent States, and that as free and independent States they shall have full power to levy war, conclude peace, contract alliances, establish commerce, and do all other acts and things which independent States may of right do.

And for the support of this declaration we mutually pledge to each other our lives, our fortunes, and our sacred honor.

THE DECLARATION OF INDEPENDENCE
JULY 4, 1776

A Declaration by the Representatives of the United States of America, in General Congress assembled.

When in the course of human events it becomes necessary for one people to dissolve the political bands which have connected them with another, and to assume among the powers of the earth the separate and equal station to which the laws of nature and of nature's God entitle them, a decent respect to the opinions of mankind requires that they should declare the causes which impel them to the separation.

We hold these truths to be self-evident: that all men are created equal; that they are endowed by their Creator with certain unalienable rights; that among these are life, liberty and the pursuit of happiness; that to secure these rights, governments are instituted among men, deriving their just powers from the consent of the governed; that whenever any form of government becomes destructive of these ends, it is the right of the people to alter or to abolish it, and to institute new government, laying its foundation on such principles, and organizing its powers in such form, as to them shall seem most likely to effect their safety and happiness. Prudence, indeed, will dictate that governments long established should not be changed for light and transient causes; and accordingly all experience hath shewn, that mankind are more disposed to suffer while evils are sufferable, than to right themselves by abolishing the forms to which they are accustomed. But when a long train of abuses and usurpations pursuing invariably the same object, evinces a design to reduce them under absolute despotism, it is their right, it is their duty to throw off such government, and to provide new guards for their future security. Such has been the patient sufferance of these colonies; and such is now the necessity which constrains them to alter their former systems of government. The history of the present King of Great Britain is a history of repeated injuries and usurpations, all having in direct object the establishment of an absolute tyranny over these States. To prove this, let facts be submitted to a candid world.

He has refused his assent to laws the most wholesome and necessary for the public good.

He has forbidden his governors to pass laws of immediate and pressing importance, unless suspended in their operation till his assent should be obtained; and, when so suspended, he has utterly neglected to attend to them.

He has refused to pass other laws for the accommodation of large districts of people, unless those people would relinquish the right of representation in the Legislature, a right inestimable to them, and formidable to tyrants only.

He has called together legislative bodies at places unusual, uncomfortable, and distant from the depository of their public records, for the sole purpose of fatiguing them into compliance with his measures.

He has dissolved representative houses repeatedly for opposing with manly firmness his invasions on the rights of the people.

He has refused for a long time after such dissolutions to cause others to be elected, whereby the legislative powers, incapable of annihilation, have returned to the people at large for their exercise, the State remaining, in the meantime, exposed to all the dangers of invasion from without and convulsions within.

He has endeavored to prevent the population of these States; for that purpose obstructing the laws for naturalization of foreigners, refusing to pass others to encourage their migrations hither, and raising the conditions of new appropriations of lands.

He has obstructed the administration of justice by refusing his assent to laws for establishing judiciary powers.

He has made judges dependent on his will alone for the tenure of their offices, and the amount and payment of their salaries.

He has erected a multitude of new offices and sent hither swarms of officers to harass our people and eat out their substance.

He has kept among us in times of peace standing armies, without the consent of our Legislatures.

He has effected to render the military independent of, and superior to, the civil power.

He has combined with others to subject us to a jurisdiction foreign to our constitution and unacknowledged by our laws, giving his assent to their acts of pretended legislation: for quartering large bodies of armed troops among us; for protecting them by a mock trial from punishment for any murders which they should commit on the inhabitants of these States; for cutting off our trade with all parts of the world; for imposing taxes on us without our consent; for depriving us in many cases of the benefits of trial by jury; for transporting us beyond seas to be tried for pretended offenses; for abolishing the free system of English laws in a neighboring province, establishing therein an arbitrary government, and enlarging its boundaries, so as to render it at once an example and fit instrument for introducing the same absolute rule into these Colonies; for taking away our charters, abolishing our most valuable laws, and altering fundamentally the forms of our governments; for suspending our own Legislatures, and declaring themselves invested with power to legislate for us in all cases whatsoever.

He has abdicated government here by declaring us out of his protection and waging war against us.

He has plundered our seas, ravaged our coasts, burnt our towns, and destroyed the lives of our people.

He is at this time transporting large armies of foreign mercenaries to complete the work of death, desolation, and tyranny already begun with circumstances of cruelty and perfidy scarcely paralleled in the most barbarous ages and totally unworthy the head of a civilized nation.

He has constrained our fellow-citizens taken captive on the high seas to bear arms against their country, to become the executioners of their friends and brethren, or to fall themselves by their hands.

He has excited domestic insurrections amongst us, and has endeavored to bring on the inhabitants of our frontiers, the merciless Indian savages, whose known rule of warfare, is an undistinguished destruction, of all ages, sexes and conditions.

In every stage of these oppressions we have petitioned for redress in the most humble terms; our repeated petitions have been answered only by repeated injury.

A Prince, whose character is thus marked by every act which may define a tyrant, is unfit to be the ruler of a free people.

Nor have we been wanting in attentions to our British brethren. We have warned them from time to time of attempts by their legislature to extend an unwarrantable jurisdiction over us. We have reminded them of the circumstances of our emigration and settlement here. We have appealed to their native justice and magnanimity, and we have conjured them by the ties of our common kindred to disavow these usurpations, which, would inevitably interrupt our connections and correspondence. They, too, have been deaf to the voice of justice and of consanguinity. We must therefore acquiesce in the necessity, which denounces our separation, and hold them, as we hold the rest of mankind, enemies in war, in peace, friends.

We, therefore, the representatives of the United States of America, in General Congress, assembled, appealing to the supreme judge of the world, for the rectitude of our intention, do, in the name, and by authority of the good people of these Colonies, solemnly publish and declare, that these united Colonies are, and of right ought to be, free and independent States; that they are absolved from all allegiance to the British Crown, and that all political connection between them and the State of Great Britain, is and ought to be totally dissolved; and that as free and independent States, they have full power to levy war, conclude peace, contract alliances, establish commerce, and to do all other acts and things which independent States may of right do.

And for the support of this declaration, with a firm reliance on the protection of divine Providence, we mutually pledge to each other our lives, our fortunes, and our sacred honor.

Thomas Jefferson was one of the fifty-six signers of the Declaration of Independence.

THE VIRGINIA STATUTE OF
RELIGIOUS FREEDOM

THE VIRGINIA STATUTE OF RELIGIOUS FREEDOM
1779

Well aware that Almighty God hath created the mind free; that all attempts to influence it by temporal punishments or burdens, or by civil incapacitations, tend only to beget habits of hypocrisy and meanness, and are a departure from the plan of the Holy Author of our religion, who being Lord both of body and mind, yet chose not to propagate it by coercions on either, as was in his Almighty power to do; that the impious presumption of legislators and rulers, civil as well as ecclesiastical, who, being themselves but fallible and uninspired men have assumed dominion over the faith of others, setting up their own opinions and modes of thinking as the only true and infallible, and as such endeavoring to impose them on others, hath established and maintained false religions over the greatest part of the world, and through all time; that to compel a man to furnish contributions of money for the propagation of opinions which he disbelieves, is sinful and tyrannical; that even the forcing him to support this or that teacher of his own religious persuasion, is depriving him of the comfortable liberty of giving his contributions to the particular pastor whose morals he would make his pattern, and whose powers he feels most persuasive to righteousness, and is withdrawing from the ministry those temporal rewards, which proceeding from an approbation of their personal conduct, are an additional incitement to earnest and unremitting labors for the instruction of mankind; that our civil rights have no dependence on our religious opinions, more than our opinions in physics or geometry; that, therefore, the proscribing any citizen as unworthy the public confidence by laying upon him an incapacity of being called to the offices of trust and emolument, unless he profess or renounce this or that religious opinion, is depriving him injuriously of those privileges and advantages to which in common with his fellow citizens he has a natural right; that it tends also to corrupt the principles of that very religion it is meant to encourage, by bribing, with a monopoly of worldly honors and emoluments, those who will externally profess and conform to it; that though indeed these are criminal who do not withstand such temptation, yet neither are those innocent who lay the bait in their way; that to suffer the civil magistrate to intrude his powers into the field of opinion and to restrain the profession or propagation of principles, on the supposition of their ill tendency, is a dangerous fallacy, which at once destroys all religious liberty, because he being of course judge of that tendency, will make his opinions the rule of judgment, and approve or condemn the sentiments of others only as they shall square with or differ from his own; that it is time enough for the rightful purposes of civil government, for its offices to interfere when principles break out into overt acts against peace and good order; and finally, that truth is great and will prevail if left to herself, that she is the proper and sufficient antagonist to error, and has nothing to fear from the conflict, unless by human interposition disarmed of her natural weapons, free argument and debate, errors ceasing to be dangerous when it is permitted freely to contradict them.

Be it therefore enacted by the General Assembly, That no man shall be compelled to frequent or support any religious worship, place or ministry whatsoever, nor shall be enforced, restrained, molested, or burthened in his body or goods, nor shall otherwise suffer on account of his religious opinions or belief; but that all men shall be free to profess, and by argument to maintain, their opinions in matters of religion, and that the same shall in nowise diminish, enlarge, or affect their civil capacities. And though we well know this Assembly, elected by the people for the ordinary purposes of legislation only, have no power to restrain the acts of succeeding assemblies, constituted with the powers equal to our own, and that therefore to declare this act irrevocable, would be of no effect in law, yet we are free to declare, and do declare, that the rights hereby asserted are of the natural rights of mankind, and that if any act shall be hereafter passed to repeal the present or to narrow its operation, such act will be an infringement of natural right.

THE PRESIDENTIAL PAPERS OF THOMAS JEFFERSON

FIRST INAUGURAL ADDRESS
MARCH 4, 1801

Friends and Fellow-Citizens: Called upon to undertake the duties of the first executive office of our country, I avail myself of the presence of that portion of my fellow-citizens which is here assembled to express my grateful thanks for the favor with which they have been pleased to look toward me, to declare a sincere consciousness that the task is above my talents, and that I approach it with those anxious and awful presentiments which the greatness of the charge and the weakness of my powers so justly inspire. A rising nation, spread over a wide and fruitful land, traversing all the seas with the rich productions of their industry, engaged in commerce with nations who feel power and forget right, advancing rapidly to destinies beyond the reach of mortal eye - when I contemplate these transcendent objects, and see the honor, the happiness, and the hopes of this beloved country committed to the issue and the auspices of this day, I shrink from the contemplation, and humble myself before the magnitude of the undertaking. Utterly, indeed, should I despair did not the presence of many whom I here see remind me that in the other high authorities provided by our Constitution I shall find resources of wisdom, of virtue, and of zeal on which to rely under all difficulties. To you, then, gentlemen, who are charged with the sovereign functions of legislation, and to those associated with you, I look with encouragement for that guidance and support which may enable us to steer with safety the vessel in which we are all embarked amidst the conflicting elements of a troubled world.

During the contest of opinion through which we have passed the animation of discussions and of exertions has sometimes worn an aspect which might impose on strangers unused to think freely and to speak and to write what they think; but this being now decided by the voice of the nation, announced according to the rules of the Constitution, all will, of course, arrange themselves under the will of the law, and unite in common efforts for the common good. All, too, will bear in mind this sacred principle, that though the will of the majority is in all cases to prevail, that will to be rightful must be reasonable; that the minority possess their equal rights, which equal law must protect, and to violate would be oppression. Let us, then, fellow-citizens, unite with one heart and one mind. Let us restore to social intercourse that harmony and affection without which liberty and even life itself are but dreary things. And let us reflect that, having banished from our land that religious intolerance under which mankind so long bled and suffered, we have yet gained little if we countenance a political intolerance as despotic, as wicked, and capable of as bitter and bloody persecutions. During the throes and convulsions of the ancient world, during the agonizing spasms of infuriated man, seeking through blood and slaughter his long-lost liberty, it was not wonderful that the agitation of the billows should reach even this distant and peaceful shore; that this should be more felt and feared by some and less by others, and should divide opinions as to measures of safety. But every difference of opinion is not a difference of principle. We have called by different names brethren of the same principle. We are all Republicans, we are all Federalists. If there be any among us who would wish to dissolve this Union or to change its republican form, let them stand undisturbed as monuments of the safety with which error of opinion may be tolerated where reason is left free to combat it. I know, indeed, that some honest men fear that a republican government can not be strong, that this Government is not strong enough; but would the honest patriot, in the full tide of successful experiment, abandon a government which has so far kept us free and firm on the theoretic and visionary fear that this Government, the world's best hope, may by possibility want energy to preserve itself? I trust not. I believe this, on the contrary, the strongest Government on earth. I believe it the only one where every man, at the call of the law, would fly to the standard of the law, and would meet invasions of the public order as his own personal concern. Sometimes it is said that man can not be trusted with the government of himself. Can he, then, be trusted with the government of others? Or have we found angels in the forms of kings to govern him? Let history answer this question.

Let us, then, with courage and confidence pursue our own Federal and Republican principles, our attachment to union and representative government. Kindly separated by nature and a wide ocean from the exterminating havoc of one quarter of the globe; too high-minded to endure the degradations of the others; possessing a chosen country, with room enough for our descendants to the thousandth and thousandth generation; entertaining a due sense of our equal right to the use of our own faculties, to the acquisitions of our own industry, to honor and confidence from our fellow-citizens, resulting not from birth, but from our actions and their sense of them; enlightened by a benign religion, professed, indeed, and practiced in various forms, yet all of them inculcating honesty, truth, temperance, gratitude, and the love of man; acknowledging and adoring an overruling Providence, which by all its dispensations proves that it delights in the happiness of man here and his greater happiness hereafter with all these blessings, what more is necessary to make us a happy and a prosperous people? Still one thing more, fellow-citizens - a wise and frugal Government, which shall restrain men from injuring one another, shall leave them otherwise free to regulate their own pursuits of industry and improvement, and shall not take from the mouth of labor the bread it has earned. This is the sum of good government, and this is necessary to close the circle of our felicities.

About to enter, fellow-citizens, on the exercise of duties which comprehend everything dear and valuable to you, it is proper you should understand what I deem the essential principles of our Government, and consequently those which ought to shape its Administration. I will compress them within the narrowest compass they will bear, stating the general principle, but not all its limitations. Equal and exact justice to all men, of whatever state or persuasion, religious or political; peace, commerce, and honest friendship with all nations, entangling alliances with none; the support of the State governments in all their rights, as the most competent administrations for our domestic concerns and the surest bulwarks against anti-republican tendencies; the preservation of the General Government in its whole constitutional vigor, as the sheet anchor of our peace at home and safety abroad; a jealous care of the right of election by the people - a mild and safe corrective of abuses which are lopped by the sword of revolution where peaceable remedies are unprovided; absolute acquiescence in the decisions of the majority, the vital principle of republics, from which is no appeal but to force, the vital principle and immediate parent of despotism; a well-disciplined militia, our best reliance in peace and for the first moments of war, till regulars may relieve them; the supremacy of the civil over the military authority; economy in the public expense, that labor may be lightly burthened; the honest payment of our debts and sacred preservation of the public faith; encouragement of agriculture, and of commerce as its handmaid; the diffusion of information and arraignment of all abuses at the bar of the public reason; freedom of religion; freedom of the press, and freedom of person under the protection of the habeas corpus, and trial by juries impartially selected. These principles form the bright constellation which has gone before us and guided our steps through an age of revolution and reformation. The wisdom of our sages and blood of our heroes have been devoted to their attainment. They should be the creed of our political faith, the text of civic instruction, the touchstone by which to try the services of those we trust; and should we wander from them in moments of error or of alarm, let us hasten to retrace our steps and to regain the road which alone leads to peace, liberty, and safety.

I repair, then, fellow-citizens, to the post you have assigned me. With experience enough in subordinate offices to have seen the difficulties of this the greatest of all, I have learnt to expect that it will rarely fall to the lot of imperfect man to retire from this station with the reputation and the favor which bring him into it. Without pretensions to that high confidence you reposed in our first and greatest revolutionary character, whose preeminent services had entitled him to the first place in his country's love and destined for him the fairest page in the volume of faithful history, I ask so much confidence only as may give firmness and effect to the legal administration of your affairs. I shall often go wrong through defect of judgment. When right, I shall often be thought wrong by those whose positions will not command a view of the whole ground. I ask your indulgence for my own errors, which will never be intentional, and your support against the errors of others, who may condemn what they would not if seen in all its parts. The approbation implied by your suffrage is a great consolation to me for the past, and my future solicitude will be to retain the good opinion of those who have bestowed it in advance, to conciliate that of others by doing them all the good in my power, and to be instrumental to the happiness and freedom of all.

Relying, then, on the patronage of your good will, I advance with obedience to the work, ready to retire from it whenever you become sensible how much better choice it is in your power to make. And may that Infinite Power which rules the destinies of the universe lead our councils to what is best, and give them a favorable issue for your peace and prosperity.

FIRST ANNUAL MESSAGE
DECEMBER 8, 1801

Fellow-Citizens of the Senate and House of Representatives: It is a circumstance of sincere gratification to me that on meeting the great council of our nation I am able to announce to them on grounds of reasonable certainty that the wars and troubles which have for so many years afflicted our sister nations have at length come to an end, and that the communications of peace and commerce are once more opening among them. Whilst we devoutly return thanks to the beneficent Being who has been pleased to breathe into them the spirit of conciliation and forgiveness, we are bound with peculiar gratitude to be thankful to Him that our own peace has been preserved through so perilous a season, and ourselves permitted quietly to cultivate the earth and to practice and improve those arts which tend to increase our comforts. The assurances, indeed, of friendly disposition received from all the powers with whom we have principal relations had inspired a confidence that our peace with them would not have been disturbed. But a cessation of irregularities which had affected the commerce of neutral nations and of the irritations and injuries produced by them can not but add to this confidence, and strengthens at the same time the hope that wrongs committed on unoffending friends under a pressure of circumstances will now be reviewed with candor, and will be considered as founding just claims of retribution for the past and new assurance for the future.

Among our Indian neighbors also a spirit of peace and friendship generally prevails, and I am happy to inform you that the continued efforts to introduce among them the implements and the practice of husbandry and of the household arts have not been without success; that they are becoming more and more sensible of the superiority of this dependence for clothing and subsistence over the precarious resources of hunting and fishing, and already we are able to announce that instead of that constant diminution of their numbers produced by their wars and their wants, some of them begin to experience an increase of population.

To this state of general peace with which we have been blessed, one only exception exists. Tripoli, the least considerable of the Barbary States, had come forward with demands unfounded either in right or in compact, and had permitted itself to denounce war on our failure to comply before a given day. The style of the demand admitted but one answer. I sent a small squadron of frigates into the Mediterranean, with assurances to that power of our sincere desire to remain in peace, but with orders to protect our commerce against the threatened attack. The measure was seasonable and salutary. The Bey had already declared war. His cruisers were out. Two had arrived at Gibraltar. Our commerce in the Mediterranean was blockaded and that of the Atlantic in peril. The arrival of our squadron dispelled the danger. One of the Tripolitan cruisers having fallen in with and engaged the small schooner *Enterprise*, commanded by Lieutenant Sterret, which had gone as a tender to our larger vessels, was captured, after a heavy slaughter of her men, without the loss of a single one on our part. The bravery exhibited by our citizens on that element will, I trust, be a testimony to the world that it is not the want of that virtue which makes us seek their peace, but a conscientious desire to direct the energies of our nation to the multiplication of the human race, and not to its destruction. Unauthorized by the Constitution, without the sanction of Congress, to go beyond the line of defense, the vessel, being disabled from committing further hostilities, was liberated with its crew. The Legislature will doubtless consider whether, by authorizing measures of offense also, they will place our force on an equal footing with that of its adversaries. I communicate all material information on this subject, that in the exercise of this important function confided by the Constitution to the Legislature exclusively their judgment may form itself on a knowledge and consideration of every circumstance of weight.

I wish I could say that our situation with all the other Barbary States was entirely satisfactory. Discovering that some delays had taken place in the performance of certain articles stipulated by us, I thought it my duty, by immediate measures for fulfilling them, to vindicate to ourselves the right of considering the effect of departure from stipulation on their side. From the papers which will be laid before you will be enabled to judge whether our treaties are regarded by them as fixing at all the measure of their demands or as guarding from the exercise of force our vessels within their power, and to consider how far it will be safe and expedient to leave our affairs with them in their present posture.

I lay before you the result of the census lately taken of our inhabitants, to a conformity with which we are now to reduce the ensuing ratio of representation and taxation. You will perceive that the increase of numbers during the last ten years, proceeding in geometrical ratio, promises a duplication in little more than twenty-two years. We contemplate this rapid growth and the prospect it holds up to us, not with a view to the injuries it may enable us to do others in some future day, but to the settlement of the extensive country still remaining vacant within our limits to the multiplication of men susceptible of happiness, educated in the love of order, habituated to self-government, and valuing its blessings above all price.

Other circumstances, combined with the increase of numbers, have produced an augmentation of revenue arising from consumption in a ratio far beyond that of population alone; and though the changes in foreign relations now taking place so desirably for the whole world may for a season affect this branch of revenue, yet weighing all probabilities of expense as well as of income, there is reasonable ground of confidence that we may now safely dispense with all the internal taxes, comprehending excise, stamps, auctions, licenses, carriages, and refined sugars, to which the postage on newspapers may be added to facilitate the progress of information, and that the remaining sources of revenue will be sufficient to provide for the support of Government, to pay the interest of the public debts, and to discharge the principals within shorter periods than the laws or the general expectation had contemplated. War, indeed, and untoward events may change this prospect of things and call for expenses which the imposts could not meet; but sound principles will not justify our taxing the industry of our fellow-citizens to accumulate treasure for wars to happen we know not when, and which might not, perhaps, happen but from the temptations offered by that treasure.

These views, however, of reducing our burthens are formed on the expectation that a sensible and at the same time a salutary reduction may take place in our habitual expenditures. For this purpose those of the civil Government, the Army, and Navy will need revisal.

When we consider that this Government is charged with the external and mutual relations only of these States; that the States themselves have principal care of our persons, our property, and our reputation, constituting the great field of human concerns, we may well doubt whether our organization is not too complicated, too expensive; whether offices and officers have not been multiplied unnecessarily and sometimes injuriously to the service they were meant to promote. I will cause to be laid before you an essay toward a statement of those who, under public employment of various kinds, draw money from the Treasury or from our citizens. Time has not permitted a perfect enumeration, the ramifications of office being too multiplied and remote to be completely traced in a first trial. Among those who are dependent on Executive discretion I have begun the reduction of what was deemed unnecessary. The expenses of diplomatic agency have been considerably diminished. The inspectors of internal revenue who were found to obstruct the accountability of the institution have been discontinued. Several agencies created by Executive authority, on salaries fixed by that also, have been suppressed, and should suggest the expediency of regulating that power by law, so as to subject its exercises to legislative inspection and sanction. Other reformations of the same kind will be pursued with that caution which is requisite in removing useless things, not to injure what is retained. But the great mass of public offices is established by law, and therefore by law alone can be abolished. Should the Legislature think it expedient to pass this roll in review and try all its parts by the test of public utility, they may be assured of every aid and light which Executive information can yield. Considering the general tendency to multiply offices and dependencies and to increase expense to the ultimate term of burthen which the citizen can bear, it behooves us to avail ourselves of every occasion which presents itself for taking off the surcharge, that it never may be seen here that after leaving to labor the smallest portion of its earnings on which it can subsist, Government shall itself consume the whole residue of what it was instituted to guard.

In our care, too, of the public contributions intrusted to our direction it would be prudent to multiply barriers against their dissipation by appropriating specific sums to every specific purpose susceptible of definition; by disallowing all applications of money varying from the appropriation in object or transcending it in amount; by reducing the undefined field of contingencies and thereby circumscribing discretionary powers over money, and by bringing back to a single department all accountabilities for money, where the examinations may be prompt, efficacious, and uniform.

An account of the receipts and expenditures of the last year, as prepared by the Secretary of the Treasury, will, as usual, be laid before you. The success which has attended the late sales of the public lands shews that with attention they may be made an important source of receipt. Among the payments those made in discharge of the principal and interest of the national debt will shew that the public faith has been exactly maintained. To these will be added an estimate of appropriations necessary for the ensuing year. This last will, of course, be affected by such modifications of the system of expense as you shall think proper to adopt.

A statement has been formed by the Secretary of War, on mature consideration, of all the posts and stations where garrisons will be expedient and of the number of men requisite for each garrison. The whole amount is considerably short of the present military establishment. For the surplus no particular use can be pointed out. For defense against invasion their number is as nothing, nor is it conceived needful or safe that a standing army should be kept up in time of peace for that purpose. Uncertain as we must ever be of the particular point in our circumference where an enemy may choose to invade us, the only force which can be ready at every point and competent to oppose them is the body of neighboring citizens as formed into a militia. On these, collected from the parts most convenient in numbers proportioned to the invading force, it is best to rely not only to meet the first attack, but if it threatens to be permanent to maintain the defense until regulars may be engaged to relieve them. These considerations render it important that we should at every session continue to amend the defects which from time to time shew themselves in the laws for regulating the militia until they are sufficiently perfect. Nor should we now or at any time separate until we can say we have done everything for the militia which we could do were an enemy at our door.

The provision of military stores on hand will be laid before you, that you may judge of the additions still requisite.

With respect to the extent to which our naval preparations should be carried some difference of opinion may be expected to appear, but just attention to the circumstances of every part of the Union will doubtless reconcile all. A small force will probably continue to be wanted for actual service in the Mediterranean. Whatever annual sum beyond that you may think proper to appropriate to naval preparations would perhaps be better employed in providing those articles which may be kept without waste or consumption, and be in readiness when any exigence calls them into use. Progress has been made, as will appear by papers now communicated, in providing materials for 74-gun ships as directed by law.

How far the authority given by the Legislature for procuring and establishing sites for naval purposes has been perfectly understood and pursued in the execution admits of some doubt. A statement of the expenses already incurred on that subject is now laid before you. I have in certain cases suspended or slackened these expenditures, that the Legislature might determine whether so many yards are necessary as have been contemplated. The works at this place are among those permitted to go on, and five of the seven frigates directed to be laid up have been brought and laid up here, where, besides the safety of their position, they are under the eye of the Executive Administration, as well as of its agents, where yourselves also will be guided by your own view in the legislative provisions respecting them which may from time to time be necessary. They are preserved in such condition, as well the vessels as whatever belongs to them, as to be at all times ready for sea on a short warning. Two others are yet to be laid up so soon as they shall have received the repairs requisite to put them also into sound condition. As a superintending officer will be necessary at each yard, his duties and emoluments, hitherto fixed by the Executive, will be a more proper subject for legislation. A communication will also be made of our progress in the execution of the law respecting the vessels directed to be sold.

The fortifications of our harbors, more or less advanced, present considerations of great difficulty. While some of them are on a scale sufficiently proportioned to the advantages of their position, to the efficacy of their protection, and the importance of the points within it, others are so extensive, will cost so much in their first erection, so much in their maintenance, and require such a force to garrison them as to make it questionable what is best now to be done. A statement of those commenced or projected, of the expenses already incurred, and estimates of their future cost, as far as can be foreseen, shall be laid before you, that you may be enabled to judge whether any alteration is necessary in the laws respecting this subject. Agriculture, manufactures, commerce, and navigation, the four pillars of our prosperity, are then most thriving when left most free to individual enterprise. Protection from casual embarrassments, however, may sometimes be seasonably interposed. If in the course of your observations or inquiries they should appear to need any aid within the limits of our constitutional powers, your sense of their importance is a sufficient assurance they will occupy your attention. We can not, indeed, but all feel an anxious solicitude for the difficulties under which our carrying trade will soon be placed. How far it can be relieved, otherwise than by time, is a subject of important consideration.

The judiciary system of the United States, and especially that portion of it recently erected, will of course present itself to the contemplation of Congress, and, that they may be able to judge of the proportion which the institution bears to the business it has to perform, I have caused to be procured from the several States and now lay before Congress an exact statement of all the causes decided since the first establishment of the courts, and of those which were depending when additional courts and judges were brought in to their aid.

And while on the judiciary organization it will be worthy your consideration whether the protection of the inestimable institution of juries has been extended to all the cases involving the security of our persons and property. Their impartial selection also being essential to their value, we ought further to consider whether that is sufficiently secured in those States where they are named by a marshal depending on Executive will or designated by the court or by officers dependent on them.

I can not omit recommending a revisal of the laws on the subject of naturalization. Considering the ordinary chances of human life, a denial of citizenship under a residence of fourteen years is a denial to a great proportion of those who ask it, and controls a policy pursued from their first settlement by many of these States, and still believed of consequence to their prosperity; and shall we refuse to the unhappy fugitives from distress that hospitality which the savages of the wilderness extended to our fathers arriving in this land? Shall oppressed humanity find no asylum on this globe? The Constitution indeed has wisely provided that for admission to certain offices of important trust a residence shall be required sufficient to develop character and design. But might not the general character and capabilities of a citizen be safely communicated to every-one manifesting a bona fide purpose of embarking his life and fortunes permanently with us, with restrictions, perhaps, to guard against the fraudulent usurpation of our flag, an abuse which brings so much embarrassment and loss on the genuine citizen and so much danger to the nation of being involved in war that no endeavor should be spared to detect and suppress it?

These, fellow-citizens, are the matters respecting the state of the nation which I have thought of importance to be submitted to your consideration at this time. Some others of less moment or not yet ready for communication will be the subject of separate messages. I am happy in this opportunity of committing the arduous affairs of our Government to the collected wisdom of the Union. Nothing shall be wanting on my part to inform as far as in my power the legislative judgment, nor to carry that judgment into faithful execution. The prudence and temperance of your discussions will promote within your own walls that conciliation which so much befriends rational conclusion, and by its example will encourage among our constituents that progress of opinion which is tending to unite them in object and in will. That all should be satisfied with any one order of things is not to be expected; but I indulge the pleasing persuasion that the great body of our citizens will cordially concur in honest and disinterested efforts which have for their object to preserve the General and State Governments in their constitutional form and equilibrium; to maintain peace abroad, and order and obedience to the laws at home; to establish principles and practices of administration favorable to the security of liberty and property, and to reduce expenses to what is necessary for the useful purposes of Government.

SECOND ANNUAL MESSAGE
DECEMBER 15, 1802

To the Senate and House of Representatives of the United States: When we assemble together, fellow-citizens, to consider the state of our beloved country, our just attentions are first drawn to those pleasing circumstances which mark the goodness of that Being from whose favor they flow and the large measure of thankfulness we owe for His bounty. Another year has come around, and finds us still blessed with peace and friendship abroad; law, order, and religion at home; good affection and harmony with our Indian neighbors; our burthens lightened, yet our income sufficient for the public wants, and the produce of the year great beyond example. These, fellow-citizens, are the circumstances under which we meet, and we remark with special satisfaction those which under the smiles of Providence result from the skill, industry, and order of our citizens, managing their own affairs in their own way and for their own use, unembarrassed by too much regulation, unoppressed by fiscal exactions.

On the restoration of peace in Europe that portion of the general carrying trade which had fallen to our share during the war was abridged by the returning competition of the belligerent powers. This was to be expected, and was just. But in addition we find in some parts of Europe monopolizing discriminations, which in the form of duties tend effectually to prohibit the carrying thither our own produce in our own vessels. From existing amities and a spirit of justice it is hoped that friendly discussion will produce a fair and adequate reciprocity. But should false calculations of interest defeat our hope, it rests with the Legislature to decide whether they will meet inequalities abroad with countervailing inequalities at home, or provide for the evil in any other way.

It is with satisfaction I lay before you an act of the British Parliament anticipating this subject so far as to authorize a mutual abolition of the duties and countervailing duties permitted under the treaty of 1794. It shows on their part a spirit of justice and friendly accommodation which it is our duty and our interest to cultivate with all nations. Whether this would produce a due equality in the navigation between the two countries is a subject for your consideration.

Another circumstance which claims attention as directly affecting the very source of our navigation is the defect or the evasion of the law providing for the return of seamen, and particularly of those belonging to vessels sold abroad. Numbers of them, discharged in foreign ports, have been thrown on the hands of our consuls, who, to rescue them from the dangers into which their distresses might plunge them and save them to their country, have found it necessary in some cases to return them at the public charge.

The cession of the Spanish Province of Louisiana to France, which took place in the course of the late war, will, if carried into effect, make a change in the aspect of our foreign relations which will doubtless have just weight in any deliberations of the Legislature connected with that subject.

There was reason not long since to apprehend that the warfare in which we were engaged with Tripoli might be taken up by some other of the Barbary Powers. A reenforcement, therefore, was immediately ordered to the vessels already there. Subsequent information, however, has removed these apprehensions for the present. To secure our commerce in that sea with the smallest force competent, we have supposed it best to watch strictly the harbor of Tripoli. Still, however, the shallowness of their coast and the want of smaller vessels on our part has permitted some cruisers to escape unobserved, and to one of these an American vessel unfortunately fell a prey. The captain, one American seaman, and two others of color remain prisoners with them unless exchanged under an agreement formerly made with the Bashaw, to whom, on the faith of that, some of his captive subjects have been restored.

The convention with the State of Georgia has been ratified by their legislature, and a repurchase from the Creeks has been consequently made of a part of the Talasscee country. In this purchase has been also comprehended a part of the lands within the fork of Oconee and Oakmulgee rivers. The particulars of the contract will be laid before Congress so soon as they shall be in a state of communication. In order to remove every ground of difference possible with our Indian neighbors, I have proceeded in the work of settling with them and marking the boundaries between us. That with the Choctaw Nation is fixed in one part and will be through the whole within a short time. The country to which their title had been extinguished before the Revolution is sufficient to receive a very respectable population, which Congress will probably see the expediency of encouraging so soon as the limits shall be declared. We are to view this position as an outpost of the United States, surrounded by strong neighbors and distant from its support; and how far that monopoly which prevents population should here be guarded against and actual habitation made a condition of the continuance of title will be for your consideration. A prompt settlement, too, of all existing rights and claims within this territory presents itself as a preliminary operation.

In that part of the Indiana Territory which includes Vincennes the lines settled with the neighboring tribes fix the extinction of their title at a breadth of 24 leagues from east to west and about the same length parallel with and including the Wabash. They have also ceded a tract of 4 miles square, including the salt springs near the mouth of that river.

In the Department of Finance it is with pleasure I inform you that the receipts of external duties for the last twelve months have exceeded those of any former year, and that the ratio of increase has been also greater than usual. This has enabled us to answer all the regular exigencies of Government, to pay from the Treasury within one year upward of $8,000,000, principal and interest, of the public debt, exclusive of upward of one million paid by the sale of bank stock, and making in the whole a reduction of nearly five millions and a half of principal, and to have now in the Treasury $4,500,000, which are in a course of application to the further discharge of debt and current demands. Experience, too, so far, authorizes us to believe, if no extraordinary event supervenes, and the expenses which will be actually incurred shall not be greater than were contemplated by Congress at their last session, that we shall not be disappointed in the expectations then formed. But nevertheless, as the effect of peace on the amount of duties is not yet fully ascertained, it is the more necessary to practice every useful economy and to incur no expense which may be avoided without prejudice.

The collection of the internal taxes having been completed in some of the States, the officers employed in it are of course out of commission. In others they will be so shortly. But in a few, where the arrangements for the direct tax had been retarded, it will be some time before the system is closed. It has not yet been thought necessary to employ the agent authorized by an act of the last session for transacting business in Europe relative to debts and loans. Nor have we used the power confided by the same act of prolonging the foreign debt by reloans, and of redeeming instead thereof an equal sum of the domestic debt. Should, however, the difficulties of remittance on so large a scale render it necessary at any time, the power shall be executed and the money thus unemployed abroad shall, in conformity with that law, be faithfully applied here in an equivalent extinction of domestic debt. When effects so salutary result from the plans you have already sanctioned; when merely by avoiding false objects of expense we are able, without a direct tax, without internal taxes, and without borrowing to make large and effectual payments toward the discharge of our public debt and the emancipation of our posterity from that mortal canker, it is an encouragement, fellow-citizens, of the highest order to proceed as we have begun in substituting economy for taxation, and in pursuing what is useful for a nation placed as we are, rather than what is practiced by others under different circumstances. And whensoever we are destined to meet events which shall call forth all the energies of our countrymen, we have the firmest reliance on those energies and the comfort of leaving for calls like these the extraordinary resources of loans and internal taxes. In the meantime, by payments of the principal of our debt, we are liberating annually portions of the external taxes and forming from them a growing fund still further to lessen the necessity of recurring to extraordinary resources.

The usual account of receipts and expenditures for the last year, with an estimate of the expenses of the ensuing one, will be laid before you by the Secretary of the Treasury.

No change being deemed necessary in our military establishment, an estimate of its expenses for the ensuing year on its present footing, as also of the sums to be employed in fortifications and other objects within that department, has been prepared by the Secretary of War, and will make a part of the general estimates which will be presented you.

Considering that our regular troops are employed for local purposes, and that the militia is our general reliance for great and sudden emergencies, you will doubtless think this institution worthy of a review, and give it those improvements of which you find it susceptible.

Estimates for the Naval Department, prepared by the Secretary of the Navy, for another year will in like manner be communicated with the general estimates. A small force in the Mediterranean will still be necessary to restrain the Tripoline cruisers, and the uncertain tenure of peace with some other of the Barbary Powers may eventually require that force to be augmented. The necessity of procuring some smaller vessels for that service will raise the estimate, but the difference in their maintenance will soon make it a measure of economy.

Presuming it will be deemed expedient to expend annually a convenient sum toward providing the naval defense which our situation may require, I can not but recommend that the first appropriations for that purpose may go to the saving what we already possess. No cares, no attentions, can preserve vessels from rapid decay which lie in water and exposed to the sun. These decays require great and constant repairs, and will consume, if continued, a great portion of the moneys destined to naval purposes. To avoid this waste of resources it is proposed to add to our navy-yard here a dock within which our present vessels may be laid up dry and under cover from the sun. Under these circumstances experience proves that works of wood will remain scarcely at all affected by time. The great abundance of running water which this situation possesses, at heights far above the level of the tide, if employed as is practiced for lock navigation, furnishes the means for raising and laying up our vessels on a dry and sheltered bed. And should the measure be found useful here, similar depositories for laying up as well as for building and repairing vessels may hereafter be undertaken at other navy-yards offering the same means. The plans and estimates of the work, prepared by a person of skill and experience, will be presented to you without delay, and from this it will be seen that scarcely more than has been the cost of one vessel is necessary to save the whole, and that the annual sum to be employed toward its completion may be adapted to the views of the Legislature as to naval expenditure.

To cultivate peace and maintain commerce and navigation in all their lawful enterprises; to foster our fisheries as nurseries of navigation and for the nurture of man, and protect the manufactures adapted to our circumstances; to preserve the faith of the nation by an exact discharge of its debts and contracts, expend the public money with the same care and economy we would practice with our own, and impose on our citizens no unnecessary burthens; to keep in all things within the pale of our constitutional powers, and cherish the federal union as the only rock of safety - these, fellow-citizens, are the landmarks by which we are to guide ourselves in all our proceedings. By continuing to make these the rule of our action we shall endear to our countrymen the true principles of their Constitution and promote an union of sentiment and of action equally auspicious to their happiness and safety. On my part, you may count on a cordial concurrence in every measure for the public good and on all the information I possess which may enable you to discharge to advantage the high functions with which you are invested by your country.

THIRD ANNUAL MESSAGE
OCTOBER 17, 1803

To the Senate and House of Representatives of the United States: In calling you together, fellow-citizens, at an earlier day than was contemplated by the act of the last session of Congress, I have not been insensible to the personal inconveniences necessarily resulting from an unexpected change in your arrangements. But matters of great public concernment have rendered this call necessary, and the interests you feel in these will supersede in your minds all private considerations.

Congress witnessed at their late session the extraordinary agitation produced in the public mind by the suspension of our right of deposit at the port of New Orleans, no assignment of another place having been made according to treaty. They were sensible that the continuance of that privation would be more injurious to our nation than any consequences which could flow from any mode of redress, but reposing just confidence in the good faith of the Government whose officer had committed the wrong, friendly and reasonable representations were resorted to, and the right of deposit was restored.

Previous, however, to this period we had not been unaware of the danger to which our peace would be perpetually exposed whilst so important a key to the commerce of the Western country remained under foreign power. Difficulties, too, were presenting themselves as to the navigation of other streams which, arising within our territories, pass through those adjacent. Propositions had therefore been authorized for obtaining on fair conditions the sovereignty of New Orleans and of other possessions in that quarter interesting to our quiet to such extent as was deemed practicable, and the provisional appropriation of $2,000,000 to be applied and accounted for by the President of the United States, intended as part of the price, was considered as conveying the sanction of Congress to the acquisition proposed. The enlightened Government of France saw with just discernment the importance to both nations of such liberal arrangements as might best and permanently promote the peace, friendship, and interests of both, and the property and sovereignty of all Louisiana which had been restored to them have on certain conditions been transferred to the United States by instruments bearing date the 30th of April last. When these shall have received the constitutional sanction of the Senate, they will without delay be communicated to the Representatives also for the exercise of their functions as to those conditions which are within the powers vested by the Constitution in Congress.

Whilst the property and sovereignty of the Mississippi and its waters secure an independent outlet for the produce of the Western States and an uncontrolled navigation through their whole course, free from collision with other powers and the dangers to our peace from that source, the fertility of the country, its climate and extent, promise in due season important aids to our Treasury, an ample provision for our posterity, and a wide spread for the blessings of freedom and equal laws.

With the wisdom of Congress it will rest to take those ulterior measures which may be necessary for the immediate occupation and temporary government of the country; for its incorporation into our Union; for rendering the change of government a blessing to our newly adopted brethren; for securing to them the rights of conscience and of property; for confirming to the Indian inhabitants their occupancy and self-government, establishing friendly and commercial relations with them, and for ascertaining the geography of the country acquired. Such materials, for your information, relative to its affairs in general as the short space of time has permitted me to collect will be laid before you when the subject shall be in a state for your consideration.

Another important acquisition of territory has also been made since the last session of Congress. The friendly tribe of Kaskaskia Indians, with which we have never had a difference, reduced by the wars and wants of savage life to a few individuals unable to defend themselves against the neighboring tribes, has transferred its country to the United States, reserving only for its members what is sufficient to maintain them in an agricultural way. The considerations stipulated are that we shall extend to them our patronage and protection and give them certain annual aids in money, in implements of agriculture, and other articles of their choice. This country, among the most fertile within our limits, extending along the Mississippi from the mouth of the Illinois to and up the Ohio, though not so necessary as a barrier since the acquisition of the other bank, may yet be well worthy of being laid open to immediate settlement, as its inhabitants may descend with rapidity in support of the lower country should future circumstances expose that to foreign enterprise. As the stipulations in this treaty also involve matters within the competence of both Houses only, it will be laid before Congress as soon as the Senate shall have advised its ratification.

With many of the other Indian tribes improvements in agriculture and household manufacture are advancing, and with all our peace and friendship are established on grounds much firmer than heretofore. The measure adopted of establishing trading houses among them and of furnishing them necessaries in exchange for their commodities at such moderate prices as leave no gain, but cover us from loss, has the most conciliatory and useful effect on them, and is that which will best secure their peace and good will.

The small vessels authorized by Congress with a view to the Mediterranean service have been sent into that sea, and will be able more effectually to confine the Tripoline cruisers within their harbors and supersede the necessity of convoy to our commerce in that quarter. They will sensibly lessen the expenses of that service the ensuing year.

A further knowledge of the ground in the northeastern and northwestern angles of the United States has evinced that the boundaries established by the treaty of Paris between the British territories and ours in those parts were too imperfectly described to be susceptible of execution. It has therefore been thought worthy of attention for preserving and cherishing the harmony and useful intercourse subsisting between the two nations to remove by timely arrangements what unfavorable incidents might otherwise render a ground of future misunderstanding. A convention has therefore been entered into which provides for a practicable demarcation of those limits to the satisfaction of both parties.

An account of the receipts and expenditures of the year ending the 30th of September last, with the estimates for the service of the ensuing year, will be laid before you by the Secretary of the Treasury so soon as the receipts of the last quarter shall be returned from the more distant States. It is already ascertained that the amount paid into the Treasury for that year has been between $11,000,000 and $12,000,000, and that the revenue accrued during the same term exceeds the sum counted on as sufficient for our current expenses and to extinguish the public debt within the period heretofore proposed.

The amount of debt paid for the same year is about $3,100,000, exclusive of interest, and making, with the payment of the preceding year, a discharge of more than $8,500,000 of the principal of that debt, besides the accruing interest; and there remain in the Treasury nearly $6,000,000. Of these, $880,000 have been reserved for payment of the first installment due under the British convention of January 8, 1802, and two millions are what have been before mentioned as placed by Congress under the power and accountability of the President toward the price of New Orleans and other territories acquired, which, remaining untouched, are still applicable to that object and go in diminution of the sum to be funded for it.

Should the acquisition of Louisiana be constitutionally confirmed and carried into effect, a sum of nearly $13,000,000 will then be added to our public debt, most of which is payable after fifteen years, before which term the present existing debts will all be discharged by the established operation of the sinking fund. When we contemplate the ordinary annual augmentation of impost from increasing population and wealth, the augmentation of the same revenue by its extension to the new acquisition, and the economies which may still be introduced into our public expenditures, I can not but hope that Congress in reviewing their resources will find means to meet the intermediate interest of this additional debt without recurring to new taxes, and applying to this object only the ordinary progression of our revenue. Its extraordinary increase in times of foreign war will be the proper and sufficient fund for any measures of safety or precaution which that state of things may render necessary in our neutral position.

Remittances for the installments of our foreign debt having been found practicable without loss, it has not been thought expedient to use the power given by a former act of Congress of continuing them by reloans, and of redeeming instead thereof equal sums of domestic debt, although no difficulty was found in obtaining that accommodation.

The sum of $50,000 appropriated by Congress for providing gunboats remains unexpended. The favorable and peaceable turn of affairs on the Mississippi rendered an immediate execution of that law unnecessary, and time was desirable in order that the institution of that branch of our force might begin on models the most approved by experience. The same issue of events dispensed with a resort to the appropriation of $1,500,000, contemplated for purposes which were effected by happier means.

We have seen with sincere concern the flames of war lighted up again in Europe, and nations with which we have the most friendly and useful relations engaged in mutual destruction. While we regret the miseries in which we see others involved, let us bow with gratitude to that kind Providence which, inspiring with wisdom and moderation our late legislative councils while placed under the urgency of the greatest wrongs guarded us from hastily entering into the sanguinary contest and left us only to look on and to pity its ravages. These will be heaviest on those immediately engaged. Yet the nations pursuing peace will not be exempt from all evil. In the course of this conflict let it be our endeavor, as it is our interest and desire, to cultivate the friendship of the belligerent nations by every act of justice and of innocent kindness; to receive their armed vessels with hospitality from the distresses of the sea, but to administer the means of annoyance to none; to establish in our harbors such a police as may maintain law and order; to restrain our citizens from embarking individually in a war in which their country takes no part; to punish severely those persons, citizen or alien, who shall usurp the cover of our flag for vessels not entitled to it, infecting thereby with suspicion those of real Americans and committing us into controversies for the redress of wrongs not our own; to exact from every nation the observance toward our vessels and citizens of those principles and practices which all civilized people acknowledge; to merit the character of a just nation, and maintain that of an independent one, preferring every consequence to insult and habitual wrong. Congress will consider whether the existing laws enable us efficaciously to maintain this course with our citizens in all places and with others while within the limits of our jurisdiction, and will give them the new modifications necessary for these objects. Some contraventions of right have already taken place, both within our jurisdictional limits and on the high seas. The friendly disposition of the Governments from whose agents they have proceeded, as well as their wisdom and regard for justice, leave us in reasonable expectation that they will be rectified and prevented in future, and that no act will be countenanced by them which threatens to disturb our friendly intercourse. Separated by a wide ocean from the nations of Europe and from the political interests which entangle them together, with productions and wants which render our commerce and friendship useful to them and theirs to us, it can not be the interest of any to assail us, nor ours to disturb them. We should be most unwise, indeed, were we to cast away the singular blessings of the position in which nature has placed us, the opportunity she has endowed us with of pursuing, at a distance from foreign contentions, the paths of industry, peace, and happiness, of cultivating general friendship, and of bringing collisions of interest to the umpirage of reason rather than of force. How desirable, then, must it be in a Government like ours to see its citizens adopt individually the views, the interests, and the conduct which their country should pursue, divesting themselves of those passions and partialities which tend to lessen useful friendships and to embarrass and embroil us in the calamitous scenes of Europe. Confident, fellow-citizens, that you will duly estimate the importance of neutral dispositions toward the observance of neutral conduct, that you will be sensible how much it is our duty to look on the bloody arena spread before us with commiseration indeed, but with no other wish than to see it closed, I am persuaded you will cordially cherish these dispositions in all discussions among yourselves and in all communications with your constituents; and I anticipate with satisfaction the measures of wisdom which the great interests now committed to you will give *you* an opportunity of providing, and *myself* that of approving and of carrying into execution with the fidelity I owe to my country.

FOURTH ANNUAL MESSAGE
NOVEMBER 8, 1804

To the Senate and House of Representatives of the United States: To a people, fellow-citizens, who sincerely desire the happiness and prosperity of other nations; to those who justly calculate that their own well-being is advanced by that of the nations with which they have intercourse, it will be a satisfaction to observe that the war which was lighted up in Europe a little before our last meeting has not yet extended its flames to other nations, nor been marked by the calamities which sometimes stain the footsteps of war. The irregularities, too, on the ocean, which generally harass the commerce of neutral nations, have, in distant parts, disturbed ours less than on former occasions; but in the American seas they have been greater from peculiar causes, and even within our harbors and jurisdiction infringements on the authority of the laws have been committed which have called for serious attention. The friendly conduct of the Governments from whose officers and subjects these acts have proceeded, in other respects and in places more under their observation and control, gives us confidence that our representations on this subject will have been properly regarded.

While noticing the irregularities committed on the ocean by others, those on our own part should not be omitted nor left unprovided for. Complaints have been received that persons residing within the United States have taken on themselves to arm merchant vessels and to force a commerce into certain ports and countries in defiance of the laws of those countries. That individuals should undertake to wage private war, independently of the authority of their country, can not be permitted in a well-ordered society. Its tendency to produce aggression

on the laws and rights of other nations and to endanger
the peace of our own is so obvious that I doubt not you
will adopt measures for restraining it effectually in
future.

Soon after the passage of the act of the last session
authorizing the establishment of a district and port of
entry on the waters of the Mobile we learnt that its object
was misunderstood on the part of Spain.   Candid
explanations were immediately given and assurances that,
reserving our claims in that quarter as a subject of
discussion and arrangement with Spain, no act was
mediated in the meantime inconsistent with the peace and
friendship existing between the two nations, and that
conformably to these intentions would be the execution of
the law.   That Government had, however, thought proper
to suspend the ratification of the convention of 1802; but
the explanations which would reach them soon after, and
still more the confirmation of them by the tenor of the
instrument establishing the port and district, may
reasonably be expected to replace them in the dispositions
and views of the whole subject which originally dictated
the convention.

I have the satisfaction to inform you that the objections
which had been urged by that Government against the
validity of our title to the country of Louisiana have been
withdrawn, its exact limits, however, remaining still to be
settled between us; and to this is to be added that, having
prepared and delivered the stock created in execution of
the convention of Paris of April 30, 1803, in
consideration of the cession of that country, we have
received from the Government of France an
acknowledgment, in due form, of the fulfillment of that
stipulation.

With the nations of Europe in general our friendship and intercourse are undisturbed, and from the Governments of the belligerent powers especially we continue to receive those friendly manifestations which are justly due to an honest neutrality and to such good offices consistent with that as we have opportunities of rendering.

The activity and success of the small force employed in the Mediterranean in the early part of the present year, the reenforcements sent into that sea, and the energy of the officers having command in the several vessels will, I trust, by the sufferings of war, reduce the barbarians of Tripoli to the desire of peace on proper terms. Great injury, however, ensues to ourselves, as well as to others interested, from the distance to which prizes must be brought for adjudication and from the impracticability of bringing hither such as are not seaworthy.

The Bey of Tunis having made requisitions unauthorized by our treaty, their rejection has produced from him some expressions of discontent. But to those who expect us to calculate whether a compliance with unjust demands will not cost us less than a war we must leave as a question of calculation for them also whether to retire from unjust demands will not cost them less than a war. We can do to each other very sensible injuries by war, but the mutual advantages of peace make that the best interest of both.

Peace and intercourse with the other powers on the same coast continue on the footing on which they are established by treaty.

In pursuance of the act providing for the temporary government of Louisiana, the necessary officers for the Territory of Orleans were appointed in due time to commence the exercise of their functions on the 1st day of October. The distance, however, of some of them and indispensable previous arrangements may have retarded its commencement in some of its parts. The form of government thus provided having been considered but as temporary, and open to such future improvements as further information of the circumstances of our brethren there might suggest, it will of course be subject to your consideration.

In the district of Louisiana it has been thought best to adopt the division into subordinate districts which had been established under its former government. These being five in number, a commanding officer has been appointed to each, according to the provisions of the law, and so soon as they can be at their stations that district will also be in its due state of organization. In the meantime their places are supplied by the officers before commanding there. And the functions of the governor and judges of Indiana having commenced, the government, we presume, is proceeding in its new form. The lead mines in that district offer so rich a supply of that metal as to merit attention. The report now communicated will inform you of their state and of the necessity of immediate inquiry into their occupation and titles.

With the Indian tribes established within our newly acquired limits, I have deemed it necessary to open conferences for the purpose of establishing a good understanding and neighborly relations between us. So far as we have yet learned, we have reason to believe that their dispositions are generally favorable and friendly; and with these dispositions on their part, we have in our own hands means which can not fail us for preserving their peace and friendship. By pursuing an uniform course of justice toward them, by aiding them in all the improvements which may better their condition, and especially by establishing a commerce on terms which shall be advantageous to them and only not losing to us, and so regulated as that no incendiaries of our own or any other nation may be permitted to disturb the natural effects of our just and friendly offices, we may render ourselves so necessary to their comfort and prosperity that the protection of our citizens from their disorderly members will become their interest and their voluntary care. Instead, therefore, of an augmentation of military force proportioned to our extension of frontier, I propose a moderate enlargement of the capital employed in that commerce as a more effectual, economical, and humane instrument for preserving peace and good neighborhood with them.

On this side the Mississippi an important relinquishment of native title has been received from the Delawares. That tribe, desiring to extinguish in their people the spirit of hunting and to convert superfluous lands into the means of improving what they retain, has ceded to us all the country between the Wabash and Ohio south of and including the road from the rapids toward Vincennes, for which they are to receive annuities in animals and implements for agriculture and in other necessaries. This acquisition is important, not only for its extent and fertility, but as fronting 300 miles on the Ohio, and near half that on the Wabash. The produce of the settled country descending those rivers will no longer pass in review of the Indian frontier but in a small portion, and, with the cession heretofore made by the Kaskaskias, nearly consolidates our possessions north of the Ohio, in a very respectable breadth - from Lake Erie to the Mississippi. The Piankeshaws having some claim to the country ceded by the Delawares, it has been thought best to quiet that by fair purchase also. So soon as the treaties on this subject shall have received their constitutional sanctions they shall be laid before both Houses.

The act of Congress of February 28, 1803, for building and employing a number of gunboats, is now in a course of execution to the extent there provided for. The obstacle to naval enterprise which vessels of this construction offer for our seaport towns, their utility toward supporting within our waters the authority of the laws, the promptness with which they will be manned by the seamen and militia of the place in the moment they are wanting, the facility of their assembling from different parts of the coast to any point where they are required in greater force than ordinary, the economy of their maintenance and preservation from decay when not in actual service, and the competence of our finances to this defensive provision without any new burthen are considerations which will have due weight with Congress in deciding on the expediency of adding to their number from year to year, as experience shall test their utility, until all our important harbors, by these and auxiliary means, shall be secured against insult and opposition to the laws.

No circumstance has arisen since your last session which calls for any augmentation of our regular military force. Should any improvement occur in the militia system, that will be always seasonable.

Accounts of the receipts and expenditures of the last year, with estimates for the ensuing one, will as usual be laid before you.

The state of our finances continues to fulfill our expectations. Eleven millions and a half of dollars, received in the course of the year ending the 30th of September last, have enabled us, after meeting all the ordinary expenses of the year, to pay upward of $3,600,000 of the public debt, exclusive of interest. This payment, with those of the two preceding years, has extinguished upward of twelve millions of the principal and a greater sum of interest within that period, and by a proportionate diminution of interest renders already sensible the effect of the growing sum yearly applicable to the discharge of the principal.

It is also ascertained that the revenue accrued during the last year exceeds that of the preceding, and the probable receipts of the ensuing year may safely be relied on as sufficient, with the sum already in the Treasury, to meet all the current demands of the year, to discharge upward of three millions and a half of the engagements incurred under the British and French conventions, and to advance in the further redemption of the funded debt as rapidly as had been contemplated. These, fellow-citizens, are the principal matters which I have thought it necessary at this time to communicate for your consideration and attention. Some others will be laid before you in the course of the session; but in the discharge of the great duties confided to you by our country you will take a broader view of the field of legislation. Whether the great interests of agriculture, manufactures, commerce, or navigation can within the pale of your constitutional powers be aided in any of their relations; whether laws are provided in all cases where they are wanting; whether those provided are exactly what they should be; whether any abuses take place in their administration, or in that of the public revenues; whether the organization of the public agents or of the public force is perfect in all its parts; in fine, whether anything can be done to advance the general good, are questions within the limits of your functions which will necessarily occupy your attention. In these and all other matters which you in your wisdom may propose for the good of our country you may count with assurance on my hearty cooperation and faithful execution.

SECOND INAUGURAL ADDRESS
MARCH 4, 1805

Proceeding, fellow-citizens, to that qualification which the Constitution requires before my entrance on the charge again conferred on me, it is my duty to express the deep sense I entertain of this new proof of confidence from my fellow-citizens at large, and the zeal with which it inspires me so to conduct myself as may best satisfy their just expectations.

On taking this station on a former occasion I declared the principles on which I believed it my duty to administer the affairs of our Commonwealth. My conscience tells me I have on every occasion acted up to that declaration according to its obvious import and to the understanding of every candid mind.

In the transaction of your foreign affairs we have endeavored to cultivate the friendship of all nations, and especially of those with which we have the most important relations. We have done them justice on all occasions, favored where favor was lawful, and cherished mutual interests and intercourse on fair and equal terms. We are firmly convinced, and we act on that conviction, that with nations as with individuals our interests soundly calculated will ever be found inseparable from our moral duties, and history bears witness to the fact that a just nation is trusted on its word when recourse is had to armaments and wars to bridle others.

At home, fellow-citizens, you best know whether we have done well or ill. The suppression of unnecessary offices, of useless establishments and expenses, enabled us to discontinue our internal taxes. These, covering our land with officers and opening our doors to their intrusions, had already begun that process of domiciliary vexation which once entered is scarcely to be restrained from reaching successively every article of property and produce. If among these taxes some minor ones fell which had not been inconvenient, it was because their amount would not have paid the officers who collected them, and because, if they had any merit, the State authorities might adopt them instead of others less approved.

The remaining revenue on the consumption of foreign articles is paid chiefly by those who can afford to add foreign luxuries to domestic comforts, being collected on our seaboard and frontiers only, and, incorporated with the transactions of our mercantile citizens, it may be the pleasure and the pride of an American to ask, What farmer, what mechanic, what laborer ever sees a taxgatherer of the United States? These contributions enable us to support the current expenses of the Government, to fulfill contracts with foreign nations, to extinguish the native right of soil within our limits, to extend those limits, and to apply such a surplus to our public debts as places at a short day their final redemption, and that redemption once effected the revenue thereby liberated may, by a just reparation of it among the States and a corresponding amendment of the Constitution, be applied *in time of peace* to rivers, canals, roads, arts, manufactures, education, and other great objects within each State. *In time of war*, if injustice by ourselves or others must sometimes produce war, increased as the same revenue will be by increased population and consumption, and aided by other resources reserved for that crisis, it may meet within the year all the expenses of the year without encroaching on the rights of future generations by burthening them with the debts of the past. War will then be but a suspension of useful works, and a return to a state of peace a return to the progress of improvement.

I have said, fellow-citizens, that the income reserved had enabled us to extend our limits, but that extension may possibly pay for itself before we are called on, and in the meantime may keep down the accruing interest; in all events, it will replace the advances we shall have made. I know that the acquisition of Louisiana has been disapproved by some from a candid apprehension that the enlargement of our territory would endanger its union. But who can limit the extent to which the federative principle may operate effectively? The larger our association the less will it be shaken by local passions; and in any view is it not better that the opposite bank of the Mississippi should be settled by our own brethren and children than by strangers of another family? With which should we be most likely to live in harmony and friendly intercourse?

In matters of religion I have considered that its free exercise is placed by the Constitution independent of the powers of the General Government. I have therefore undertaken on no occasion to prescribe the religious exercises suited to it, but have left them, as the Constitution found them, under the direction and discipline of the church or state authorities acknowledged by the several religious societies.

The aboriginal inhabitants of these countries I have regarded with the commiseration their history inspires. Endowed with the faculties and the rights of men, breathing an ardent love of liberty and independence, and occupying a country which left them no desire but to be undisturbed, the stream of overflowing population from other regions directed itself on these shores; without power to divert or habits to contend against it, they have been overwhelmed by the current or driven before it; now reduced within limits too narrow for the hunter's state, humanity enjoins us to teach them agriculture and the domestic arts; to encourage them to that industry which alone can enable them to maintain their place in existence and to prepare them in time for that state of society which to bodily comforts adds the improvement of the mind and morals. We have therefore liberally furnished them with the implements of husbandry and household use; we have placed among them instructors in the arts of first necessity, and they are covered with the aegis of the law against aggressors from among ourselves.

But the endeavors to enlighten them on the fate which awaits their present course of life, to induce them to exercise their reason, follow its dictates, and change their pursuits with the change of circumstances have powerful obstacles to encounter; they are combated by the habits of their bodies, prejudices of their minds, ignorance, pride, and the influence of interested and crafty individuals among them who feel themselves something in the present order of things and fear to become nothing in any other. These persons inculcate a sanctimonious reverence for the customs of their ancestors; that whatsoever they did must be done through all time; that reason is a false guide, and to advance under its counsel in their physical, moral, or political condition is perilous innovation; that their duty is to remain as their Creator made them, ignorance being safety and knowledge full of danger; in short, my friends, among them also is seen the action and counteraction of good sense and of bigotry; they too have their antiphilosophists who find an interest in keeping things in their present state, who dread reformation, and exert all their faculties to maintain the ascendency of habit over the duty of improving our reason and obeying its mandates.

In giving these outlines I do not mean, fellow-citizens, to arrogate to myself the merit of the measures. That is due, in the first place, to the reflecting character of our citizens at large, who, by the weight of public opinion, influence and strengthen the public measures. It is due to the sound discretion with which they select from among themselves those to whom they confide the legislative duties. It is due to the zeal and wisdom of the characters thus selected, who lay the foundations of public happiness in wholesome laws, the execution of which alone remains for others, and it is due to the able and faithful auxiliaries, whose patriotism has associated them with me in the executive functions.

During this course of administration, and in order to disturb it, the artillery of the press has been leveled against us, charged with whatsoever its licentiousness could devise or dare. These abuses of an institution so important to freedom and science are deeply to be regretted, inasmuch as they tend to lessen its usefulness and to sap its safety. They might, indeed, have been corrected by the wholesome punishments reserved to and provided by the laws of the several States against falsehood and defamation, but public duties more urgent press on the time of public servants, and the offenders have therefore been left to find their punishment in the public indignation.

Nor was it uninteresting to the world that an experiment should be fairly and fully made, whether freedom of discussion, unaided by power, is not sufficient for the propagation and protection of truth - whether a government conducting itself in the true spirit of its constitution, with zeal and purity, and doing no act which it would be unwilling the whole world should witness, can be written down by falsehood and defamation. The experiment has been tried; you have witnessed the scene; our fellow-citizens looked on, cool and collected; they saw the latent source from which these outrages proceeded; they gathered around their public functionaries, and when the Constitution called them to the decision by suffrage, they pronounced their verdict, honorable to those who had served them and consolatory to the friend of man who believes that he may be trusted with the control of his own affairs.

No inference is here intended that the laws provided by the States against false and defamatory publications should not be enforced; he who has time renders a service to public morals and public tranquillity in reforming these abuses by the salutary coercions of the law; but the experiment is noted to prove that, since truth and reason have maintained their ground against false opinions in league with false facts, the press, confined to truth, needs no other legal restraint; the public judgment will correct false reasonings and opinions on a full hearing of all parties; and no other definite line can be drawn between the inestimable liberty of the press and its demoralizing licentiousness. If there be still improprieties which this rule would not restrain, its supplement must be sought in the censorship of public opinion.

Contemplating the union of sentiment now manifested so generally as auguring harmony and happiness to our future course, I offer to our country sincere congratulations. With those, too, not yet rallied to the same point the disposition to do so is gaining strength; facts are piercing through the veil drawn over them, and our doubting brethren will at length see that the mass of their fellow-citizens with whom they can not yet resolve to act as to principles and measures, think as they think and desire what they desire; that our wish as well as theirs is that the public efforts may be directed honestly to the public good, that peace be cultivated, civil and religious liberty unassailed, law and order preserved, equality of rights maintained, and that state of property, equal or unequal, which results to every man from his own industry or that of his father's. When satisfied of these views it is not in human nature that they should not approve and support them. In the meantime let us cherish them with patient affection, let us do them justice, and more than justice, in all competitions of interest, and we need not doubt that truth, reason, and their own interests will at length prevail, will gather them into the fold of their country, and will complete that entire union of opinion which gives to a nation the blessing of harmony and the benefit of all its strength.

I shall now enter on the duties to which my fellow-citizens have again called me, and shall proceed in the spirit of those principles which they have approved. I fear not that any motives of interest may lead me astray; I am sensible of no passion which could seduce me knowingly from the path of justice, but the weaknesses of human nature and the limits of my own understanding will produce errors of judgment sometimes injurious to your interests. I shall need, therefore, all the indulgence which I have heretofore experienced from my constituents; the want of it will certainly not lessen with increasing years. I shall need, too, the favor of that Being in whose hands we are, who led our fathers, as Israel of old, from their native land and planted them in a country flowing with all the necessaries and comforts of life; who has covered our infancy with His providence and our riper years with His wisdom and power, and to whose goodness I ask you to join in supplications with me that He will so enlighten the minds of your servants, guide their councils, and prosper their measures that whatsoever they do shall result in your good, and shall secure to you the peace, friendship, and approbation of all nations.

FIFTH ANNUAL MESSAGE
DECEMBER 3, 1805

To the Senate and House of Representatives of the United States: At a moment when the nations of Europe are in commotion and arming against each other, and when those with whom we have principal intercourse are engaged in the general contest, and when the countenance of some of them toward our peaceable country threatens that even that may not be unaffected by what is passing on the general theater, a meeting of the representatives of the nation in both Houses of Congress has become more than usually desirable. Coming from every section of our country, they bring with them the sentiments and the information of the whole, and will be enabled to give a direction to the public affairs which the will and the wisdom of the whole will approve and support.

In taking a view of the state of our country we in the first place notice the late affliction of two of our cities under the fatal fever which in latter times has occasionally visited our shores. Providence in His goodness gave it an early termination on this occasion and lessened the number of victims which have usually fallen before it. In the course of the several visitations by this disease it has appeared that it is strictly local, incident to cities and on the tide waters only, incommunicable in the country either by persons under the disease or by goods carried from diseased places; that its access is with the autumn and it disappears with the early frosts. These restrictions within narrow limits of time and space give security even to our maritime cities during three-fourths of the year, and to the country always. Although from these facts it appears unnecessary, yet to satisfy the fears of foreign nations and cautions on their part not to be complained of in a danger whose limits are yet unknown to them I have strictly enjoined on the officers at the head of the customs to certify with exact truth for every vessel sailing for a foreign port the state of health respecting this fever which prevails at the place from which she sails. Under every motive from character and duty to certify the truth, I have no doubt they have faithfully executed this injunction. Much real injury has, however, been sustained from a propensity to identify with this endemic and to call by the same name fevers of very different kinds, which have been known at all times and in all countries, and never have been placed among those deemed contagious. As we advance in our knowledge of this disease, as facts develop the source from which individuals receive it, the State authorities charged with the care of the public health, and Congress with that of the general commerce, will become able to regulate with effect their respective functions in these departments. The burthen of quarantines is felt at home as well as abroad; their efficacy merits examination. Although the health laws of the States should be found to need no present revisal by Congress, yet commerce claims that their attention be ever awake to them.

Since our last meeting the aspect of our foreign relations has considerably changed. Our coasts have been infested and our harbors watched by private armed vessels, some of them without commissions, some with illegal commissions, others with those of legal form, but committing piratical acts beyond the authority of their commissions. They have captured in the very entrance of our harbors, as well as on the high seas, not only the vessels of our friends coming to trade with us, but our own also. They have carried them off under pretense of legal adjudication, but not daring to approach a court of justice, they have plundered and sunk them by the way or in obscure places where no evidence could arise against them, maltreated the crews, and abandoned them in boats in the open sea or on desert shores without food or covering. These enormities appearing to be unreached by any control of their sovereigns, I found it necessary to equip a force to cruise within our own seas, to arrest all vessels of these descriptions found hovering on our coasts within the limits of the Gulf Stream and to bring the offenders in for trial as pirates.

The same system of hovering on our coasts and harbors under color of seeking enemies has been also carried on by public armed ships to the great annoyance and oppression of our commerce. New principles, too, have been interpolated into the law of nations, founded neither in justice nor the usage or acknowledgment of nations. According to these a belligerent takes to itself a commerce with its own enemy which it denies to a neutral on the ground of its aiding that enemy in the war; but reason revolts at such an inconsistency, and the neutral having equal right with the belligerent to decide the question, the interests of our constituents and the duty of maintaining the authority of reason, the only umpire between just nations, impose on us the obligation of providing an effectual and determined opposition to a doctrine so injurious to the rights of peaceable nations. Indeed, the confidence we ought to have in the justice of others still countenances the hope that a sounder view of those rights will of itself induce from every belligerent a more correct observance of them.

With Spain our negotiations for a settlement of differences have not had a satisfactory issue. Spoliations during a former war, for which she had formally acknowledged herself responsible, have been refused to be compensated but on conditions affecting other claims in no wise connected with them. Yet the same practices are renewed in the present war and are already of great amount. On the Mobile, our commerce passing through that river continues to be obstructed by arbitrary duties and vexatious searches. Propositions for adjusting amicably the boundaries of Louisiana have not been acceded to. While, however, the right is unsettled, we have avoided changing the state of things by taking new posts or strengthening ourselves in the disputed territories, in the hope that the other power would not by a contrary conduct oblige us to meet their example and endanger conflicts of authority the issue of which may not be easily controlled. But in this hope we have now reason to lessen our confidence. Inroads have been recently made into the Territories of Orleans and the Mississippi, our citizens have been seized and their property plundered in the very parts of the former which had been actually delivered up by Spain, and this by the regular officers and soldiers of that Government. I have therefore found it necessary at length to give orders to our troops on that frontier to be in readiness to protect our citizens, and to repel by arms any similar aggressions in future. Other details necessary for your full information of the state of things between this country and that shall be the subject of another communication.

In reviewing these injuries from some of the belligerent powers the moderation, the firmness, and the wisdom of the Legislature will all be called into action. We ought still to hope that time and a more correct estimate of interest as well as of character will produce the justice we are bound to expect. But should any nation deceive itself by false calculations, and disappoint that expectation, we

must join in the unprofitable contest of trying which
party can do the other the most harm. Some of these
injuries may perhaps admit a peaceable remedy. Where
that is competent it is always the most desirable. But
some of them are of a nature to be met by force only, and
all of them may lead to it. I can not, therefore, but
recommend such preparations as circumstances call for.
The first object is to place our seaport towns out of the
danger of insult. Measures have been already taken for
furnishing them with heavy cannon for the service of
such land batteries as may make a part of their defense
against armed vessels approaching them. In aid of these it
is desirable we should have a competent number of
gunboats, and the number, to be competent, must be
considerable. If immediately begun, they may be in
readiness for service at the opening of the next season.
Whether it will be necessary to augment our land forces
will be decided by occurrences probably in the course of
your session. In the meantime you will consider whether
it would not be expedient for a state of peace as well as of
war so to organize or class the militia as would enable us
on any sudden emergency to call for the services of the
younger portions, unencumbered with the old and those
having families. Upward of 300,000 able-bodied men
between the ages of 18 and 26 years, which the last census
shews we may now count within our limits, will furnish a
competent number of offense or defense in any point
where they may be wanted, and will give time for raising
regular forces after the necessity of them shall become
certain; and the reducing to the early period of life all its
active service can not but be desirable to our younger
citizens of the present as well as future times, inasmuch as
it engages to them in more advanced age a quiet and
undisturbed repose in the bosom of their families. I can
not, then, but earnestly recommend to your early

consideration the expediency of so modifying our militia system as, by a separation of the more active part from that which is less so, we may draw from it when necessary an efficient corps fit for real and active service, and to be called to it in regular rotation.

Considerable provision has been made under former authorities from Congress of materials for the construction of ships of war of 74 guns. These materials are on hand subject to the further will of the Legislature.

An immediate prohibition of the exportation of arms and ammunition is also submitted to your determination.

Turning from these unpleasant views of violence and wrong, I congratulate you on the liberation of our fellow-citizens who were stranded on the coast of Tripoli and made prisoners of war. In a government bottomed on the will of all the life and liberty of every individual citizen become interesting to all. In the treaty,therefore, which has concluded our warfare with that State an article for the ransom of our citizens has been agreed to. An operation by land by a small band of our countrymen and others, engaged for the occasion in conjunction with the troops of the ex-Bashaw of that country, gallantly conducted by our late consul, Eaton, and their successful enterprise on the city of Derne, contributed doubtless to the impression which produced peace, and the conclusion of this prevented opportunities of which the officers and men of our squadron destined for Tripoli would have availed themselves to emulate the acts of valor exhibited by their brethren in the attack of the last year. Reflecting with high satisfaction on the distinguished bravery displayed whenever occasions permitted in the late Mediterranean service, I think it would be an useful encouragement as well as a just reward to make an opening for some present promotion by enlarging our peace establishment of captains and lieutenants.

With Tunis some misunderstandings have arisen not yet sufficiently explained, but friendly discussions with their ambassador recently arrived and a mutual disposition to do whatever is just and reasonable can not fail of dissipating these, so that we may consider our peace on that coast, generally, to be on as sound a footing as it has been at any preceding time. Still, it will not be expedient to withdraw immediately the whole of our force from that sea.

The law providing for a naval peace establishment fixes the number of frigates which shall be kept in constant service in time of peace, and prescribes that they shall be manned by not more than two-thirds of their complement of seamen and ordinary seaman. Whether a frigate may be trusted to two-thirds only of her proper complement of men must depend on the nature of the service on which she is ordered; that may sometimes, for her safety as well as to insure her object, require her fullest complement. In adverting to this subject Congress will perhaps consider whether the best limitation on the Executive discretion in this case would not be by the number of seamen which may be employed in the whole service rather than by the number of the vessels. Occasions oftener arise for the employment of small than of large vessels, and it would lessen risk as well as expense to be authorized to employ them of preference. The limitation suggested by the number of seamen would admit a selection of vessels best adapted to the service.

Our Indian neighbors are advancing, many of them with spirit, and others beginning to engage in the pursuits of agriculture and household manufacture. They are becoming sensible that the earth yields subsistence with less labor and more certainty than the forest, and find it their interest from time to time to dispose of parts of their surplus and waste lands for the means of improving those they occupy and of subsisting their families while they are preparing their farms. Since your last session the Northern tribes have sold to us the lands between the Connecticut Reserve and the former Indian boundary and those on the Ohio from the same boundary to the rapids and for a considerable depth inland. The Chickasaws and Cherokees have sold us the country between and adjacent to the two districts of Tennessee, and the Creeks the residue of their lands in the fork of Ocmulgee up to the Ulcofauhatche. The three former purchases are important, inasmuch as they consolidate disjoined parts of our settled country and render their intercourse secure; and the second particularly so, as, with the small point on the river which we expect is by this time ceded by the Piankeshaws, it completes our possession of the whole of both banks of the Ohio from its source to near its mouth, and the navigation of that river is thereby rendered forever safe to our citizens settled and settling on its extensive waters. The purchase from the Creeks, too, has been for some time particularly interesting to the State of Georgia.

The several treaties which have been mentioned will be submitted to both Houses of Congress for the exercise of their respective functions.

Deputations now on their way to the seat of Government from various nations of Indians inhabiting the Missouri and other parts beyond the Mississippi come charged with assurances of their satisfaction with the new relations in which they are placed with us, of their dispositions to cultivate our peace and friendship, and their desire to enter into commercial intercourse with us. A state of our progress in exploring the principal rivers of that country, and of the information respecting them hitherto obtained, will be communicated so soon as we shall receive some further relations which we have reason shortly to expect.

The receipts at the Treasury during the year ending on the 30th day of September last have exceeded the sum of $13,000,000, which, with not quite five millions in the Treasury at the beginning of the year, have enabled us after meeting other demands to pay nearly two millions of the debt contracted under the British treaty and convention, upward of four millions of principal of the public debt, and four millions of interest. These payments, with those which had been made in three years and a half preceding, have extinguished of the funded debt nearly eighteen millions of principal. Congress by their act of November 10, 1803, authorized us to borrow $1,750,000 toward meeting the claims of our citizens assumed by the convention with France. We have not, however, made use of this authority, because the sum of four millions and a half, which remained in the Treasury on the same 30th day of September last, with the receipts which we may calculate on for the ensuing year, besides paying the annual sum of $8,000,000 appropriated to the funded debt and meeting all the current demands which may be expected, will enable us to pay the whole sum of $3,750,000 assumed by the French convention and still leave us a surplus of nearly $1,000,000 at our free disposal. Should you concur in the provisions of arms and armed vessels recommended by the circumstances of the times, this surplus will furnish the means of doing so.

On this first occasion of addressing Congress since, by the choice of my constituents, I have entered on a second term of administration, I embrace the opportunity to give this public assurance that I will exert my best endeavors to administer faithfully the executive department, and will zealously cooperate with you in every measure which may tend to secure the liberty, property, and personal safety of our fellow-citizens, and to consolidate the republican forms and principles of our Government.

In the course of your session you shall receive all the aid which I can give for the dispatch of public business, and all the information necessary for your deliberations, of which the interests of our own country and the confidence reposed in us by others will admit a communication.

SIXTH ANNUAL MESSAGE
DECEMBER 2, 1806

To the Senate and House of Representatives of the United States of America in Congress assembled: It would have given me, fellow-citizens, great satisfaction to announce in the moment of your meeting that the difficulties in our foreign relations existing at the time of your last separation had been amicably and justly terminated. I lost no time in taking those measures which were most likely to bring them to such a termination - by special missions charged with such powers and instructions as in the event of failure could leave no imputation on either our moderation or forbearance. The delays which have since taken place in our negotiations with the British Government appear to have proceeded from causes which do not forbid the expectation that during the course of the session I may be enabled to lay before you their final issue. What will be that of the negotiations for settling our differences with Spain nothing which had taken place at the date of the last dispatches enables us to pronounce. On the western side of the Mississippi she advanced in considerable force, and took post at the settlement of Bayou Pierre, on the Red River. This village was originally settled by France, was held by her as long as she held Louisiana, and was delivered to Spain only as a part of Louisiana. Being small, insulated, and distant, it was not observed at the moment of redelivery to France and the United States that she continued a guard of half a dozen men which had been stationed there. A proposition, however, having been lately made by our commander in chief to assume the Sabine River as a temporary line of separation between the troops of the two nations until the issue of our negotiations shall be known, this has been referred by the Spanish commandant to this superior, and in the meantime he has withdrawn his force to the western side of the Sabine River. The correspondence on this subject now communicated will exhibit more particularly the present state of things in that quarter.

The nature of that country requires indispensably that an unusual proportion of the force employed there should be cavalry or mounted infantry. In order, therefore, that the commanding officer might be enabled to act with effect, I had authorized him to call on the governors of Orleans and Mississippi for a corps of 500 volunteer cavalry. The temporary arrangement he has proposed may perhaps render this unnecessary; but I inform you with great pleasure of the promptitude with which the inhabitants of those Territories have tendered their services in defense of their country. It has done honor to themselves, entitled them to the confidence of their fellow-citizens in every part of the Union, and must strengthen the general determination to protect them efficaciously under all circumstances which may occur.

Having received information that in another part of the United States a great number of private individuals were combining together, arming and organizing themselves contrary to law, to carry on a military expedition against the territories of Spain, I thought it necessary, by proclamation as well as by special orders, to take measures for preventing and suppressing this enterprise, for seizing the vessels, arms, and other means provided for it, and for arresting and bringing to justice to its authors and abettors. It was due to that good faith which ought ever to be the rule of action in public as well as in private transactions, it was due to good order and regular government, that while the public force was acting strictly on the defensive and merely to protect our citizens from aggression the criminal attempts of private individuals to decide for their country the question of peace or war by commencing active and unauthorized hostilities should be promptly and efficaciously suppressed.

Whether it will be necessary to enlarge our regular force will depend on the result of our negotiations with Spain; but as it is uncertain where that result will be known, the provisional measures requisite for that, and to meet any pressure intervening in that quarter, will be a subject for your early consideration.

The possession of both banks of the Mississippi reducing to a single point the defense of that river, its waters, and the country adjacent, it becomes highly necessary to provide for that point a more adequate security. Some position above its mouth, commanding the passage of the river, should be rendered sufficiently strong to cover the armed vessels which may be stationed there for defense, and in conjunction with them to present an insuperable obstacle to any force attempting to pass. The approaches to the city of New Orleans from the eastern quarter also will require to be examined and more effectually guarded. For the internal support of the country the encouragement of a strong settlement on the western side of the Mississippi, within reach of New Orleans, will be worthy the consideration of the Legislature.

The gunboats authorized by an act of the last session are so advanced that they will be ready for service in the ensuing spring. Circumstances permitted us to allow the time necessary for their more solid construction. As a much larger number will still be wanting to place our seaport towns and waters in that state of defense to which

we are competent and they entitled, a similar
appropriation for a further provision for them is
recommended for the ensuing year.

A further appropriation will also be necessary for
repairing fortifications already established and the
erection of such other works as may have real effect in
obstructing the approach of an enemy to our seaport
towns, or their remaining before them.

In a country whose constitutions derived from the will of
the people, directly expressed by their free suffrages;
where the principal executive functionaries and those of
the legislature are renewed by them at short periods;
where under the character of jurors they exercise in
person the greatest portion of the judiciary powers; where
the laws are consequently so formed and administered as
to bear with equal weight and favor on all, restraining no
man in the pursuits of honest industry and securing to
everyone the property which that acquires, it would not
be supposed that any safeguards could be needed against
insurrection or enterprise on the public peace or
authority. The laws, however, aware that these should not
be trusted to moral restraints only, have wisely provided
punishment for these crimes when committed. But would
it not be salutary to give also the means of preventing
their commission? Where an enterprise is meditated by
private individuals against a foreign nation in amity with
the United States, powers of prevention to a certain extent
are given by the laws. Would they not be as reasonable
and useful where the enterprise preparing is against the
United States? While adverting to this branch of law it is
proper to observe that in enterprises mediated against
foreign nations the ordinary process of binding to the
observance of the peace and good behaviour, could it be

extended to acts to be done out of the jurisdiction of the United States, would be effectual in some cases where the offender is able to keep out of sight every indication of his purpose which could draw on him the exercise of the powers now given by law.

The States on the coast of Barbary seem generally disposed at present to respect our peace and friendship; with Tunis alone some uncertainty remains. Persuaded that it is our interest to maintain our peace with them on equal terms or not at all, I propose to send in due time a reenforcement into the Mediterranean unless previous information shall shew it to be unnecessary.

We continue to receive proofs of the growing attachment of our Indian neighbors and of their disposition to place all their interests under the patronage of the United States. These dispositions are inspired by their confidence in our justice and in the sincere concern we feel for their welfare; and as long as we discharge these high and honorable functions with the integrity and good faith which alone can entitle us to their continuance we may expect to reap the just reward in their peace and friendship.

The expedition of Messrs. Lewis and Clarke for exploring the river Missouri and the best communication from that to the Pacific Ocean has had all the success which could have been expected. They have traced the Missouri nearly to its source, descended the Columbia to the Pacific Ocean, ascertained with accuracy the geography of that interesting communication across our continent, learnt the character of the country, of its commerce and inhabitants; and it is but justice to say that Messrs. Lewis and Clarke and their brave companions have by this arduous service deserved well of their country.

The attempt to explore the Red River, under the direction of Mr. Freeman, though conducted with a zeal and prudence meriting entire approbation, has not been equally successful. After proceeding up it about 600 miles, nearly as far as the French settlements had extended while the country was in their possession, our geographers were obliged to return without completing their work. Very useful additions have also been made to our knowledge of the Mississippi by Lieutenant Pike, who has ascended it to its source, and whose journal and map, giving the details of his journey, will shortly be ready for communication to both Houses of Congress. Those of Messrs. Lewis, Clarke, and Freeman will require further time to be digested and prepared. These important surveys, in addition to those before possessed, furnish materials for commencing an accurate map of the Mississippi and its western waters. Some principal rivers, however, remain still to be explored, toward which the authorization of Congress by moderate appropriations will be requisite.

I congratulate you, fellow-citizens, on the approach of the period at which you may interpose your authority constitutionally to withdraw the citizens of the United States from all further participation in those violations of human rights which have been so long continued on the unoffending inhabitants of Africa, and which the morality, the reputation, and the best interests of our country have long been eager to proscribe. Although no law you may pass can take prohibitory effect till the first day of the year 1808, yet the intervening period is not too long to prevent by timely notice expeditions which can not be completed before that day.

The receipts at the Treasury during the year ending on the 30th day of September last have amounted to near $15,000,000, which have enabled us, after meeting the current demands, to pay $2,700,000 of the American claims in part of the price of Louisiana; to pay of the funded debt upward of three millions of principal and nearly four of interest, and, in addition, to reimburse in the course of the present month near two millions of 5-1/2 per cent stock. These payments and reimbursements of the funded debt, with those which had been made in the four years and a half preceding, will at the close of the present year have extinguished upward of twenty-three millions of principal.

The duties composing the Mediterranean fund will cease by law at the end of the present session. Considering, however, that they are levied chiefly on luxuries and that we have an impost on salt, a necessary of life, the free use of which otherwise is so important, I recommend to your consideration the suppression of the duties on salt and the continuation of the Mediterranean fund instead thereof for a short time, after which that also will become unnecessary for any purpose now within contemplation.

When both of these branches of revenue shall in this way be relinquished there will still ere long be an accumulation of moneys in the Treasury beyond the installments of public debt which we are permitted by contract to pay. They can not then, without a modification assented to by the public creditors, be applied to the extinguishment of this debt and the complete liberation of our revenues, the most desirable of

all objects. Nor, if our peace continues, will they be
wanting for any other existing purpose. The question
therefore now comes forward, To what other objects shall
these surpluses be appropriated, and the whole surplus of
impost, after the entire discharge of the public debt, and
during those intervals when the purposes of war shall not
call for them? Shall we suppress the impost and give that
advantage to foreign over domestic manufactures? On a
few articles of more general and necessary use the
suppression in due season will doubtless be right, but the
great mass of the articles on which impost is paid are
foreign luxuries, purchased by those only who are rich
enough to afford themselves the use of them. Their
patriotism would certainly prefer its continuance and
application to the great purposes of the public education,
roads, rivers, canals, and such other objects of public
improvement as it may be thought proper to add to the
constitutional enumeration of Federal powers. By these
operations new channels of communication will be opened
between the States, the lines of separation will disappear,
their interests will be identified, and their union cemented
by new and indissoluble ties. Education is here placed
among the articles of public care, not that it would be
proposed to take its ordinary branches out of the hands of
private enterprise, which manages so much better all the
concerns to which it is equal, but a public institution can
alone supply those sciences which though rarely called for
are yet necessary to complete the circle, all the parts of
which contribute to the improvement of the country and
some of them to its preservation. The subject is now
proposed for the consideration of Congress, because if
approved by the time the State legislatures shall have
deliberated on this extension of the Federal trusts, and the
laws shall be passed and other arrangements made for
their execution, the necessary funds will be on hand and

without employment. I suppose an amendment to the Constitution, by consent of the States, necessary, because the objects now recommended are not among those enumerated in the Constitution, and to which it permits the public moneys to be applied.

The present consideration of a national establishment for education particularly is rendered proper by this circumstance also, that if Congress, approving the proposition, shall yet think it more eligible to found it on a donation of lands, they have it now in their power to endow it with those which will be among the earliest to produce the necessary income. This foundation would have the advantage of being independent of war, which may suspend other improvements by requiring for its own purposes the resources destined for them.

This, fellow-citizens, is the state of the public interests at the present moment and according to the information now possessed. But such is the situation of the nations of Europe and such, too, the predicament in which we stand with some of them that we can not rely with certainty on the present aspect of our affairs, that may change from moment to moment during the course of your session or after you shall have separated. Our duty is, therefore, to act upon things as they are and to make a reasonable provision for whatever they may be. Were armies to be raised whenever a speck of war is visible in our horizon, we never should have been without them. Our resources would have been exhausted on dangers which have never happened, instead of being reserved for what is really to take place. A steady, perhaps a quickened, pace in preparations for the defense of our seaport towns and waters; an early settlement of the most exposed and vulnerable parts of our country; a militia so organized that its effective portions can be called to any point in the Union, or volunteers instead of them to serve a sufficient time, are means which may always be ready, yet never preying on our resources until actually called into use. They will maintain the public interests while a more permanent force shall be in course of preparation. But much will depend on the promptitude with which these means can be brought into activity. If war be forced upon us, in spite of our long and vain appeals to the justice of nations, rapid and vigorous movements in its outset will go far toward securing us in its course and issue, and toward throwing its burthens on those who render necessary the resort from reason to force.

The result of our negotiations, or such incidents in their course as may enable us to infer their probable issue; such further movements also on our western frontiers as may shew whether war is to be pressed there while negotiation is protracted elsewhere, shall be communicated to you from time to time as they become known to me, with whatever other information I possess or may receive, which may aid your deliberations on the great national interests committed to your charge.

SEVENTH ANNUAL MESSAGE
OCTOBER 27, 1807

To the Senate and House of Representatives of the United States: Circumstances, fellow-citizens, which seriously threatened the peace of our country have made it a duty to convene you at an earlier period than usual. The love of peace so much cherished in the bosoms of our citizens, which has so long guided the proceedings of their public councils and induced forbearance under so many wrongs, may not insure our continuance in the quiet pursuits of industry. The many injuries and depredations committed on our commerce and navigation upon the high seas for years past, the successive innovations on those principles of public law which have been established by the reason and usage of nations as the rule of their intercourse and the umpire and security of their rights and peace, and all the circumstances which induced the extraordinary mission to London are already known to you. The instructions given to our ministers were framed in the sincerest spirit of amity and moderation. They accordingly proceeded, in conformity therewith, to propose arrangements which might embrace and settle all the points in difference between us, which might bring us to a mutual understanding on our neutral and national rights and provide for a commercial intercourse on conditions of some equality. After long and fruitless endeavors to effect the purposes of their mission and to obtain arrangements within the limits of their instructions, they concluded to sign such as could be obtained and to send them for consideration, candidly declaring to the other negotiators at the same time that they were acting against their instructions, and that their Government, therefore, could not be pledged for ratification. Some of the articles proposed might have been admitted on a principle of compromise, but others were too highly disadvantageous, and no sufficient provision was made against the principal source of the irritations and collisions which were constantly endangering the peace of the two nations. The question, therefore, whether a treaty should be accepted in that form could have admitted but of one decision, even had no declarations of the other party impaired our confidence in it. Still anxious not to close the door against friendly adjustment, new modifications were framed and further concessions authorized than could before have been supposed necessary; and our ministers were instructed to resume their negotiations on these grounds. On this new reference to amicable discussion we were reposing in confidence, when on the 22d day of June last by a formal order from a British admiral the frigate *Chesapeake*, leaving her port for a distant service, was attacked by one of those vessels which had been lying in our harbors under the indulgences of hospitality, was disabled from proceeding, had several of her crew killed and four taken away. On this outrage no commentaries are necessary. Its character has been pronounced by the indignant voice of our citizens with an emphasis and unanimity never exceeded. I immediately, by proclamation, interdicted our harbors and waters to all British armed vessels, forbade intercourse with them, and uncertain how far hostilities were intended, and the town of Norfolk, indeed, being threatened with immediate attack, a sufficient force was ordered for the protection of that place, and such other preparations commenced and pursued as the prospect rendered proper. An armed vessel of the United States was dispatched with instructions to our ministers at London to call on that Government for the satisfaction and security required by the outrage. A very short interval ought now to bring the answer, which shall be communicated to you as soon as received; then also, or as soon after as the public interests shall be found to admit, the unratified treaty and proceedings relative to it shall be made known to you.

The aggression thus begun has been continued on the part of the British commanders by remaining within our waters in defiance of the authority of the country, by habitual violations of its jurisdiction, and at length by putting to death one of the persons whom they had forcibly taken from on board the *Chesapeake.* These aggravations necessarily lead to the polity either of never admitting an armed vessel into our harbors or of maintaining in every harbor such an armed force as may constrain obedience to the laws and protect the lives and property of our citizens against their armed guests; but the expense of such a standing force and its inconsistence with our principles dispense with those courtesies which would necessarily call for it, and leave us equally free to exclude the navy, as we are the army, of a foreign power from entering our limits.

To former violations of maritime rights another is now added of very extensive effect. The Government of that nation has issued an order interdicting all trade by neutrals between ports not in amity with them; and being now at war with nearly every nation on the Atlantic and Mediterranean seas, our vessels are required to sacrifice their cargoes at the first port they touch or to return home without the benefit of going to any other market. Under this new law of the ocean our trade on the Mediterranean has been swept away by seizures and condemnations, and that in other seas is threatened with the same fate.

Our differences with Spain remain still unsettled, no measure having been taken on her part since my last communications to Congress to bring them to a close. But under a state of things which may favor reconsideration they have been recently pressed, and an expectation is entertained that they may now soon be brought to an issue of some sort. With their subjects on our borders no new collisions have taken place nor seem immediately to be apprehended. To our former grounds of complaint has been added a very serious one, as you will see by the decree a copy of which is now communicated. Whether this decree, which professes to be conformable to that of the French Government of November 21, 1806, heretofore communicated to Congress, will also be conformed to that in its construction and application in relation to the United States had not been ascertained at the date of our last communications. These, however, gave reason to expect such a conformity.

With the other nations of Europe our harmony has been uninterrupted, and commerce and friendly intercourse have been maintained on their usual footing.

Our peace with the several states on the coast of Barbary appears as firm as at any former period and as likely to continue as that of any other nation.

Among our Indian neighbors in the northwestern quarter some fermentation was observed soon after the late occurrences, threatening the continuance of our peace. Messages were said to be interchanged and tokens to be passing, which usually denote a state of restlessness among them, and the character of the agitators pointed to the sources of excitement. Measures were immediately taken for providing against that danger; instructions were given to require explanations, and, with assurances of our continued friendship, to admonish the tribes to remain quiet at home, taking no part in quarrels not belonging to them. As far as we are yet informed, the tribes in our vicinity, who are most advanced in the pursuits of industry, are sincerely disposed to adhere to their friendship with us and to their peace with all others, while those more remote do not present appearances sufficiently quiet to justify the intermission of military precaution on our part.

The great tribes on our southwestern quarter, much advanced beyond the others in agriculture and household arts, appear tranquil and identifying their views with ours in proportion to their advancement. With the whole of these people, in every quarter, I shall continue to inculcate peace and friendship with all their neighbors and perseverance in those occupations and pursuits which will best promote their own well-being.

The appropriations of the last session for the defense of our seaport towns and harbors were made under expectation that a continuance of our peace would permit us to proceed in that work according to our convenience. It has been thought better to apply the sums then given toward the defense of New York, Charleston, and New Orleans chiefly, as most open and most likely first to need protection, and to leave places less immediately in danger to the provisions of the present session.

The gunboats, too, already provided have on a like principle been chiefly assigned to New York, New Orleans, and the Chesapeake. Whether our movable force on the water, so material in aid of the defensive works on the land, should be augmented in this or any other form is left to the wisdom of the Legislature. For the purpose of manning these vessels in sudden attacks on our harbors it is a matter for consideration whether the seamen of the United States may not justly be formed into a special militia, to be called on for tours of duty in defense of the harbors where they shall happen to be, the ordinary militia of the place furnishing that portion which may consist of landsmen.

The moment our peace was threatened I deemed it indispensable to secure a greater provision of those articles of military stores with which our magazines were not sufficiently furnished. To have awaited a previous and special sanction by law would have lost occasions which might not be retrieved. I did not hesitate, therefore, to authorize engagements for such supplements to our existing stock as would render it adequate to the emergencies threatening us, and I trust that the Legislature, feeling the same anxiety for the safety of our country, so materially advanced by this precaution, will approve, when done, what they would have seen so important to be done if then assembled. Expenses, also unprovided for, arose out of the necessity of calling all our gunboats into actual service for the defense of our harbors; of all which accounts will be laid before you.

Whether a regular army is to be raised, and to what extent, must depend on the information so shortly expected. In the meantime I have called on the States for quotas of militia, to be in readiness for present defense, and have, moreover, encouraged the acceptance of volunteers; and I am happy to inform you that these have offered themselves with great alacrity in every part of the Union. They are ordered to be organized and ready at a moment's warning to proceed on any service to which they may be called, and every preparation within the Executive powers has been made to insure us the benefit of early exertions.

I informed Congress at their last session of the enterprises against the public peace which were believed to be in preparation by Aaron Burr and his associates, of the measures taken to defeat them and to bring the offenders to justice. Their enterprises were happily defeated by the patriotic exertions of the militia whenever called into action, by the fidelity of the Army, and energy of the commander in chief in promptly arranging the difficulties presenting themselves on the Sabine, repairing to meet those arising on the Mississippi, and dissipating before their explosion plots engendering there. I shall think it my duty to lay before you the proceedings and the evidence publicly exhibited on the arraignment of the principal offenders before the circuit court of Virginia. You will be enabled to judge whether the defect was in the testimony, in the law, or in the administration of the law; and wherever it shall be found, the Legislature alone can apply or originate the remedy. The framers of our Constitution certainly supposed they had guarded as well their Government against destruction by treason as their citizens against oppression under pretense of it, and if these ends are not attained it is of importance to inquire by what means more effectual they may be secured.

The accounts of the receipts of revenue during the year ending on the 30th day of September last being not yet made up, a correct statement will be hereafter transmitted from the Treasury. In the meantime, it is ascertained that the receipts have amounted to near $16,000,000, which, with the five millions and a half in the Treasury at the beginning of the year, have enabled us, after meeting the current demands and interest incurred, to pay more than four millions of the principal of our funded debt. These payments,with those of the preceding five and a half years, have extinguished of the funded debt $25,500,000, being the whole which could be paid or purchased within the limits of the law and of our contracts, and have left us in the Treasury $8,500,000. A portion of this sum may be considered as a commencement of accumulation of the surpluses of revenue which, after paying the installments of debt as they shall become payable, will remain without any specific object. It may partly, indeed, be applied toward completing the defense of the exposed points of our country, on such a scale as shall be adapted to our principles and circumstances. This object is doubtless among the first entitled to attention in such a state of our finances, and it is one which, whether we have peace or war, will provide security where it is due. Whether what shall remain of this, with the future surpluses, may be usefully applied to purposes already authorized or more usefully to others requiring new authorities, or how otherwise they shall be disposed of, are questions calling for the notice of Congress, unless, indeed, they shall be superseded by a change in our public relations now awaiting the determination of others. Whatever be that determination, it is a great consolation that it will become known at a moment when the supreme council of the nation is assembled at its post, and ready to give the aids of its wisdom and authority to whatever course the good of our country shall then call us to pursue.

Matters of minor importance will be the subjects of future communications, and nothing shall be wanting on my part which may give information or dispatch to the proceedings of the Legislature in the exercise of their high duties, and at a moment so interesting to the public welfare.

EIGHTH ANNUAL MESSAGE
NOVEMBER 8, 1808

To the Senate and House of Representatives of the United States: It would have been a source, fellow-citizens, of much gratification if our last communications from Europe had enabled me to inform you that the belligerent nations, whose disregard of neutral rights has been so destructive to our commerce, had become awakened to the duty and true policy of revoking their unrighteous edicts. That no means might be omitted to produce this salutary effect, I lost no time in availing myself of the act authorizing a suspension, in whole or in part, of the several embargo laws. Our ministers at London and Paris were instructed to explain to the respective Governments there our disposition to exercise the authority in such manner as would withdraw the pretext on which the aggressions were originally founded and open the way for a renewal of that commercial intercourse which it was alleged on all sides had been reluctantly obstructed. As each of those Governments had pledged its readiness to concur in renouncing a measure which reached its adversary through the incontestable rights of neutrals only, and as the measure had been assumed by each as a retaliation for an asserted acquiescence in the aggressions of the other, it was reasonably expected that the occasion would have been seized by both for evincing the sincerity of their professions, and for restoring to the commerce of the United States its legitimate freedom. The instructions to our ministers with respect to the different belligerents were necessarily modified with a reference to their different circumstances, and to the condition annexed by law to the Executive power of suspension, requiring a decree of security to our commerce which would not result from a repeal of the decrees of France. Instead of a pledge, therefore, of a suspension of the embargo as to her in case of such a repeal, it was presumed that a sufficient inducement might be found in other considerations, and particularly in the change produced by a compliance with our just demands by one belligerent and a refusal by the other in the relations between the other and the United States. To Great Britain, whose power on the ocean is so ascendant, it was deemed not inconsistent with that condition to state explicitly that on her rescinding her orders in relation to the United States their trade would be opened with her, and remain shut to her enemy in case of his failure to rescind his decrees also. From France no answer has been received, nor any indication that the requisite change in her decrees is contemplated. The favorable reception of the proposition to Great Britain was the less to be doubted, as her orders of council had not only been referred for their vindication to an acquiescence on the part of the United States no longer to be pretended, but as the arrangement proposed, whilst it resisted the illegal decrees of France, involved, moreover, substantially the precise advantages professedly aimed at by the British orders. The arrangement has nevertheless been rejected.

This candid and liberal experiment having thus failed, and no other event having occurred on which a suspension of the embargo by the Executive was authorized, it necessarily remains in the extent originally given to it. We have the satisfaction, however, to reflect that in return for the privations imposed by the measure, and which our fellow-citizens in general have borne with patriotism, it has had the important effects of saving our mariners and our vast mercantile property, as well as of affording time for prosecuting the defensive and provisional measures called for by the occasion. It has demonstrated to foreign nations the moderation and firmness which govern our councils, and to our citizens the necessity of uniting in support of the laws and the rights of their country, and has thus long frustrated those usurpations and spoliations which, if resisted, involved war; if submitted to, sacrificed a vital principle of our national independence.

Under a continuance of the belligerent measures which, in defiance of laws which consecrate the rights of neutrals, overspread the ocean with danger, it will rest with the wisdom of Congress to decide on the course best adapted to such a state of things; and bringing with them, as they do, from every part of the Union the sentiments of our constituents, my confidence is strengthened that in forming this decision they will, with an unerring regard to the essential rights and interests of the nation, weigh and compare the painful alternatives out of which a choice is to be made. Nor should I do justice to the virtues which on other occasions have marked the character of our fellow-citizens if I did not cherish an equal confidence that the alternative chosen, whatever it may be, will be maintained with all the fortitude and patriotism which the crisis ought to inspire.

The documents containing the correspondences on the subject of the foreign edicts against our commerce, with the instructions given to our ministers at London and Paris, are now laid before you.

The communications made to Congress at their last session explained the posture in which the close of the discussions relating to the attack by a British ship of war on the frigate *Chesapeake* left a subject on which the nation had manifested so honorable a sensibility. Every view of what had passed authorized a belief that immediate steps would be taken by the British Government for redressing a wrong which the more it was investigated appeared the more clearly to require what had not been provided for in the special mission. It is found that no steps have been taken for the purpose. On the contrary, it will be seen in the documents laid before you that the inadmissible preliminary which obstructed the adjustment is still adhered to, and, moreover, that it is now brought into connection with the distinct and irrelative case of the orders in council. The instructions which had been given to our minister at London with a view to facilitate, if necessary, the reparation claimed by the United States are included in the documents communicated.

Our relations with the other powers of Europe have undergone no material changes since your last session. The important negotiations with Spain which had been alternately suspended and resumed necessarily experience a pause under the extraordinary and interesting crisis which distinguishes her internal situation.

With the Barbary Powers we continue in harmony, with the exception of an unjustifiable proceeding of the Dey of Algiers toward our consul to that Regency. Its character and circumstances are now laid before you, and will enable you to decide how far it may, either now or hereafter, call for any measures not within the limits of the Executive authority.

With our Indian neighbors the public peace has been steadily maintained. Some instances of individual wrong have, as at other times, taken place, but in no wise implicating the will of the nation. Beyond the Mississippi the Ioways, the Sacs, and the Alabamas have delivered up for trial and punishment individuals from among themselves accused of murdering citizens of the United States. On this side of the Mississippi the Creeks are exerting themselves to arrest offenders of the same kind, and the Choctaws have manifested their readiness and desire for amicable and just arrangements respecting depredations committed by disorderly persons of their tribe. And, generally, from a conviction that we consider them as a part of ourselves, and cherish with sincerity their rights and interests, the attachment of the Indian tribes is gaining strength daily - is extending from the nearer to the more remote, and will amply requite us for the justice and friendship practiced toward them. Husbandry and household manufacture are advancing among them more rapidly with the Southern than Northern tribes, from circumstances of soil and climate, and one of the two great divisions of the Cherokee Nation have now under consideration to solicit the citizenship of the United States, and to be identified with us in laws and government in such progressive manner as we shall think best.

In consequence of the appropriations of the last session of Congress for the security of our seaport towns and harbors, such works of defense have been erected as seemed to be called for by the situation of the several places, their relative importance, and the scale of expense indicated by the amount of the appropriation. These works will chiefly be finished in the course of the present season, except at New York and New Orleans, where most was to be done; and although a great proportion of the last appropriation has been expended on the former place, yet some further views will be submitted to Congress for rendering its security entirely adequate against naval enterprise. A view of what has been done at the several places, and of what is proposed to be done, shall be communicated as soon as the several reports are received.

Of the gunboats authorized by the act of December last, it has been thought necessary to build only 103 in the present year. These, with those before possessed, are sufficient for the harbors and waters most exposed, and the residue will require little time for their construction when it shall be deemed necessary.

Under the act of the last session for raising an additional military force so many officers were immediately appointed as were necessary for carrying on the business of recruiting, and in proportion as it advanced others have been added. We have reason to believe their success has been satisfactory, although such returns have not yet been received as enable me to present you a statement of the numbers engaged.

I have not thought it necessary in the course of the last season to call for any general detachments of militia or of volunteers under the laws passed for that purpose. For the ensuing season, however, they will be required to be in readiness should their service be wanted. Some small and special detachments have been necessary to maintain the laws of embargo on that portion of our northern frontier which offered peculiar facilities for evasion, but these were replaced as soon as it could be done by bodies of new recruits. By the aid of these and of the armed vessels called into service in other quarters the spirit of disobedience and abuse, which manifested itself early and with sensible effect while we were unprepared to meet it, has been considerably repressed.

Considering the extraordinary character of the times in which we live, our attention should unremittingly be fixed on the safety of our country. For a people who are free, and who mean to remain so, a well organized and armed militia is their best security. It is therefore incumbent on us at every meeting to revise the condition of the militia, and to ask ourselves if it is prepared to repel a powerful enemy at every point of our territories exposed to invasion. Some of the States have paid a laudable attention to this object, but every degree of neglect is to be found among others. Congress alone having the power to produce an uniform state of preparation in this great organ of defense, the interests which they so deeply feel in their own and their country's security will present this as among the most important objects of their deliberation.

Under the acts of March 11 and April 23 respecting arms, the difficulty of procuring them from abroad during the present situation and dispositions of Europe induced us to direct our whole efforts to the means of internal supply. The public factories have therefore been enlarged, additional machineries erected, and, in proportion as artificers can be found or formed, their effect, already more than doubled, may be increased so as to keep pace with the yearly increase of the militia. The annual sums appropriated by the latter act have been directed to the encouragement of private factories of arms, and contracts have been entered into with individual undertakers to nearly the amount of the first year's appropriation.

The suspension of our foreign commerce, produced by the injustice of the belligerent powers and the consequent losses and sacrifices of our citizens are subjects of just concern. The situation into which we have thus been forced has impelled us to apply a portion of our industry and capital to internal manufactures and improvements. The extent of this conversion is daily increasing, and little doubt remains that the establishments formed and forming will, under the auspices of cheaper materials and subsistence, the freedom of labor from taxation with us, and of protecting duties and prohibitions, become permanent. The commerce with the Indians, too, within our own boundaries is likely to receive abundant aliment from the same internal source, and will secure to them peace and the progress of civilization, undisturbed by practices hostile to both.

The accounts of the receipts and expenditures during the year ending the 30th of September last being not yet made up, a correct statement will hereafter be transmitted from the Treasury. In the meantime it is ascertained that the receipts have amounted to near $18,000,000, which, with the eight millions and a half in the Treasury at the beginning of the year, have enabled us, after meeting the current demands and interest incurred, to pay $2,300,000 of the principal of our funded debt, and left us in the Treasury on that day near $14,000,000. Of these, $5,350,000 will be necessary to pay what will be due on the 1st day of January next, which will complete the reimbursement of the 8 per cent stock. These payments, with those made in the six years and a half preceding, will have extinguished $33,580,000 of the principal of the funded debt, being the whole which could be paid or purchased within the limits of the law and of our contracts, and the amount of principal thus discharged will have liberated the revenue from about $2,000,000 of interest and added that sum annually to the disposable surplus. The probable accumulation of the surpluses of revenue beyond what can be applied to the payment of the public debt whenever the freedom and safety of our

commerce shall be restored merits the consideration of
Congress. Shall it lie unproductive in the public vaults?
Shall the revenue be reduced? Or shall it not rather be
appropriated to the improvements of roads, canals, rivers,
education, and other great foundations of prosperity and
union under the powers which Congress may already
possess or such amendment of the Constitution as may be
approved by the States? While uncertain of the course of
things, the time may be advantageously employed in
obtaining the powers necessary for a system of
improvement, should that be thought best.

Availing myself of this the last occasion which will occur
of addressing the two Houses of the Legislature at their
meeting, I can not omit the expression of my sincere
gratitude for the repeated proofs of confidence
manifested to me by themselves and their predecessors
since my call to the administration and the many
indulgences experienced at their hands. The same
grateful acknowledgements are due to my fellow-citizens
generally, whose support has been my great
encouragement under all embarrassments. In the
transaction of their business I can not have escaped error.
it is incident to our imperfect nature. But I may say with
truth my errors have been of the understanding, not of
intention, , and that the advancement of their rights and
interests has been the constant motive for every measure.
On these considerations I solicit their indulgence.
Looking forward with anxiety to their future destinies, I
trust that in their steady character, unshaken by
difficulties, in their love of liberty, obedience to law, and
support of the public authorities I see a sure guaranty of
the permanence of our Republic; and, retiring from the
charge of their affairs, I carry with me the consolation of

a firm persuasion that Heaven has in store for our beloved country long ages to come of prosperity and happiness.

THE AUTOBIOGRAPHY OF
THOMAS JEFFERSON

THE AUTOBIOGRAPHY OF
THOMAS JEFFERSON

January 6, 1821

At the age of 77, I begin to make some memoranda, and state some recollections of dates and facts concerning myself, for my own more ready reference, and for the information of my family.

The tradition in my father's family was, that their ancestor came to this country from Wales, and from near the mountain of Snowdon, the highest in Great Britain. I noted once a case from Wales, in the law reports, where a person of our name was either plaintiff or defendant; and one of the same name was secretary to the Virginia Company. These are the only instances in which I have met with the name in that country. I have found it in our early records; but the first particular information I have of any ancestor was of my grandfather, who lived at the place in Chesterfield called Ozborne's, and owned the lands afterwards the glebe of the parish. He had three sons; Thomas who died young, Field who settled on the waters of Roanoke and left numerous descendants, and Peter, my father, who settled on the lands I still own, called Shadwell, adjoining my present residence. He was born February 29, 1707-08, and intermarried 1739, with Jane Randolph, of the age of 19, daughter of Isham Randolph, one of the seven sons of that name and family settled at Dungeoness in Goochland. They trace their pedigree far back in England and Scotland, to which let every one ascribe the faith and merit he chooses.

My father's education had been quite neglected; but being of a strong mind, sound judgment, and eager after information, he read much and improved himself, insomuch that he was chosen, with Joshua Fry, Professor of Mathematics in William and Mary college, to continue the boundary line between Virginia and North Carolina, which had been begun by Colonel Byrd; and was afterwards employed with the same Mr. Fry, to make the first map of Virginia which had ever been made, that of Captain Smith being merely a conjectural sketch. They possessed excellent materials for so much of the country as is below the Blue Ridge; little being then known beyond that ridge. He was the third or fourth settler, about the year 1737, of the part of the country in which I live. He died, August 17th, 1757, leaving my mother a widow, who lived till 1776, with six daughters and two sons, myself the elder. To my younger brother he left his estate on James River, called Snowdon, after the supposed birth-place of the family: to myself, the lands on which I was born and live.

He placed me at the English school at five years of age; and at the Latin at nine, where I continued until his death. My teacher, Mr. Douglas, a clergyman from Scotland, with the rudiments of the Latin and Greek languages, taught me the French; and on the death of my father, I went to the Reverend Mr. Maury, a correct classical scholar, with whom I continued two years; and then, to wit, in the spring of 1760, went to William and Mary college, where I continued two years. It was my great good fortune, and what probably fixed the destinies of my life, that Dr. William Small of Scotland, was then Professor of Mathematics, a man profound in most of the useful branches of science, with a happy talent of communication, correct and gentlemanly manners, and an enlarged and liberal mind. He, most happily for me, became soon attached to me, and made me his daily companion when not engaged in the school; and from his conversation I got my first views of the expansion of science, and of the system of things in which we are placed. Fortunately, the philosophical chair became vacant soon after my arrival at college, and he was appointed to fill it *per interim* and he was the first who ever gave, in that college, regular lectures in Ethics, Rhetoric and Belles Lettres. He returned to Europe in 1762, having previously filled up the measure of his goodness to me, by procuring for me, from his most intimate friend, George Wythe, a reception as a student of law; under his direction, and introduced me to the acquaintance and familiar table of Governor Fauquier, the ablest man who had ever filled that office. With him, and at his table, Dr. Small and Mr. Wythe, his *amici omnium horarum,* (friends of all hours) and myself, formed *a partie quaree,* and to the habitual conversations on these occasions I owed much instruction. Mr. Wythe continued to be my faithful and beloved mentor in youth, and my most affectionate friend through life. In 1767, he led me into the practice of the law at the bar of the General court, at which I continued until the Revolution shut up the courts of justice.

In 1769, I became a member of the legislature by the choice of the county in which I live, and so continued until it was closed by the Revolution. I made one effort in that body for the permission of the emancipation of slaves, which was rejected: and indeed, during the regal government, nothing liberal could expect success. Our minds were circumscribed within narrow limits, by an habitual belief that it was our duty to be subordinate to the mother country in all matters of government, to direct all our labors in subservience to her interests, and even to observe a bigoted intolerance for all religions but hers. The difficulties with our representatives were of habit and despair, not of reflection and conviction. Experience soon proved that they could bring their minds to rights, on the first summons of their attention. But the King's Council, which acted as another house of legislature, held their places at will, and were in most humble obedience to that will: the Governor too, who had a negative on our laws, held by the same tenure, and with still greater devotedness to it: and, last of all, the Royal negative closed the last door to every hope of amelioration.

On the first of January, 1772, I was married to Martha Skelton, widow of Bathurst Skelton, and daughter of John Wayles, then twenty-three years old. Mr. Wayles was a lawyer of much practice, to which he was introduced more by his great industry, punctuality, and practical readiness, than by eminence in the science of his profession. He was a most agreeable companion, full of pleasantry and good humor, and welcomed in every society. He acquired a handsome fortune, and died in May, 1773, leaving three daughters: the portion which came on that event to Mrs. Jefferson, after the debts should be paid, which were very considerable, was about equal to my own patrimony, and consequently doubled the ease of our circumstances.

When the famous Resolutions of 1765, against the Stamp act, were proposed, I was yet a student of law in Williamsburg. I attended the debate, however, at the door of the lobby of the House of Burgesses, and heard the splendid display of Mr. Henry's talents as a popular orator. They were great indeed; such as I have never heard from any other man. He appeared to me to speak as Homer wrote. Mr. Johnson, a lawyer, and member from the Northern Neck, seconded the resolutions, and by him the learning and the logic of the case were chiefly maintained. My recollections of these transactions may be seen on page 60 of the life of Patrick Henry, by Wirt, to whom I furnished them.

In May, 1769, a meeting of the General Assembly was called by the Governor, Lord Botetourt. I had then become a member; and to that meeting became known the joint resolutions and address of the Lords and Commons, of 1768-9, on the proceedings in Massachusetts. Counter-resolutions, and an address to the King by the House of Burgesses, were agreed to with little opposition, and a spirit manifestly displayed itself of considering the cause of Massachusetts as a common one. The Governor dissolved us: but we met the next day in the Apollo (public room) of the Raleigh tavern, formed ourselves into a voluntary convention, drew up articles of association against the use of any merchandise imported from Great Britain, signed and recommended them to the people, repaired to our several counties, and were re-elected without any other exception than of the very few who had declined assent to our proceedings.

Nothing of particular excitement occurring for a considerable time, our countrymen seemed to fall into a state of insensibility to our situation; the duty on tea, not yet repealed, and the declaratory act of a right in the British Parliament to bind us by their laws in all cases whatsoever, still suspended over us. But a court of inquiry held on Rhode Island in 1762, with a power to send persons to England to be tried for offenses committed here, was considered, at our session of the spring of 1773, as demanding attention. Not thinking our old and leading members up to the point of forwardness and zeal which the times required, Mr. Henry, Richard Henry Lee, Francis L. Lee, Mr. Carr and myself agreed to meet in the evening, in a private room of the Raleigh, to consult on the state of things. There may have been a member or two more whom I do not recollect. We were all sensible that the most urgent of all measures was that of coming to an understanding with all the other colonies, to consider the British claims as a common cause to all, and to produce a unity of action: and, for this purpose, that a committee of correspondence in each colony would be the best instrument of intercommunication: and that their first measure would probably be, to propose a meeting of deputies from every colony, at some central place, who should be charged with the direction of the measures which should be taken by all. We, therefore, drew up the resolutions which may be seen in Wirt, page 87. The consulting members proposed to me to move them, but I urged that it should be done by Mr. Carr, my friend and brother-in-law, then a new member, to whom I wished an opportunity should be given of making known to the house his great worth and talents. It was so agreed; he moved them, they were agreed to *nem. con.* (unanimously), and a committee of correspondence appointed, of whom Peyton Randolph, the speaker, was chairman. The Governor (then Lord Dunmore) dissolved us, but the committee met the next day, prepared a circular letter to the speakers of the other colonies, inclosing to each a copy of the resolutions, and left it in charge with their chairman to forward them by expresses.

The origination of these committees of correspondence between the colonies has been since claimed for Massachusetts, and Marshall has given into this error, although the very note of his appendix to which he refers, shows that their establishment was confined to their own towns. This matter will be seen clearly stated in a letter of Samuel Adams Wells to me of April 2nd, 1819, and my answer of May 12th. I was corrected by the letter of Mr. Wells in the information I had given Mr. Wirt, as stated in his note, page 87, that the messengers of Massachusetts and Virginia crossed each other on the way, bearing similar propositions; for Mr. Wells shows that Massachusetts did not adopt the measure, but on the receipt of our proposition, delivered at their next session. Their message, therefore, which passed ours, must have related to something else, for I well remember Peyton Randolph's informing me of the crossing of our messengers.

The next event which excited our sympathies for Massachusetts, was the Boston port bill, by which that port was to be shut up on the 1st of June, 1774. This arrived while we were in session in the spring of that year. The lead in the House, on these subjects, being no longer left to the old members, Mr. Henry, R.H. Lee, Fr. L. Lee, three or four other members, whom I do not recollect, and myself, agreeing that we must boldly take an unequivocal stand in the line with Massachusetts, determined to meet and consult on the proper measures, in the council chamber, for the benefit of the library in that room. We were under conviction of the necessity of arousing our people from the lethargy into which they had fallen, as to passing events; and thought that the appointment of a day of general fasting and prayer would be most likely to call up and alarm their attention. No example of such a solemnity had existed since the days of our distresses in the war of '55, since which a new generation had grown up. With the help, therefore, of Rushworth, whom we rummaged over for the revolutionary precedents and forms of the Puritans of that day, preserved by him, we cooked up a resolution, somewhat modernizing their phrases, for appointing the

1st day of June, on which the portbill was to commence, for a day of fasting, humiliation, and prayer, to implore Heaven to avert from us the evils of civil war, to inspire us with firmness in support of our rights, and to turn the hearts of the King and Parliament to moderation and justice. To give greater emphasis to our proposition, we agreed to wait the next morning on Mr. Nicholas, whose grave and religious character was more in unison with the tone of our resolution, and solicit him to move it. We accordingly went to him in the morning. He moved it the same day; the 1st of June was proposed; and it passed without opposition. The Governor dissolved us, as usual. We retired to the Apollo, as before, agreed to an association, and instructed the committee of correspondence to propose to the corresponding committees of the other colonies, to appoint deputies to meet in Congress at such place, *annually*, as should be convenient, to direct, from time to time, the measures required by the general interest: and we declared that an attack on any one colony, should be considered as an attack on the whole. This was in May. We further recommended to the several counties to elect deputies to meet at Williamsburg, the 1st of August ensuing, to consider the state of the colony, and particularly to appoint delegates to a general Congress, should that measure be acceded to by the committees of correspondence generally. It was acceded to; Philadelphia was appointed for the place, and the 5th of September for the time of meeting. We returned home, and in our several counties invited the clergy to meet assemblies of the people on the 1st of June, to perform the ceremonies of the day, and to address to them discourses suited to the occasion. The people met generally, with anxiety and alarm in their countenances, and the effect of the day, through the whole colony, was like a shock of electricity, arousing every man, and placing him erect and solidly on his centre. They chose, universally, delegates for the convention. Being elected one for my own county, I prepared a draught of instructions to be given to the delegates whom we should send to the Congress, which I meant to propose at our meeting. In this I took the ground that, from the beginning, I had thought the only one orthodox or tenable, which was, that the relation between Great Britain and these colonies was exactly the same as that of England and Scotland, after the accession of James, and until the union, and the same as her present relations with Hanover, having the same executive chief, but no other necessary political connection; and that our emigration from England to this country gave her no more rights over us, than the emigrations of the Danes and Saxons gave to the present authorities of the mother country, over England. In this doctrine, however, I had never been able to get any one to agree with me but Mr. Wythe. He concurred in it from the first dawn of the question, What was the political relation between us and England? Our other patriots, Randolph, the Lees, Nicholas, Pendleton, stopped at the half-way house of John Dickinson, who admitted that England has a right to regulate our commerce, and to lay duties on it for the purposes of regulation, but not of raising revenue. But for this ground there was no foundation in compact, in any acknowledged principles of colonization, nor in reason: expatriation being a natural right, and acted on as such, by all nations, in all ages. I set out for Williamsburg some days before that appointed for our meeting, but was taken ill of a dysentery on the road, and was unable to proceed. I sent on, therefore, to Williamsburg, two copies of my draught, the one under cover to Peyton Randolph, who I knew would be in the chair of the convention, the other to Patrick Henry. Whether Mr. Henry disapproved the ground taken, or was too lazy to read it (for he was the laziest man in reading I ever knew) I never learned: but he communicated it to nobody. Peyton Randolph informed the convention he had received such a paper from a member, prevented by sickness from offering it in his place, and he laid it on the table for perusal. It was read generally by the members, approved by many, though thought too bold for the present state of things; but they printed it in pamphlet form, under the title of "A Summary View of the Rights of British America." It found its way to England, was taken up by the opposition, interpolated a little by Mr. Burke so as to make it answer opposition purposes, and in that form ran rapidly through several editions. This information I had from Parson Hurt, who happened at the time to be in London, whither he had gone to receive clerical orders; and I was informed afterwards by Peyton Randolph, that it had procured me the honor of having my name inserted in a long list of proscriptions, enrolled in a bill of attainder commenced in one of the Houses of Parliament, but suppressed in embryo by the hasty step of events, which warned them to be a little cautious. Montague, agent of the House of Burgesses in England, made extracts from the bill, copied the names, and sent them to Peyton Randolph. The names, I think, were about twenty, which he repeated to me, but I recollect those only of Hancock, the two Adamses, Peyton Randolph himself and myself. The convention met on the 1st of August, renewed their association, appointed delegates to the Congress, gave them instructions very temperately and properly expressed, both as to style and matter; and they repaired to Philadelphia at the time appointed. The splendid proceedings of that Congress, at their first session, belong to general history, are known to every one, and need not therefore be noted here. They terminated their session on the 26th of October, to meet again on the 10th of May ensuing. The convention, at their ensuing session of March '75, approved of the proceedings of Congress, thanked their delegates, and reappointed the same persons to represent the colony at the meeting to be held in May: and foreseeing the probability that Peyton Randolph, their president, and speaker also of the House of Burgesses, might be called off, they added me, in that event, to the delegation.

Mr. Randolph was, according to expectation, obliged to leave the chair of Congress, to attend the General Assembly summoned by Lord Dunmore, to meet on the 1st day of June, 1775. Lord North's conciliatory propositions, as they were called, had been received by the Governor, and furnished the subject for which this assembly was convened. Mr. Randolph accordingly attended, and the tenor of these propositions being generally known, as having been addressed to all the governors, he was anxious that the answer of our Assembly, likely to be the first, should harmonize with what he knew to be the sentiments and wishes of the body he had recently left. He feared that Mr. Nicholas, whose mind was not yet up to the mark of the times, would undertake the answer, and therefore pressed me to prepare it. I did so, and, with his aid, carried it through the House, with long and doubtful scruples from Mr. Nicholas and James Mercer, and a dash of cold water on it here and there, enfeebling it somewhat, but finally with unanimity, or a vote approaching it. This being passed, I repaired immediately to Philadelphia, and conveyed to Congress the first notice they had of it. It was entirely approved there. I took my seat with them on the 21st of June. On the 24th, a committee which had been appointed to prepare a declaration of the causes of taking up arms, brought in their report (drawn I believe by J. Rutledge) which, not being liked, the House recommitted it, on the 26th, and added Mr. Dickinson and myself to the committee. On the rising of the House, the committee having not yet met, I happened to find myself near Governor W. Livingston, and proposed to him to draw the paper. He excused himself and proposed that I should draw it. On my pressing him with urgency, "We are as yet but new acquaintances, sir," said he; "why are you so earnest for my doing it?" "Because," said I, "I have been informed that you drew the Address to the people of Great Britain, a production, certainly, of the finest pen in America." "On that," says he, "perhaps, sir, you may not have been correctly informed." I had received the information in Virginia from Colonel Harrison on his return from that Congress. Lee, Livingston, and Jay had been the committee for the draught. The first, prepared by Lee, had been disapproved and recommitted. The second was drawn by Jay, but being presented by Governor Livingston, had led Colonel Harrison into the error. The next morning, walking in the hall of Congress, many members being assembled, but the House not yet formed, I observed Mr. Jay speaking to R.H. Lee, and leading him by the button of his coat to me. "I understand, sir," said he to me, "that this gentlemen informed you, that Governor Livingston drew the Address to the people of Great Britain." I assured him, at once, that I had not received that information from Mr. Lee, and that not a word had ever passed on the subject between Mr. Lee and myself; and after some explanations the subject was dropped. These gentlemen had had some sparrings in debate before, and continued ever very hostile to each other.

I prepared a draught of the declaration committed to us. It was too strong for Mr. Dickinson. He still retained the hope of reconciliation with the mother country, and was unwilling it should be lessened by offensive statements. He was so honest a man, and so able a one, that he was greatly indulged even by those who could not feel his scruples. We therefore requested him to take the paper, and put it into a form he could approve. He did so, preparing an entire new statement, and preserving of the former only the last four paragraphs and half of the preceding one. We approved and reported it to Congress, who accepted it. Congress gave a signal proof of their indulgence to Mr. Dickinson, and of their great desire not to go too fast for any respectable part of our body, in permitting him to draw their second petition to the King according to his own ideas, and passing it with scarcely any amendment. The disgust against this humility was general; and Mr. Dickinson's delight at its passage was the only circumstance which reconciled them to it. The vote being passed, although further observation on it was out of order, he could not refrain from rising and expressing his satisfaction, and concluded by saying, "There is but one word, Mr. President, in the paper which I disapprove, and that is the word *Congress*"; on which Ben Harrison rose and said, "There is but one word in the paper, Mr. President, of which I approve, and that is the word *Congress*."

On the 22nd of July, Dr Franklin, Mr. Adams, R.H. Lee, and myself, were appointed a committee to consider and report on Lord North's conciliatory resolution. The answer of the Virginia Assembly on that subject having been approved, I was requested by the committee to prepare this report, which will account for the similarity of feature in the two instruments.

On the 15th of May, 1776, the convention of Virginia instructed their delegates in Congress, to propose to that body to declare the colonies independent of Great Britain, and appoint a committee to prepare a declaration of rights and plan of government.

In Congress, Friday, June 7, 1776

The delegates from Virginia moved, in obedience to instructions from their constituents, that the Congress should declare that these United colonies are, and of right ought to be, free and independent states, that they are absolved from all allegiance to the British crown, and that all political connection between them and the state of Great Britain is, and ought to be, totally dissolved; that measures should be immediately taken for procuring the assistance of foreign powers, and a Confederation be formed to bind the colonies more closely together.

The House being obliged to attend at that time to some other business, the proposition was referred to the next day, when the members were ordered to attend punctually at ten o'clock.

Saturday, June 8

They proceeded to take it into consideration, and referred it to a committee of the whole, into which they immediately resolved themselves, and passed that day and Monday, the 10th, in debating on the subject.

It was argued by Wilson, Robert R. Livingston, E. Rutledge, Dickinson, and others -

That, though they were friends to the measures themselves, and saw the impossibility that we should ever again be united with Great Britain, yet they were against adopting them at this time:

That the conduct we had formerly observed was wise and proper now, of deferring to take any capital step till the voice of the people drove us into it:

That they were our power, and without them our declarations could not be carried into effect:

That the people of the middle colonies (Maryland, Delaware, Pennsylvania, the Jerseys and New York) were not yet ripe for bidding adieu to British connection, but that they were fast ripening, and, in a short time, would join in the general voice of America:

That the resolution, entered into by this House on the 15th of May, for suppressing the exercise of all powers derived from the crown, had shown, by the ferment into which it had thrown these middle colonies, that they had not yet accommodated their minds to a separation from the mother country:

That some of them had expressly forbidden their delegates to consent to such a declaration, and others had given no instructions, and consequently no powers to give such consent:

That if the delegates of any particular colony had no power to declare such colony independent, certain they were, the others could not declare it for them; the colonies being as yet perfectly independent of each other:

That the assembly of Pennsylvania was now sitting above stairs, their convention would sit within a few days, the convention of New York was now sitting, and those of the Jerseys and Delaware counties would meet on the Monday following, and it was probable these bodies would take up the question of Independence, and would declare to their delegates the voice of their state:

That if such a declaration should now be agreed to, these delegates must retire, and possibly their colonies might secede from the Union:

That such a secession would weaken us more than could be compensated by any foreign alliance:

That in the event of such a division, foreign powers would either refuse to join themselves to our fortunes, or, having us so much in their power as that desperate declaration would place us, they would insist on terms proportionably more hard and prejudicial:

That we had little reason to expect an alliance with those to whom alone, as yet, we had cast our eyes:

That France and Spain had reason to be jealous of that rising power, which would one day certainly strip them of all their American possessions:

That it was more likely they should form a connection with the British court, who, if they should find themselves unable otherwise to extricate themselves from their difficulties, would agree to a partition of our territories, restoring Canada to France, and the Floridas to Spain, to accomplish for themselves a recovery of these colonies:

That it would not be long before we should receive certain information of the disposition of the French court from the agent whom we had sent to Paris for that purpose:

That if this disposition should be favorable, by waiting the event of the present campaign, which we all hoped would be successful, we should have reason to expect an alliance on better terms:

That this would in fact work no delay of any effectual aid from such ally, as, from the advance of the season and distance of our situation, it was impossible we could receive any assistance during this campaign:

That it was prudent to fix among ourselves the terms on which we should form alliance, before we declared we would form one at all events:

And that if these were agreed on, and our Declaration of Independence ready by the time our Ambassador should be prepared to sail, it would be as well as to go into that Declaration at this day.

On the other side, it was urged by J. Adams, Lee, Wythe, and others, that no gentleman had argued against the policy or the right of separation from Britain, nor had supposed it possible we should ever renew our connection; that they had only opposed its being now declared:

That the question was not whether, by a Declaration of Independence, we should make ourselves what we are not; but whether we should declare a fact which already exists:

That, as to the people or parliament of England, we had always been independent of them, their restraints on our trade deriving efficacy from our acquiescence only, and not from any rights they possessed of imposing them, and that so far, our connection had been federal only, and was now dissolved by the commencement of hostilities:

That, as to the King, we had been bound to him by allegiance, but that this bond was now dissolved by his assent to the last act of Parliament, by which he declares us out of his protection, and by his levying war on us, a fact which had long ago proved us out of his protection; it being a certain position in law, that allegiance and protection are reciprocal, the one ceasing when the other is withdrawn:

That James the Second never declared the people of England out of his protection, yet his actions proved it, and the Parliament declared it:

No delegates then can be denied, or ever want, a power of declaring an existing truth:

That the delegates from the Delaware counties having declared their constituents ready to join, there are only two colonies, Pennsylvania and Maryland, whose delegates are absolutely tied up, and that these had, by their instructions, only reserved a right of confirming or rejecting the measure:

That the instructions from Pennsylvania might be accounted for from the times in which they were drawn, near a twelve-month ago, since which the face of affairs has totally changed.

That within that time, it had become apparent that Britain was determined to accept nothing less than a *carte-blanche*, and that the King's answer to the Lord Mayor, Aldermen and Common Council of London, which had come to hand four days ago, must have satisfied every one of this point:

That the people wait for us to lead the way:

That *they* are in favor of the measure, though the instructions given by some of their *representatives* are not:

That the voice of the representatives is not always consonant with the voice of the people, and that this is remarkably the case in these middle colonies:

That the effect of the resolution of the 15th of May has proved this, which, raising the murmurs of some in the colonies of Pennsylvania and Maryland, called forth the opposing voice of the freer part of the people, and proved them to be the majority even in these colonies:

That the backwardness of these two colonies might be ascribed, partly to the influence of proprietary power and connections, and partly, to their having not yet been attacked by the enemy:

That these causes were not likely to be soon removed, as there seemed no probability that the enemy would make either of these the seat of this summer's war:

That it would be vain to wait either weeks or months for perfect unanimity, since it was impossible that all men should ever become of one sentiment on any question:

That the conduct of some colonies, from the beginning of this contest, had given reason to suspect it was their settled policy to keep in the rear of the confederacy, that their particular prospect might be better, even in the worst event:

That, therefore, it was necessary for those colonies who had thrown themselves forward and hazarded all from the beginning, to come forward now also, and put all again to their own hazard:

That the history of the Dutch Revolution, of whom three states only confederated at first, proved that a secession of some colonies would not be so dangerous as some apprehended:

That a Declaration of Independence alone could render it consistent with European delicacy, for European powers to treat with us, or even to receive an Ambassador from us:

That till this, they would not receive our vessels into their ports, nor acknowledge the adjudications of our courts of admiralty to be legitimate, in cases of capture of British vessels:

That though France and Spain may be jealous of our rising power, they must think it will be much more formidable with the addition of Great Britain; and will therefore see it their interest to prevent a coalition; but should they refuse, we shall be but where we are; whereas without trying, we shall never know whether they will aid us or not:

That the present campaign may be unsuccessful, and therefore we had better propose an alliance while our affairs wear a hopeful aspect:

That to wait the event of this campaign will certainly work delay, because, during the summer, France may assist us effectually, by cutting off those supplies of provisions from England and Ireland, on which the enemy's armies here are to depend; or by setting in motion the great power they have collected in the West Indies. and calling our enemy to the defence of the possessions they have there:

That it would be idle to lose time in settling the terms of alliance, till we had first determined we would enter into alliance:

That it is necessary to lose no time in opening a trade for our people, who will want clothes, and will want money too, for the payment of taxes:

And that the only misfortune is, that we did not enter into alliance with France six months sooner, as, besides opening her ports for the vent of our last year's produce, she might have marched an army into Germany, and prevented the petty princes there, from selling their unhappy subjects to subdue us.

It appearing in the course of these debates, that the colonies of New York, New Jersey, Pennsylvania, Delaware, Maryland, and South Carolina were not yet matured for falling from the parent stem, but that they were fast advancing to that state, it was thought most prudent to wait a while for them, and to postpone the final decision to July 1st; but, that this might occasion as little delay as possible, a committee was appointed to prepare a Declaration of Independence. The committee were John Adams, Dr. Franklin, Roger Sherman, Robert R. Livingston, and myself. Committees were also appointed, at the same time, to prepare a plan of confederation for the colonies, and to state the terms proper to be proposed for foreign alliance. The committee for drawing the Declaration of Independence, desired me to do it. it was accordingly done, and being approved by them, I reported it to the House on Friday, the 28th of June, when it was read, and ordered to lie on the table. On Monday, the 1st of July, the House resolved itself into a committee of the whole, and resumed the consideration of the original motion made by the delegates of Virginia, which, being again debated through the day, was carried in the affirmative by the votes of New Hampshire, Connecticut, Massachusetts, Rhode Island, New Jersey, Maryland, Virginia, North Carolina and Georgia. South Carolina and Pennsylvania voted against it. Delaware had but two members present, and they were divided. The delegates from New York declared they were for it themselves, and were assured their constituents were for it; but that their instructions having been drawn near a twelve-month before, when reconciliation was still the general object, they were enjoined by them to do nothing which should impede that object. They, therefore, thought themselves not justifiable in voting on either side, and asked leave to withdraw from the question; which was given them. The committee rose and reported their resolution to the House. Mr. Edward Rutledge, of South Carolina, then requested the determination might be put off to the next day, as he believed his colleagues, though they disapproved of the resolution, would then join in it for the sake of unanimity. The ultimate question, whether the House would agree to the resolution of the committee, was accordingly postponed to the next day, when it was again moved, and South Carolina concurred in voting for it. In the meantime, a third member had come post from the Delaware counties, and turned the vote of that colony in favor of the resolution. Members of a different sentiment attending that morning from Pennsylvania also, her vote was changed, so that the whole twelve colonies who were authorized to vote at all, gave their voices for it; and, within a few days, the convention of New York approved of it, and thus supplied the void occasioned by the withdrawing of her delegates from the vote.

Congress proceeded the same day to consider the Declaration of Independence, which had been reported and lain on the table the Friday preceding, and on Monday referred to a committee of the whole. The pusillanimous idea that we had friends in England worth keeping terms with, still haunted the minds of many. For this reason, those passages which conveyed censures on the people of England were struck out, lest they should give them offence. The clause too, reprobating the enslaving the inhabitants of Africa, was struck out in complaisance to South Carolina and Georgia, who had never attempted to restrain the importation of slaves, and who, on the contrary, still wished to continue it. Our northern brethren also, I believe, felt a little tender under those censures; for though their people had very few slaves themselves, yet they had been pretty considerable carriers of them to others. The debates, having taken up the greater parts of the 2d, 3d, and 4th days of July, were, on the evening of the last, closed; the Declaration was reported by the committee, agreed to by the House, and signed by every member present, except Mr. Dickinson. As the sentiments of men are known not only by what they receive, but what they reject also, I will state the form of the Declaration as originally reported.

[See page 39 for Jefferson's original draft of the Declaration of Independence, and page 47 for the final version.]

Some erroneous statements of the proceedings on the Declaration of Independence having got before the public in latter times. Mr. Samuel A. Wells asked explanations of me, which are given in my letter to him of May 12, '19, before and now again referred to. I took notes in my place while these things were going on, and at their close wrote them out in form and with correctness, and from 1 to 7 of the two preceding sheets, are the originals then written; as the two following are of the earlier debates on the Confederation, which I took in like manner.

On Friday, July 12, the committee appointed to draw the articles of Confederation reported them, and, on the 22d, the House resolved themselves into a committee to take them into consideration. On the 30th and 31st of that month, and 1st of the ensuing, those articles were debated which determined the proportion, or quota, of money which each state should furnish to the common treasury, and the manner of voting in Congress. The first of these articles was expressed in the original draught in these words." Art. XI. All charges of war and all other expenses that shall be incurred for the common defence, or general welfare, and allowed by the United States assembled, shall be defrayed out of a common treasury, which shall be supplied by the several colonies in proportion to the number of inhabitants of every age, sex, and quality, except Indians not paying taxes, in each colony, a true account of which, distinguishing the white inhabitants, shall be triennially taken and transmitted to the Assembly of the United States."

Mr. Chase moved that the quotas should be fixed, not by the number of inhabitants of every condition, but by that of the "white inhabitants." He admitted that taxation should be always in proportion to property, that this was, in theory, the true rule; but that, from a variety of difficulties, it was a rule which could never be adopted in practice. The value of the property in every State, could never be estimated justly and equally. Some other measure for the wealth of the State must therefore be devised, some standard referred to, which would be more simple. He considered the number of inhabitants as a tolerably good criterion of property, and that this might always be obtained. He therefore thought it the best mode which we could adopt, with one exception only: he observed that negroes are property, and as such, cannot be distinguished from the lands or personalities held in those States where there are few slaves; that the surplus of profit which a Northern farmer is able to lay by, he invests in cattle, horses, etc., whereas a Southern farmer lays out the same surplus in slaves. There is no more reason, therefore, for taxing the Southern States on the farmer's head, and on his slave's head, than the Northern ones on their farmer's heads and the heads of their cattle; that the method proposed would, therefore, tax the Southern States according to their numbers and their wealth conjunctly, while the Northern would be taxed on numbers only: that negroes, in fact, should not be considered as members of the State, more than cattle, and that they have no more interest in it.

Mr. John Adams observed, that the numbers of people were taken by this article, as an index of the wealth of the

State, and not as subjects of taxation; that, as to this matter, it was of no consequence by what name you called your people, whether by that of freemen or of slaves; that in some countries the laboring poor were called freemen, in others they were called slaves; but that the difference as to the state was imaginary only. What matters it whether a landlord, employing ten laborers on his farm, gives them annually as much money as will buy them the necessaries of life, or gives them those necessaries at short hand? The ten laborers add as much wealth annually to the State, increase its exports as much in the one case as the other. Certainly five hundred freemen produce no more profits, no greater surplus for the payment of taxes, than five hundred slaves. Therefore, the State in which are the laborers called freemen, should be taxed no more than that in which are those called slaves. Suppose, by an extraordinary operation of nature or of law, one-half the laborers of a State could in the course of one night be transformed into slaves; would the State be made poorer or the less able to pay taxes? That the condition of the laboring poor in most countries, that of the fishermen particularly of the Northern States, is as abject as that of slaves. It is the number of laborers which produces the surplus for taxation, and numbers, therefore, indiscriminately, are the fair index of wealth; that it is the use of the word "property" here, and its application to some of the people of the State, which produces the fallacy. How does the Southern farmer procure slaves? Either by importation or by purchase from his neighbor. If he imports a slave, he adds one to the number of laborers in his country, and proportionably to its profits and abilities to pay taxes; if he buys from his neighbor, it is only a transfer of a laborer from one farm to another, which does not change the annual produce of the State, and therefore, should not change its tax: that if a

Northern farmer works ten laborers on his farm, he can, it is true, invest the surplus of ten men's labor in cattle; but so may the Southern farmer, working ten slaves; that a State of one hundred thousand freemen can maintain no more cattle, than one of one hundred thousand slaves. Therefore, they have no more of that kind of property; that a slave may indeed, from the custom of speech, be more properly called the wealth of his master, than the free laborer might be called the wealth of his employer; but as to the State, both were equally its wealth, and should, therefore, equally add to the quota of its tax.

Mr. Harrison proposed, as a compromise, that two slaves should be counted as one freeman. He affirmed that slaves did not do as much work as freemen, and doubted if two effected more than one; that this was proved by the price of labor; the hire of a laborer in the Southern colonies being from 8 pounds to 12 pounds, while in the Northern it was generally 24 pounds.

Mr. Wilson said, that if this amendment should take place, the Southern colonies would have all the benefit of slaves, whilst the Northern ones would bear the burthen: that slaves increase the profits of a State, which the Southern States mean to take to themselves; that they also increase the burthen of defence, which would of course fall so much the heavier on the Northern: that slaves occupy the places of freemen, and eat their food. Dismiss your slaves, and freemen will take their places. It is our duty to lay every discouragement on the importation of slaves; but this amendment would give the *jus trium liberorum* (right of three freemen) to him who would import slaves: that other kinds of property were pretty equally distributed through all the colonies: there were as many cattle, horses and sheep, in the North as the South, and South as the

North; but not so as to slaves: that experience has shown that those colonies have been always able to pay most, which have the most inhabitants, whether they be black or white; and the practice of the Southern colonies has always been to make every farmer pay poll taxes upon all his laborers, whether black or white. He acknowledges, indeed, that freemen work the most; but they consume the most also. They do not produce a greater surplus for taxation. The slave is neither fed nor clothed so expensively as a freeman. Again, white women are exempted from labor generally, but negro women are not. In this, then, the Southern States have an advantage as the article now stands. It has sometimes been said, that slavery is necessary, because the commodities they raise would be too dear for market if cultivated by freemen; but now it is said that the labor of the slave is the dearest.

Mr. Payne urged the original resolution of Congress, to proportion the quotas of the States to the number of souls.

Dr. Witherspoon was of opinion, that the value of lands and houses was the best estimate of the wealth of a nation, and that it was practicable to obtain such a valuation. This is the true barometer of wealth. The one now proposed is imperfect in itself, and unequal between the States. It has been objected that negroes eat the food of freemen, and, therefore, should be taxed; horses also eat the food of freemen; therefore they also should be taxed. It has been said too, that in carrying slaves into the estimate of the taxes the State is to pay, we do no more than those States themselves do, who always take slaves into the estimate of the taxes the individual is to pay. But the cases are not parallel. In the Southern colonies slaves pervade the whole colony; but they do not pervade the whole continent. That as to the original resolution of Congress, to proportion the quotas according to the souls, it was temporary only, and related to the moneys heretofore emitted: whereas we are now entering into a new compact, and therefore stand on original ground.

August 1.

The question being put, the amendment proposed was rejected by the votes of New Hampshire, Massachusetts, Rhode Island, Connecticut, New York, New Jersey, and Pennsylvania, against those of Delaware, Maryland, Virginia, North and South Carolina. Georgia was divided.

The other article was in these words. "Art. XVIII. In determining questions, each colony shall have one vote."

July 30, 31, August 1.

Present forty-one members. Mr. Chase observed this article was the most likely to divide us, of any one proposed in the draught then under consideration: that the larger colonies had threatened they would not confederate at all, if their weight in Congress should not be equal to the numbers of people they added to the confederacy; while the smaller ones declared against a union, if they did not retain an equal vote for the protection of their rights. That it was of the utmost consequence to bring the parties together, as, should we sever from each other, either no foreign power will ally with us at all, or the different States will form different alliances, and thus increase the horrors of those scenes of civil war and bloodshed, which in such a state of separation and independence, would render us a miserable people. That our importance, our interests, our peace required that we should confederate, and that mutual sacrifices should be made to effect a compromise of this difficult question. He was of opinion, the smaller colonies would lose their rights, if they were not in some instances allowed an equal vote; and, therefore, that a discrimination should take place among the questions which would come before Congress. That the smaller States should be secured in all questions concerning life or liberty, and the greater ones, in all respecting property. He, therefore, proposed, that in votes relating to money, the voice of each colony should be proportioned to the number of its inhabitants.

Dr. Franklin thought, that the votes should be so proportioned in all cases. He took notice that the Delaware counties had bound up their delegates to disagree to this article. He thought it a very extraordinary language to be held by any State, that they would not confederate with us, unless we would let them dispose of our money. Certainly, if we vote equally, we ought to pay equally; but the smaller States will hardly purchase the privilege at this price. That had he lived in a State where the representation, originally equal, had become unequal by time and accident, he might have submitted rather than disturb government; but that we should be very wrong to set out in this practice, when it is in our power to establish what is right. That at the time of the Union between England and Scotland, the latter had made the objection which the smaller States now do; but experience had proved that no unfairness had ever been shown them: that their advocates had prognosticated that it would again happen, as in times of old, that the whale would swallow Jonas [*sic*], but he thought the prediction reversed in event, and that Jonas had swallowed the whale, for the Scotch had in fact got possession of the government, and gave laws to the English. He reprobated the original agreement of Congress to vote by colonies, and, therefore, was for their voting, in all cases, according to the number of taxables.

Dr. Witherspoon opposed every alteration of the article. All men admit that a confederacy is necessary. Should the idea get abroad that there is likely to be no union among us, it will damp the minds of the people, diminish the glory of our struggle, and lessen its importance; because it will open to our view future prospects of war and dissension among ourselves. If an equal vote be refused, the smaller States will become vassals to the larger; and all experience has shown that the vassals and subjects of free States are the most enslaved. He instanced the Helots of Sparta, and the provinces of Rome. He observed that foreign powers, discovering this blemish, would make it a handle for disengaging the smaller States from so unequal a confederacy. That the colonies should in fact be considered as individuals; and that, as such, in all disputes, they should have an equal vote; that they are now collected as individuals making a bargain with each other, and, of course, had a right to vote as individuals. That in the East India Company they voted by persons, and not by their proportion of stock. That the Belgic confederacy voted by provinces. That in questions of war the smaller States were as much interested as the larger, and, therefore, should vote equally; and indeed, that the larger States were more likely to bring war on the confederacy, in proportion as their frontier was more extensive. He admitted that equality of representation was an excellent principle, but then it must be of things which are coordinate; that is, of things similar, and of the same nature: that nothing relating to individuals could ever come before Congress; nothing but what would respect colonies. He distinguished between an incorporating and a federal union. The union of England was an incorporating one, yet Scotland had suffered by that union; for that its inhabitants were drawn from it by the hopes of places and employments: nor was it an instance of equality of representation; because, while Scotland was allowed nearly a thirteenth of representation they were to pay only one-fortieth of the land tax. He expressed his hopes, that in the present enlightened state of men's minds, we might expect a lasting confederacy, if it was founded on fair principles.

John Adams advocated the voting in proportion to numbers. He said that we stand here as the representatives of the people: that in some States the people are many, in others they are few; that therefore, their vote here should be proportioned to the numbers from whom it comes. Reason, justice and equity never had weight enough on the face of the earth, to govern the councils of men. It is interest alone which does it, and it is interest alone which can be trusted: that therefore the interests within doors, should be the mathematical representatives of the interests without doors: that the individuality of the colonies is a mere sound. Does the individuality of a colony increase its wealth or numbers? If it does, pay equally. If it does not add weight in the scale of the confederacy, it cannot add to their rights, nor weigh in argument. A. has 50 pounds, B. 500 pounds, C. 1000 pounds in partnership. Is it just they should equally dispose of the moneys of the partnership? It has been said, we are independent individuals making a bargain together. The question is not what we are now, but what we ought to be when our bargain shall be made. The confederacy is to make us one individual only; it is to form us like separate parcels of metal, into one common mass. We shall no longer retain our separate

individuality, but become a single individual as to all
questions submitted to the confederacy.   Therefore, all
those reasons, which prove the justice and expediency of
equal representation in other assemblies, hold good here.
It has been objected that a proportional vote will
endanger the smaller States. We answer that an equal vote
will endanger the larger.   Virginia, Pennsylvania, and
Massachusetts, are the three greater colonies.

Consider their distance, their difference of produce, of
interests, and of manners, and it is apparent they can
never have an interest or inclination to combine for the
oppression of the smaller: that the smaller will naturally
divide on all questions with the larger.   Rhode Island,
from its relation, similarity and intercourse, will generally
pursue the same objects with Massachusetts; Jersey,
Delaware, and Maryland, with Pennsylvania.

Dr. Rush took notice, that the decay of the liberties of the
Dutch republic proceeded from three causes.   1.   The
perfect unanimity requisite on all occasions.   2.   Their
obligation to consult their constituents.   3.   Their voting
by provinces.   This last destroyed the equality of
representation, and the liberties of Great Britain also are
sinking from the same defect.   That a part of our rights is
deposited in the hands of our legislatures. There, it was
admitted, there should be an equality of representation.
Another part of our rights is deposited in the hands of
Congress: why is it not equally necessary there should be
an equal representation there? Were it possible to collect
the whole body of the people together, they would
determine the questions submitted to them by their
majority.   Why should not the same majority decide when
voting here, by their representatives?   The larger colonies
are so providentially divided in situation, as to render

every fear of their combining visionary. Their interests are different, and their circumstances dissimilar. It is more probable they will become rivals, and leave it in the power of the smaller States to give preponderance to any scale they please. The voting by the number of free inhabitants, will have one excellent effect, that of inducing the colonies to discourage slavery, and to encourage the increase of their free inhabitants.

Mr. Hopkins observed, there were four larger, four smaller, and four middle-sized colonies. That the four largest would contain more than half the inhabitants of the confederated States, and therefore, would govern the others as they should please. That history affords no instance of such a thing as equal representation. The Germanic body votes by States. The Helvetic body does the same; and so does the Belgic confederacy. That too little is known of the ancient confederations, to say what was their practice.

Mr. Wilson thought, that taxation should be in proportion to wealth, but that representation should accord with the number of freemen. That government is a collection or result of the wills of all: that if any government could speak the will of all, it would be perfect; and that, so far as it departs from this, it becomes imperfect. It has been said that Congress is a representation of States, not of individuals. I say, that the objects of its care are all the individuals of the States. It is strange that annexing the name of "State" to ten thousand men, should give them an equal right with forty thousand. This must be the effect of magic, not of reason. As to those matters which are referred to Congress, we are not so many States; we are one large State. We lay aside our individuality, whenever we come here. The Germanic body is a burlesque on government; and their practice, on any point, is a sufficient authority and proof that it is wrong. The greatest imperfection in the constitution of the Belgic confederacy is their voting by provinces. The interest of the whole is constantly sacrificed to that of the small States. The history of the war in the reign of Queen Anne sufficiently proves this. It is asked, shall nine colonies put it into the power of four to govern them as they please? I invert the question, and ask, shall two millions of people put it in the power of one million to govern them as they please? It is pretended, too, that the smaller colonies will be in danger from the greater. Speak in honest language and say, the minority will be in danger from the majority. And is there an assembly on earth, where this danger may not be equally pretended? The truth is, that our proceedings will then be consentaneous with the interests of the majority, and so they ought to be. The probability is much greater, that the larger States will disagree, than that they will combine. I defy the wit of man to invent a possible case, or to suggest any one thing on earth, which shall be for the interests of Virginia, Pennsylvania and Massachusetts, and which will not also be for the interest of the other States.

These articles, reported July 12, '76, were debated from day to day, and time to time, for two years, were ratified July 9, '78, by ten States, by New Jersey on the 26th of November of the same year, and by Delaware on the 23rd of February following. Maryland alone held off two years more, acceding to them March 1, '81, and thus closing the obligation.

Our delegation had been renewed for the ensuing year, commencing August 11; but the new government was now organized, a meeting of the legislature was to be held in

October, and I had been elected a member by my county. I knew that our legislation, under the regal government, had many very vicious points which urgently required reformation, and I thought I could be of more use in forwarding that work. I therefore retired from my seat in Congress on the 2d of September, resigned it, and took my place in the legislature of my State, on the 7th of October.

On the 11th, I moved for leave to bring in a bill for the establishment of courts of justice, the organization of which was of importance. I drew the bill; it was approved by the committee, reported and passed, after going through its due course.

On the 12th, I obtained leave to bring in a bill declaring tenants in tail to hold their lands in fee simple. In the earlier times of the colony, when lands were to be obtained for little or nothing, some provident individuals procured large grants; and, desirous of founding great families for themselves, settled them on their descendants in fee tail. The transmission of this property from generation to generation, in the same name, raised up a distinct set of families, who, being privileged by law in the perpetuation of their wealth, were thus formed into a Patrician order, distinguished by the splendor and luxury of their establishments. From this order, too, the king habitually selected his counsellors of State; the hope of which distinction devoted the whole corps to the interests and will of the crown. To annul this privilege, and instead of an aristocracy of wealth, of more harm and danger, than benefit, to society, to make an opening for the aristocracy of virtue and talent, which nature has wisely provided for the direction of the interests of society, and scattered with equal hand through all its conditions, was deemed essential to a well-ordered republic. To effect it, no violence was necessary, no deprivation of natural right, but rather an enlargement of it by a repeal of the law. For this would authorize the present holder to divide the property among his children equally, as his affections were divided; and would place them, by natural generation, on the level of their fellow citizens. But this repeal was strongly opposed by Mr. Pendleton, who was zealously attached to ancient establishments; and who, taken all in all, was the ablest man in debate I have ever met with. He had not indeed the poetical fancy of Mr. Henry, his sublime imagination, his lofty and overwhelming diction; but he was cool, smooth and persuasive; his language flowing, chaste and embellished; his conceptions quick, acute and full of resource; never vanquished: for if he lost the main battle, he returned upon you, and regained so much of it as to make it a drawn one, by dexterous manoeuvres, skirmishes in detail, and the recovery of small advantages which, little singly, were important all together. You never knew when you were clear of him, but were harassed by his perseverance, until the patience was worn down of all who had less of it than himself. Add to this, that he was one of the most virtuous and benevolent of men, the kindest friend, the most amiable and pleasant of companions, which ensured a favorable reception to whatever came from him. Finding that the general principle of entails could not be maintained, he took his stand on an amendment which he proposed, instead of an absolute abolition, to permit the tenant in tail to convey in fee simple, if he chose it; and he was within a few votes of saving so much of the old law. But the bill passed finally for entire abolition.

In that one of the bills for organizing our judiciary system, which proposed a court of Chancery, I had provided for a trial by jury of all matters of fact, in that as well as in the courts of law. He defeated it by the introduction of four words only, "*if either party choose.*" The consequence has been, that as no suitor will say to his judge, "Sir, I distrust you, give me a jury," juries are rarely, I might say, perhaps, never, seen in that court,but when called for by the Chancellor of his own accord.

The first establishment in Virginia which became permanent, was made in 1607. I have found no mention of negroes in the colony until about 1650. The first brought here as slaves were by a Dutch ship; after which the English commenced the trade, and continued it until the revolutionary war. That suspended, *ipso facto,* their importation for the present, and the business of the war pressing constantly on the legislature, this subject was not acted on finally until the year '78, when I brought in a bill to prevent their further importation. This passed without opposition, and stopped the increase of the evil by importation, leaving to future efforts its final eradication.

The first settlers of this colony were Englishmen, loyal subjects to their king and church, and the grant to Sir Walter Raleigh contained an express proviso that their laws "should not be against the true Christian faith, now professed in the church of England." As soon as the state of the colony admitted, it was divided into parishes, in each of which was established a minister of the Anglican church, endowed with a fixed salary, in tobacco, a glebe house and land with the other necessary appendages. To meet these expenses, all the inhabitants of the parishes were assessed, whether they were or not, members of the established church. Towards Quakers who came here, they were most cruelly intolerant, driving them from the colony by the severest penalties. In process of time, however, other sectarisms were introduced, chiefly of the Presbyterian family; and the established clergy, secure for life in their glebes and salaries, adding to these, generally, the emoluments of a classical school, found employment enough, in their farms and schoolrooms, for the rest of the week, and devoted Sunday only to the edification of their flock, by service, and a sermon at their parish church. Their other pastoral functions were little attended to. Against this inactivity, the zeal and industry of sectarian preachers had an open and undisputed field; and by the time of the revolution, a majority of the inhabitants had become dissenters from the established church, but were still obliged to pay contributions to support the pastors of the minority. This unrighteous compulsion, to maintain teachers of what they deemed religious errors, was grievously felt during the regal government, and without a hope of relief. But the first republican legislature, which met in '76, was crowded with petitions to abolish this spiritual tyranny. These brought on the severest contests in which I have ever been engaged. Our great opponents were Mr. Pendleton and Robert Carter Nicholas; honest men, but zealous churchmen. The petitions were referred to the committee of the whole house on the state of the country; and, after desperate contests in that committee, almost daily from the 11th of October to the 5th of December, we prevailed so far only, as to repeal the laws which rendered criminal the maintenance of any religious opinions, the forbearance of repairing to church, or the exercise of any mode of worship; and further, to exempt dissenters from contributions to the support of the established church; and to suspend, only until the next session, levies on the members of that church for the salaries of their own incumbents. For although the majority of our citizens were dissenters, as has been observed, a majority of the legislature were churchmen. Among these, however, were some reasonable and liberal men, who enabled us, on some points, to obtain feeble majorities. But our opponents carried, in the general resolutions of the committee of November '79, a declaration that religious assemblies ought to be regulated, and that provision ought to be made for continuing the succession of the clergy, and superintending their conduct. And, in the bill now passed, was inserted an express reservation of the question, Whether a general assessment should not be established by law, on every one, to the support of the pastor of his choice; or whether all should be left to voluntary contributions; and on this question, debated at every session, from '76 to '79, (some of our dissenting allies, having now secured their particular object, going over to the advocates of a general assessment,) we could only obtain a suspension from session to session until '79, when the question against a general assessment was finally carried, and the establishment of the Anglican church entirely put down. In justice to the two honest but zealous opponents who have been named, I must add, that although, from their natural temperaments, they were more disposed generally to acquiesce in things as they are, than to risk innovations, yet whenever the public will had once decided, none were more faithful or exact in their obedience to it.

The seat of our government had originally been fixed in the peninsula of Jamestown, the first settlement of the colonists; and had been afterwards removed a few miles inland to Williamsburg. But this was at a time when our settlements had not extended beyond the tide waters. Now they had crossed the Alleghany; and the centre of population was very far removed from what it had been.

Yet Williamsburg was still the depository of our archives, the habitual residence of the Governor and many other of the public functionaries, the established place for the sessions of the legislature, and the magazine of our military stores; and its situation was so exposed that it might be taken at any time in war, and, at this time particularly, an enemy might in the night run up either of the rivers, between which it lies, land a force above, and take possession of the place, without the possibility of saving either persons or things. I had proposed its removal so early as October, '76; but it did not prevail until the session of May, '79.

Early in the session of May, '79, I prepared, and obtained leave to bring in a bill, declaring who should be deemed citizens, asserting the natural right of expatriation, and prescribing the mode of exercising it. This, when I withdrew from the House, on the 1st of June following, I left in the hands of George Mason, and it was passed on the 26th of that month.

In giving this account of the laws of which I was myself the mover and draughtsman, I, by no means, mean to claim to myself the merit of obtaining their passage. I had many occasional and strenuous coadjutors in debate, and one, most steadfast, able and zealous; who was himself a host. This was George Mason, a man of the first order of wisdom among those who acted on the theatre of the revolution, of expansive mind, profound judgement, cogent in argument, learned in the lore of our former constitution, and earnest for the republican change on democratic principles. His elocution was neither flowing nor smooth; but his language was strong, his manner most impressive, and strengthened by a dash of biting cynicism, when provocation made it seasonable.

Mr. Wythe, while speaker in the two sessions of 1777, between his return from Congress and his appointment to the Chancery, was an able and constant associate in whatever was before a committee of the whole. His pure integrity, judgment and reasoning powers, gave him great weight. . . .

Mr. Madison came into the House in 1776, a new member and young; which circumstances, concurring with his extreme modesty, prevented his venturing himself in debate before his removal to the Council of State, in November, '77. From thence he went to Congress, then consisting of few members. Trained in these successive schools, he acquired a habit of self-possession, which placed at ready command the rich resources of his luminous and discriminating mind, and of his extensive information, and rendered him the first of every assembly afterwards, of which he became a member. Never wandering from his subject into vain declamation, but pursuing it closely, in language pure, classical and copious, soothing always the feelings of his adversaries by civilities and softness of expression, he rose to the eminent station which he held in the great National Convention of 1787; and in that of Virginia which followed, he sustained the new constitution in all its parts, bearing off the palm against the logic of George Mason, and the fervid declamation of Mr. Henry. With these consummate powers, were united a pure and spotless virtue, which no calumny has ever attempted to sully. Of the powers and polish of his pen and of the wisdom of his administration in the highest office of the nation, I need say nothing. They have spoken, and will forever speak for themselves.

So far we were proceeding in the details of reformation only; selecting points of legislation, prominent in character and principle, urgent, and indicative of the strength of the general pulse of reformation. When I left Congress, in '76, it was in the persuasion that our whole code must be reviewed, adapted to our republican form of government; and, now that we had no negatives of Councils, Governors and Kings to restrain us from doing right, it should be corrected, in all its parts, with a single eye to reason, and the good of those for whose government it was framed. Early, therefore, in the session of '76, to which I returned, I moved and presented a bill for the revision of the laws, which was passed on the 24th of October; and on the 5th of November, Mr. Pendleton, Mr.Wythe, Gorge Mason, Thomas L. Lee, and myself, were appointed a committee to execute the work. We agreed to meet at Fredericksburg to settle the plan of operation, and to distribute the work. We met there accordingly, on the 13th of January, 1777. The first question was, whether we should propose to abolish the whole existing system of laws, and prepare a new and complete Institute, or preserve the general system, and only modify it to the present state of things. Mr. Pendleton, contrary to his usual disposition in favor of ancient things, was for the former proposition, in which he was joined by Mr. Lee. To this it was objected, that to abrogate our whole system would be a bold measure, and probably far beyond the views of the legislature; that they had been in the practice of revising, from time to time, the laws of the colony, omitting the expired, the repealed, and the obsolete, amending only those retained, and probably meant we should now do the same, only including the British statutes as well as our own: that to compose a new Institute, like those of Justinian and Bracton, or that of Blackstone, which was the model proposed by Mr. Pendleton, would be an arduous undertaking, of vast research, of great consideration and judgment; and when reduced to a text, every word of that text, from the imperfection of human language, and its incompetence to express distinctly every shade of idea, would become a subject of question and chicanery, until settled by repeated adjudications; and this would involve us for ages in litigation, and render property uncertain, until, like the statutes of old, every word had been tried and settled by numerous decisions, and by new volumes of reports and commentaries; and that no one of us, probably, would undertake such a work, which to be systematical, must be the work of one hand. This last was the opinion of Mr. Wythe, Mr. Mason, and myself. When we proceeded to the distribution of the work, Mr. Mason, and myself. When we proceeded to the distribution of the work, Mr. Mason excused himself, as, being no lawyer, he felt himself unqualified for the work, and he resigned soon after. Mr. Lee excused himself on the same ground, and died, indeed, in a short time. The other two gentlemen, therefore, and myself divided the work among us. The common law and statutes to the 4 James I. (when our separate legislature was established) were assigned to me; the British statutes, from that period to the present day, to Mr.Wythe; and the Virginia laws to Mr. Pendleton. As the law of Descents, and the criminal law fell of course within my portion, I wished the committee to settle the leading principles of these, as a guide for me in framing them; and, with respect to the first, I proposed to abolish the law of primogeniture, and to make real estate descendible in parcenary to the next of kin, as personal property is, by the statute of distribution. Mr. Pendleton wished to preserve the right of primogeniture, but seeing at once that that could not prevail, he proposed we should adopt the Hebrew principle, and give a double portion to the elder son. I observed, that if the eldest son could eat twice as much, or do double work, it might be a natural evidence of his right to a double portion; but being on a par in his powers and wants, with his brothers and sisters, he should be on a par also in the partition of the patrimony; and such was the decision of the other members.

On the subject of the Criminal law, all were agreed, that the punishment of death should be abolished, except for treason and murder; and that, for other felonies, should be substituted hard labor in the public works, and in some cases, the *Lex talionis* (the law of retaliation). How this last revolting principle came to obtain our approbation, I do not remember. There remained, indeed, in our laws, a vestige of it in a single case of a slave; it was the English law, in the time of the Anglo-Saxons, copied probably from the Hebrew law of "an eye for eye, a tooth for a tooth," and it was the law of several ancient people; but the modern mind had left it far in the rear of its advances. These points, however, being settled, we repaired to our respective homes for the preparation of the work.

In the execution of my part, I thought it material not to vary the diction of the ancient statutes by modernizing it, nor to give rise to new questions by new expressions. The text of these statutes had been so fully explained and defined, by numerous adjudications, as scarcely ever now to produce a question in our courts. I thought it would be useful, also, in all new draughts, to reform the style of the later British statutes, and of our own acts of Assembly; which, from their verbosity, their endless tautologies, their involutions of case within case, and parenthesis within parenthesis, and their multiplied efforts at certainty, by *saids* and *aforesaids*, by *ors* and by *ands*, to make them more plain, are really rendered more perplexed and incomprehensible, not only to common readers, but to the lawyers themselves. We were employed in this work from that time to February, 1779, when we met at Williamsburg, that is to say, Mr. Pendleton, Mr. Wythe and myself; and meeting day by day, we examined critically our several parts, sentence by sentence, scrutinizing and amending, until we had agreed on the whole. We then returned home, had fair copies made of our several parts, which were reported to the General Assembly, June 18, 1779, by Mr. Wythe and myself, Mr. Pendleton's residence being distant, and he having authorized us by letter to declare his approbation. We had, in this work, brought so much of the Common law as it was thought necessary to alter, all the British statutes from *Magna Charta* to the present day, and all the laws of Virginia, from the establishment of our legislature, in the 4th Jac. I. to the present time, which we thought should be retained, within the compass of one hundred and twenty-six bills, making a printed folio of ninety pages only. Some bills were taken out, occasionally, from time to time, and passed; but the main body of the work was not entered on by the legislature until after the general peace, in 1785, when, by the unwearied exertions of Mr. Madison, in opposition to the endless quibbles, chicaneries, perversions, vexations and delays of lawyers and demi-lawyers, most of the bills were passed by the legislature, with little alteration.

The bill for establishing religious freedom, the principles of which had, to a certain degree, been enacted before, I had drawn in all the latitude of reason and right. It still met with opposition; but, with some mutilations in the preamble, it was finally passed; and a singular proposition proved that its protection of opinion was meant to be universal. Where the preamble declares, that coercion is a departure from the plan of the holy author of our religion, an amendment was proposed, by inserting the word "Jesus Christ," so that is should read, "a departure from the plan of Jesus Christ, the holy author of our religion;" the insertion was rejected by a great majority, in proof that they meant to comprehend, within the mantle of its protection, the Jew and the Gentile, the Christian and Mahometan, the Hindoo, and Infidel of every denomination.

Beccaria, and other writers on crimes and punishments, had satisfied the reasonable world of the unrightfulness and inefficacy of the punishment of crimes by death; and hard labor on roads, canals and other public works, had been suggested as a proper substitute. The Revisors had adopted these opinions; but the general idea of our country had not yet advanced to that point. The bill, therefore, for proportioning crimes and punishments, was lost in the House of Delegates by a majority of a single vote. I learned afterwards, that the substitute of hard labor in public, was tried (I believe it was in Pennsylvania) without success. Exhibited as a public spectacle, with shaved heads and mean clothing, working on the high roads, produced in the criminals such a prostration of character, such an abandonment of self-respect, as, instead of reforming, plunged them into the most desperate and hardened depravity of morals and character. To pursue the subject of this law - I was written to in 1785 (being then in Paris) by directors appointed to superintending the building of a Capitol in Richmond, to advise them as to a plan, and to add to it one of a Prison. Thinking it a favorable opportunity of introducing into the State an example of architecture, in the classic style of antiquity, and the Maison Quarree of Nismes, an ancient Roman temple, being considered as the most perfect model existing of what may be called Cubic architecture, I applied to M. Clerissault, who had published drawings of the Antiquities of Nismes, to have me a model of the building made in stucco, only changing the order from Corinthian to Ionic, on account of the difficulty of the Corinthian capitals. I yielded, with reluctance, to the taste of Clerissault, in his preference of the modern capital of Scamozzi to the more noble capital of antiquity. This was executed by the artist whom Choiseul Gouffier had carried with him to Constantinople, and employed, while Ambassador there, in making those beautiful models of the remains of Grecian architecture which are to be seen at Paris. To adapt the exterior to our use, I drew a plan for the interior, with the apartments necessary for legislative, executive, and judiciary purposes; and accommodated in their size and distribution to the form and dimensions of the building. These were forwarded to the Directors, in 1786, and were carried into execution, with some variations, not for the better, the most important of which, however, admit of future correction. With respect to the plan of a Prison, requested at the same time, I had heard of a benevolent society, in England, which had been indulged by the government in an experiment of the effect of labor, in *solitary confinement,* on some of their criminals; which experiment had succeeded beyond expectation. The same idea had been suggested in France, and an Architect of Lyons had proposed a plan of a well-contrived edifice, on the principle of solitary confinement. I procured a copy, and as it was too large for our purposes, I drew one on a scale less extensive, but susceptible of additions as they should be wanting. This I sent to the Directors, instead of a plan of a common prison, in the hope that it would suggest the idea of labor in solitary confinement, instead of that on the public works, which we had adopted in our

Revised Code. Its principle, accordingly, but not its exact form, was adopted by Latrobe in carrying the plan into execution, by the erection of what is now called the Penitentiary, built under his direction. In the meanwhile, the public opinion was ripening, by time, by reflection, and by the example of Pennsylvania, where labor on the highways had been tried, without approbation, from 1786 to '89, and had been followed by their Penitentiary system on the principle of confinement and labor, which was proceeding auspiciously. In 1796, our legislature resumed the subject, and passed the law for amending the Penal laws of the commonwealth. They adopted solitary, instead of public, labor, established a gradation in the duration of the confinement, approximated the style of the law more to the modern usage, and, instead of the settled distinctions of murder and manslaughter, preserved in my bill, they introduced the new terms of murder in the first and second degree. Whether these have produced more or fewer questions of definition, I am not sufficiently informed of our judiciary transactions to say. . . .

The acts of Assembly concerning the College of William and Mary, were properly within Mr. Pendleton's portion of our work; but these related chiefly to its revenue, while its constitution, organization and scope of science, were derived from its charter. We thought that on this subject, a systematical plan of general education should be proposed, and I was requested to undertake it. I accordingly prepared three bills for the Revisal, proposing three distinct grades of education, reaching all classes. 1st. Elementary schools, for all children generally, rich and poor. 2d. Colleges, for a middle degree of instruction, calculated for the common purposes of life, and such as would be desirable for all who were in easy circumstances.

And, 3d, an ultimate grade for teaching the sciences generally, and in their highest degree. The first bill proposed to lay off every county into Hundreds, or Wards, of a proper size and population for school in which reading, writing, and common arithmetic should be taught; and that the whole State should be divided into twenty-four districts, in each of which should be a school for classical learning, grammar, geography, and the higher branches of numerical arithmetic. The second bill proposed to amend the constitution of William and Mary college, to enlarge its sphere of science, and to make it in fact a University. The third was for the establishment of a library. These bills were not acted on until the same year, '96, and then only so much of the first as provided for elementary schools. The College of William and Mary was an establishment purely of the Church of England; the Visitors were required to be all of that Church; the Professors to subscribe its thirty-nine Articles; its Students to learn its Catechism; and one of its fundamental objects was declared to be, to raise up Ministers for that church. The religious jealousies, therefore, of all the dissenters, took alarm lest this might give an ascendancy to the Anglican sect, and refused acting on that bill. Its local eccentricity, too, and unhealthy autumnal climate, lessened the general inclination towards it. And in the Elementary bill, they inserted a provision which completely defeated it; for they left it to the court of each county to determine for itself, when this act should be carried into execution, within their county. One provision of the bill was, that the expenses of these schools should be borne by the inhabitants of the county, every one in proportion to his general tax rate. This would throw on wealth the education of the poor; and the justices, being generally of the more wealthy class, were unwilling to incur that burden, and I believe it was not suffered to commence in a single county. I shall recur again to this subject, towards the close of my story, if I should have life and resolution enough to reach that term; for I am already tired of talking about myself.

The bill on the subject of slaves, was a mere digest of the existing laws respecting them, without any intimation of a plan for a future and general emancipation. It was thought better that this should be kept back, and attempted only by way of amendment, whenever the bill should be brought on. The principles of the amendment, however, were agreed on, that is to say, the freedom of all born after a certain day, and deportation at a proper age. But it was found that the public mind would not yet bear the proposition, nor will it bear it even at this day. Yet the day is not distant when it must bear and adopt it, or worse will follow. Nothing is more certainly written in the book of fate, than that these people are to be free; nor is it less certain that the two races, equally free, cannot live in the same government. Nature, habit, opinion, have drawn indelible lines of distinction between them. It is still in our power to direct the process of emancipation and deportation, peaceably, and in such slow degree, as that the evil will wear off insensibly, and their place be, *pari passu* (on an equal basis), filled up by free white laborers. If, on the contrary, it is left to force itself on, human nature must shudder at the prospect held up. We should in vain look for an example in the Spanish deportation or deletion of the Moors. This precedent would fall far short of our case.

I consider four of these bills, passed or reported, as forming a system by which every fibre would be eradicated of ancient or future aristocracy; and a foundation laid for a government truly republican. The repeal of the laws of entail would prevent the accumulation and perpetuation of wealth, in select families, and preserve the soil of the country from being daily more and more absorbed in mortmain. The abolition of primogeniture, and equal partition of inheritances, removed the feudal and unnatural distinctions which made one member of every family rich, and all the rest poor, substituting equal partition, the best of all Agrarian laws. The restoration of the rights of conscience relieved the people from taxation for the support of a religion not theirs; for the establishment was truly of the religion of the rich, the dissenting sects being entirely composed of the less wealthy people; and these, by the bill for a general education,would be qualified to understand their rights, to maintain them, and to exercise with intelligence their parts in self-government; and all this would be effected, without the violation of a single natural right of any one individual citizen. To these, too, might be added, as a further security, the introduction of the trial by jury, into the Chancery courts, which have already ingulfed, and continue to ingulf, so great a proportion of the jurisdiction over our property.

On the 1st of June, 1779, I was appointed Governor of the Commonwealth, and retired from the legislature. Being elected, also, one of the Visitors of William and Mary college, a self-electing body, I effected, during my residence in Williamsburg that year, a change in the organization of that institution, by abolishing the Grammar school, and the two professorships of Divinity and Oriental languages, and substituting a professorship of Law and Police, one of Anatomy, Medicine and Chemistry, and one of Modern languages; and the charter confining us to six professorships, we added the Law of

Nature and Nations, and the Fine Arts to the duties of the Moral professor, and Natural History to those of the professor of Mathematics and Natural Philosophy.

Being now, as it were, identified with the Commonwealth itself, to write my own history, during the two years of my administration, would be to write the public history of that portion of the revolution within this State. This has been done by others, and particularly by Mr. Girardin, who wrote his Continuation of Burke's history of Virginia, while at Milton, in this neighborhood, had free access to all my papers while composing it, and has given as faithful an account as I could myself. For this portion, therefore, of my own life, I refer altogether to his history. From a belief that, under the pressure of the invasion under which we were then laboring, the public would have more confidence in a Military chief, and that the Military commander, being invested with the Civil power also, both might be wielded with more energy, promptitude and effect for the defence of the State, I resigned the administration at the end of my second year, and General Nelson was appointed to succeed me.

Soon after my leaving Congress, September, '76, to wit, on the last day of that month, I had been appointed, with Dr. Franklin, to go to France, as a Commissioner, to negotiate treaties of alliance and commerce with that government. Silas Deane, then in France, acting as agent for procuring military stores, was joined with us in commission. But such was the state of my family that I could not leave it, nor could I expose it to the dangers of the sea, and of capture by the British ships, then covering the ocean. I saw, too, that the laboring oar was really at home, where much was to be done, of the most permanent interest, in new modeling our governments and much to defend our fanes and fire-sides from the desolations of an invading enemy, pressing on our country in every point. I declined, therefore, and Mr. Lee was appointed in my place. On the 15th of June, 1781, I had been appointed, with Mr. Adams, Mr. Franklin, Mr. Jay, and Mr. Laurence, a Minister Plenipotentiary for negotiating peace, then expected to be effected through the mediation of the Empress of Russia. The same reasons obliged me still to decline; and the negotiation was in fact never entered on. But, in the autumn of the next year, 1782, Congress receiving assurances that a general peace would be concluded in the winter and spring, they renewed my appointment on the 13th of November of that year. I had, two months before that, lost the cherished companion of my life in whose affections, unabated on both sides, I had lived the last ten years in unchequered happiness. (Jefferson is, of course, referring to the death of Mrs. Jefferson.) With the public interests, the state of my mind concurred in recommending the change of scene proposed; and I accepted the appointment, and left Monticello on the 19th of December, 1782, for Philadelphia, where I arrived on the 27th. The Minister of France, Luzerne, offered me a passage in the Romulus frigate, which I accepted; but she was then lying a few miles below Baltimore, blocked up in the ice. I remained, therefore, a month in Philadelphia, looking over the papers in the office of State, in order to possess myself of the general state of our foreign relations, and then went to Baltimore, to await the liberation of the frigate from the ice. After waiting there nearly a month, we received information that a Provisional treaty of peace had been signed by our Commissioners on the 3d of September, 1782, to become absolute, on the conclusion of peace between France and Great Britain. Considering my proceeding to Europe as now of no utility to the public, I returned immediately to Philadelphia, to take the orders of Congress, and was excused by them from further proceeding. I, therefore, returned home, where I arrived on the 15th of May, 1783.

On the 6th of the following month, I was appointed by the legislature a delegate to Congress, the appointment to take place on the 1st of November ensuing, when that of the existing delegation would expire. I, accordingly, left home on the 16th of October, arrived at Trenton, where Congress was sitting, on the 3rd day on November, and took my seat on the 4th, on which day Congress adjourned, to meet at Annapolis on the 26th.

Congress had now become a very small body, and the members very remiss in their attendance on its duties, insomuch, that a majority of the States, necessary by the Confederation to constitute a House even for minor business, did not assemble until the 13th of December.

They, as early as January 7, 1782, had turned their attention to the moneys current in the several States, and had directed the Financier, Robert Morris, to report to them a table of rates, at which the foreign coins should be received at the treasury. That officer, or rather his assistant, Gouverneur Morris, answered them on the 15th, in an able and elaborate statement of the denominations of money current in the several States, and of the comparative value of the foreign coins chiefly in circulation with us. He went into the consideration of the necessity of establishing a standard of value with us, and of the adoption of a money Unit. He proposed for that Unit, such a fraction of pure silver as would be a common measure of the penny of every State, without leaving a fraction. This common divisor he found to 1/1440 of a dollar, or 1/1600 of the crown sterling. The value of a dollar was, therefore, to be expressed by 1,440 units, and of a crown by 1,600; each Unit containing a quarter of a grain of fine silver. Congress turning again their attention to this subject the following year, the Financier, by a letter of April 30, 1783, further explained and urged the Unit he had proposed; but nothing more was done in it until the ensuing year, when it was again taken up, and referred to a committee, of which I was a member. The general views of the Financier were sound, and the principle was ingenious on which he proposed to found his Unit; but it was too minute for ordinary use, too laborious for computation, either by the head or in figures. The price of a loaf of bread, 1/20 of a dollar, would be 72 units.

A pound of butter, 1/5 of a dollar, 288 units.

A horse or bullock, of eighty dollars value, would require a notation of six figures, to wit, 115,200, and the public debt, suppose of eighty millions, would require twelve figures, to wit, 115,200,000,000 units. Such a system of money - arithmetic would be entirely unmanageable for the common purposes of society. I proposed, therefore, instead of this, to adopt the Dollar as our Unit of account and payment, and that its divisions and sub-divisions should be in the decimal ratio. I wrote some notes on the subject, which I submitted to the consideration of the Financier. I received his answer and adherence to his general system, only agreeing to take for his Unit one hundred of those he first proposed, so that a Dollar should be 1440/100, and a crown 16 units. I replied to this, and printed my notes and reply on a flying sheet, which I put into the hands of the members of Congress for consideration, and the Committee agreed to report on my principle. This was adopted the ensuing year, and is the system which now prevails. . . . The divisions into dimes, cents, and mills is now so well understood, that it would be easy of introduction into the kindred branches of weights and measures. I use when I travel, an Odometer of Clark's invention, which divides the mile into cents, and I find every one comprehends a distance readily, when stated to him in miles and cents; so he would in feet and cents, pounds and cents, &c.

The remissness of Congress, and their permanent session, began to be a subject of uneasiness; and even some of the legislatures had recommended to them intermissions, and periodical sessions. As the Confederation had made no provision for a visible head of the government, during vacations of Congress, and such a one was necessary to superintend the executive business, to receive and communicate with foreign ministers and nations, and to assemble Congress on sudden and extraordinary emergencies, I proposed, early in April, the appointment of a committee, to be called the "Committee of the States," to consist of a member from each State, who should remain in session during the recess of Congress: that the functions of Congress should be divided into executive and legislative, the latter to be reserved, and the former, by a general resolution, to be delegated to that Committee. This proposition was afterwards agreed to; a Committee appointed, who entered on duty on the subsequent adjournment of Congress, quarreled very soon, split into two parties, abandoned their post, and left the government without any visible head, until the next meeting in Congress. We have since seen the same thing take place in the Directory of France; and I believe it will forever take place in any Executive consisting of a plurality. Our plan, best, I believe, combines wisdom and practicability, by providing a plurality of Counsellors, but a single Arbiter for ultimate decision. I was in France when we heard of this schism, and separation of our Committee, and, speaking with Dr. Franklin of this singular disposition of men to quarrel, and divide into parties, he gave his sentiments, as usual, by way of Apologue. He mentioned the Eddystone lighthouse, in the British channel, as being built on a rock, in the mid-channel, totally inaccessible in winter, from the boisterous character of that sea, in that season; that, therefore, for the two keepers employed to keep up the lights, all provision for the winter were necessarily carried to them in autumn, as they could never be visited again till the return of the milder season; that, on the first practicable day in the spring, a boat put off to them with fresh supplies. The boatman met at the door one of the keepers, and accosted him with a "How goes it, friend? Very well. How is your companion? I do not know. Don't know? Is not he here? I can't tell. Have not you seen him to-day? No. When did you see him? Not since last fall. You have killed him? Not I, indeed." They were about to lay hold of him, as having certainly murdered his companion; but he desired them to go up stairs and examine for themselves. They went up, and there found the other keeper. They had quarrelled, it seems, soon after being left there, had divided into two parties, assigned the cares below to one, and those above to the other, and had never spoken to, or seen, one another since.

But to return to our Congress at Annapolis. The definitive treaty of peace which had been signed at Paris on the 3rd of September, 1783, and received here, could not be ratified without a House of nine States. On the 23rd of December, therefore, we addressed letters to the several Governors, stating the receipt of the definitive treaty; that seven States only were in attendance, while nine were necessary to its ratification; and urging them to press on their delegates the necessity of their immediate attendance. And on the 26th, to save time, I moved that the Agent of Marine (Robert Morris) should be instructed to have ready a vessel at this place, at New York, and at some Eastern port, to carry over the ratification of the treaty when agreed to. It met the general sense of the House, but was opposed by Dr. Lee, on the ground of expense, which it would authorize the Agent to incur for us; and, he said, it would be better to ratify at once, and send on the ratification. Some members had before suggested, that seven States were competent to the ratification. My motion was therefore postponed, and another brought forward by Mr. Read, of South Carolina, for an immediate ratification. This was debated the 26th and 27th. Read, Lee, Williamson and Jeremiah Chase, urged that ratification was a mere matter of form, that the treaty was conclusive from the moment it was signed by the ministers; that, although the Confederation requires the assent of *nine States* to *enter into* a treaty, yet, that its conclusion could not be called *entrance into it*, that supposing nine States requisite, it would be in the power of five States to keep us always at war; that nine States had virtually authorized the ratification, having ratified the provisional treaty, and instructed their ministers to agree to a definitive one in the same terms, and the present one was, in fact, substantially, and almost verbatim, the same; that there now remain but sixty-seven days for the ratification, for its passage across the Atlantic, and its exchange; that there was no hope of our soon having nine State present; in fact, that this was the ultimate point of time to which we could venture to wait; that if the ratification was not in Paris by the time stipulated, the treaty would become void; that if ratified by seven States, it would go under our seal, without its being known to Great Britain that only seven had concurred; that it was a question of which they had not right to take cognizance, and we were only answerable for it to our constituents; that it was like the ratification which Great Britain had received from the Dutch, by the negotiations of Sir William Temple.

On the contrary, it was argued by Monroe, Gerry, Howel, Ellery and myself, that by the modern usage of Europe, the ratification was considered as the act which gave validity to a treaty, until which, it was not obligatory. That the commission to the ministers reserved the ratification to Congress; that the treaty itself stipulated that it should be ratified; that it became a second question, who were competent to the ratification? That the Confederation expressly required nine States to enter into any treaty; that, by this, that instrument must have intended, that the assent of nine States should be necessary, as well to the *completion* as to the *commencement* of the treaty, its object having been to guard the rights of the Union in all those important cases where nine States are called for; that by the contrary construction, seven States, containing less than one-third of our whole citizens, might rivet on us a treaty, commenced indeed under commission and instructions from nine States, but formed by the minister in express contradiction to such instructions, and in direct sacrifice of the interests of so great a majority; that the definitive treaty was admitted not to be a verbal copy of the provisional one, and whether the departures from it were of substance, or not, was a question on which nine States alone were competent to decide; that the circumstances of the ratification of the provisional articles by nine States, the instructions to our ministers to form a definitive one

by them, and their actual agreement in substance, do not
render us competent to ratify in the present instance; if
these circumstances are in themselves a ratification,
nothing further is requisite than to give attested copies of
them, in exchange for the British ratification; if they are
not, we remain where we were, without a ratification by
nine States, and incompetent ourselves to ratify; that it
was but four days since the seven States, now present,
unanimously concurred in a resolution, to be forwarded to
the Governors of the absent States, in which they stated as
a cause for urging on their delegates, that nine States were
necessary to ratify the treaty; that in the case of the
Dutch ratification, Great Britain had courted it, and
therefore was glad to accept it as it was; that they knew
our Constitution, and would object to a ratification by
seven; that, if that circumstance was kept back, it would
be known hereafter, and would give them ground to deny
the validity of a ratification, into which they should have
been surprised and cheated, and it would be a
dishonorable prostitution of our seal; that there is a hope
of nine States; that if the treaty would become null, if not
ratified in time, it would not be saved by an imperfect
ratification; but that, in fact, it would not be null, and
would be placed on better ground, going in unexceptional
form, though a few days too late, and rested on the small
importance of this circumstance, and the physical
impossibilities which had prevented a punctual
compliance in point of time; that this would be approved
by all nations, and by Great Britain herself, if not
determined to renew the war, and if so determined, she
would never want excuses, were this out of the way. Mr.
Read gave notice, he should call for the yeas and nays;
whereon those in opposition, prepared a resolution,
expressing pointedly the reasons of their dissent from his
motion. It appearing, however, that his proposition could

not be carried, it was thought better to make no entry at all. Massachusetts alone would have been for it; Rhode Island, Pennsylvania and Virginia against it, Delaware, Maryland and North Carolina, would have been divided.

Our body was little numerous, but very contentious. Day after day was wasted on the most unimportant questions. A member, one of those afflicted with the morbid rage of debate, of an ardent mind, prompt imagination, and copious flow of words, who heard with impatience any logic which was not his own, sitting near me on some occasion of a trifling but wordy debate, asked me how I could sit in silence, hearing so much false reasoning, which a word should refute? I observed to him, that to refute indeed was easy, but to silence was impossible; that in measures brought forward by myself, I took the laboring oar, as was incumbent on me; but that in general, I was willing to listen; that if every sound argument or objection was used by some one or other of the numerous debaters, it was enough; if not, I thought it sufficient to suggest the omission, without going into a repetition of what had been already said by others: that this was a waste and abuse of the time and patience of the House, which could not be justified. And I believe, that if the members of deliberate bodies were to observe this course generally, they would do in a day, what takes them a week; and it is really more questionable, than may at first be thought, whether Bonaparte's dumb legislature, which said nothing, and did much, may not be preferable to one which talks much, and does nothing. I served with General Washington in the legislature of Virginia, before the revolution, and, during it, with Dr. Franklin in Congress. I never heard either of them speak ten minutes at a time, nor to any but the main point, which was to decide the question. They laid their shoulders to the great points, knowing that the little ones would follow of themselves. If the present Congress errs in too much talking, how can it be otherwise, in a body to which the people send one hundred and fifty lawyers, whose trade it is to question everything, yield nothing, and talk by the hour? That one hundred and fifty lawyers should do business together, ought not to be expected. But to return again to our subject.

Those who thought seven States competent to the ratification, being very restless under the loss of their motion, I proposed, on the third of January, to meet them on middle ground, and therefore moved a resolution, which premised, that there were but seven States present, who were unanimous for the ratification, but that they differed in opinion on the question of competency; that those however in the negative were unwilling that any powers which it might be supposed they possessed, should remain unexercised for the restoration of peace, provided it could be done, saving their good faith, and without importing any opinion of Congress, that seven States were competent, and resolving that the treaty be ratified so far as they had power; that it should be transmitted to our ministers, with instructions to keep it uncommunicated; to endeavor to obtain three months longer for exchange of ratifications; that they should be informed, that so soon as nine States shall be present, a ratification by nine shall be sent them: if this should get to them before the ultimate point of time for exchange, they were to use it, and not the other; if not, they were to offer the act of the seven States in exchange, informing them the treaty had come to hand while Congress was not in session; that but seven States were as yet assembled, and these had unanimously concurred in the ratification. This was debated on the third and fourth; and on the fifth, a vessel being to sail for England, from this port (Annapolis), the House directed the President to write to our ministers accordingly.

January 14. Delegates from Connecticut having attended yesterday, and another from South Carolina coming in this day, the treaty was ratified without a dissenting voice; and three instruments of ratification were ordered to be made out, one of which was sent by Colonel Harmer, another by Colonel Franks, and the third transmitted to the Agent of Marine, to be forwarded by any good opportunity.

Congress soon took up the consideration of their foreign relations. They deemed it necessary to get their commerce placed with every nation, on a footing as favorable as that of other nations; and for this purpose, to propose to each a distinct treaty of commerce. This act too would amount to an acknowledgment, by each, of our independence, and of our reception into the fraternity of nations; which, although as possessing our station of right, and in fact we would not condescend to ask, we were not unwilling to furnish opportunities for receiving their friendly salutations and welcome. With France, the United Netherlands, and Sweden, we had already treaties of commerce; but commissions were given for those countries also, should any amendments be thought necessary. The other States to which treaties were to be proposed, were England, Hamburg, Saxony, Prussia, Denmark, Russia, Austria, Venice, Rome, Naples, Tuscany, Sardinia, Genoa, Spain, Portugal, the Porte, Algiers, Tripoli, Tunis, and Morocco.

On the 7th of May Congress resolved that a Minister Plenipotentiary should be appointed, in addition to Mr.

Adams and Dr. Franklin, for negotiating treaties of commerce with foreign nations, and I was elected to that duty. I accordingly left Annapolis on the 11th, took with me my eldest daughter, then at Philadelphia (the two others being too young for the voyage), and proceeded to Boston, in quest of a passage. While passing through the different States, I made a point of informing myself of the state of the commerce of each; went on to New Hampshire with the same view, and returned to Boston. Thence I sailed on the 5th of July, in the Ceres, a merchant ship of Mr. Nathenial Tracey, bound to Cowes. He was himself a passenger, and, after a pleasant voyage of nineteen days, from land to land, we arrived at Cowes on the 26th. I was detained there a few days by the indisposition of my daughter. On the 30th, we embarked for Havre, arrived there on the 31st, left it on the 3d of August, and arrived at Paris on the 6th. I called immediately on Dr. Franklin, at Passy, communicated to him our charge, and we wrote to Mr. Adams, then at the Hague, to join us at Paris.

Before I had left America, that is to say, in the year 1781, I had received a letter from M. de Marbois, of the French legation in Philadelphia, informing me, he had been instructed by his government to obtain such statistical accounts of the different States of our Union, as might be useful for their information; and addressing to me a number of queries relative to the State of Virginia. I had always made it a practice, whenever an opportunity occurred of obtaining any information of our country, which might be of use to me in any station, public or private, to commit it to writing. These memoranda were on loose papers, bundled up without order, and difficult of recurrence, when I had occasion for a particular one. I thought this a good occasion to embody their substance, which I did in the order of Mr. Marbois' queries, so as to answer his wish, and to arrange them for my own use. Some friends, to whom they were occasionally communicated, wished for copies; but their volume rendering this too laborious by hand, I proposed to get a few printed, for their gratification. I was asked such a price, however, as exceeded the importance of the object. On my arrival at Paris, I found it could be done for a fourth of what I had been asked here. I therefore corrected and enlarged them, and had two hundred copies printed, under the title of "Notes on Virginia." I gave a very few copies to some particular friends in Europe, and sent the rest to my friends in America. A European copy, by the death of the owner, got into the hands of a bookseller, who engaged its translation, and when ready for the press, communicated his intentions and manuscript to me, suggesting that I should correct it, without asking any other permission for the publication. I never had seen so wretched an attempt at translation. Interverted, abridged, mutilated, and often reversing the sense of the original, I found it a blotch of errors, from beginning to end. I corrected some of the most material, and, in that form, it was printed in French. A London bookseller, on seeing the translation, requested me to permit him to print the English original. I thought it best to do so, to let the world see that it was not really so bad as the French translation had made it appear. And this is the true history of that publication.

Mr. Adams soon joined us at Paris, and our first employment was to prepare a general form, to be proposed to such nations as were disposed to treat with us. During the negotiations for peace with the British Commissioner, David Hartley, our Commissioners had proposed, on the suggestion of Dr. Franklin, to insert an article, exempting from capture by the public or private armed ships, of either belligerent, when at war, all merchant vessels and their cargoes, employed merely in carrying on the commerce between nations. It was refused by England, and unwisely, in my opinion. For, in the case of, war with us, their superior commerce places infinitely more at hazard on the ocean, than ours; and, as hawks abound in proportion to game, so our privateers would swarm, in proportion to the wealth exposed to their prize, while theirs would be few, for want of subjects of capture. We inserted this article in our form, with a provision against the molestation of fishermen, husbandmen, citizens unarmed, and following their occupations in unfortified places, for the humane treatment of prisoners of war, the abolition of contraband of war, which exposes merchant vessels to such vexatious and ruinous detentions and abuses; and for the principle of free bottoms, free goods.

In conference with the Count de Vergennes, it was thought better to leave to legislative regulation, on both sides, such modifications of our commercial intercourse, as would voluntarily flow from amicable dispositions. Without urging, we sounded the ministers of the several European nations, at the court of Versailles, on their dispositions towards mutual commerce, and the expediency of encouraging it by the protection of a treaty. Old Frederic, of Prussia, met us cordially, and without hesitation, and appointing the Baron de Thulemeyer, his minister at the Hague, to negotiate with us, we communicated to him or Projet, which, with little alteration by the King, was soon concluded. Denmark and Tuscany, entered also into negotiations with us. Other powers appearing indifferent; we did not think it proper to press them. They seemed, in fact, to know little about us, but as rebels, who had been successful in throwing off the yoke of the mother country. They were ignorant of our commerce, which had been always monopolized by England, and of the exchange of articles it might offer advantageously to both parties. They were inclined, therefore, to stand aloof, until they could see better what relations might be usefully instituted with us. The negotiations, therefore, begun with Denmark and Tuscany, we protracted designedly, until our powers had expired; and abstained from making new propositions to others having no colonies; because our commerce being an exchange of raw for wrought materials, is a competent price for admission into the colonies of those possessing them; but were we to give it, without price, to others, all would claim it, without price, on the ordinary ground of *gentis amicissimae* (most favored nation).

Mr. Adams being appointed Minister Plenipotentiary of the United States, to London, left us in June, and in July, 1785, Dr. Franklin returned to America, and I was appointed his successor at Paris. In February, 1780, Mr. Adams wrote to me, pressingly, to join him in London immediately, as he thought he discovered there some symptoms of better disposition towards us. Colonel Smith, his secretary of legation, was the bearer of his urgencies for my immediate attendance. I, accordingly, left Paris on the 1st of March, and, on my arrival in London, we agreed on a very summary form of treaty, proposing an exchange of citizenship for our citizens, our ships, and our productions generally, except as to office. On my presentation, as usual, to the King and Queen, at their levees, it was impossible for anything to be more ungracious, than their notice of Mr. Adams and myself. I saw, at once, that the ulcerations of mind in that quarter, left nothing to be expected on the subject of my attendance; and, on the first conference with the Marquis of Caermarthen, the Minister for foreign affairs, the distance and disinclination which he betrayed in his conversation, the vagueness and evasions of his answers to us, confirmed me in the belief of their aversion to have anything to do with us. We delivered him, however, our Projet, Mr. Adams not despairing as much as I did, of its effect. We afterwards, by one or more notes, requested his appointment of an interview and conference, which, without directly declining, he evaded, by pretences of other pressing occupations for the moment. After staying there seven weeks, till within a few days of the expiration of our commission, I informed the minister by note, that my duties at Paris required my return to that place, and that I should, with pleasure, be the bearer of any commands to his Ambassador there. He answered, that he had none and, wishing me a pleasant journey, I left London the 26th, and arrived at Paris the 30th of April.

While in London, we entered into negotiations with the Chevalier Pinto, Ambassador of Portugal, at that place. The only article of difficulty between us was, a stipulation that our bread stuff should be received in Portugal, in the form of flour as well as of grain. He approved of it himself, but observed that several Nobles, of great influence at their court, were the owners of wind-mills in the neighborhood of Lisbon, which depended much for their profits on manufacturing our wheat, and that this stipulation would endanger the whole treaty. He signed it, however, and its fate was what he had candidly portended.

My duties, at Paris, were confined to a few objects; the receipt of our whale-oils, salted fish, and salted meats, on favorable terms; the admission of our rice on equal terms with that of Piedmont, Egypt and the Levant; a mitigation of the monopolies of our tobacco by the Farmers-general, and a free admission of our productions into their islands, were the principal commercial objects which required attention; and, on these occasions, I was powerfully aided by all the influence and the energies of the Marquis de La Fayette, who proved himself equally zealous for the friendship and welfare of both nations; and, in justice, I must also say, that I found the government entirely disposed to befriend us on all occasions, and to yield us every indulgence, not absolutely injurious to themselves. The Count de Vergennes had the reputation, with the diplomatic corps, of being wary and slippery in his diplomatic intercourse; and so he might be with those whom he knew to be slippery, and doublefaced themselves. As he saw that I had no indirect views, practices no subtleties, meddled in no intrigues, pursued no concealed objects, I found him as frank, as honorable, as easy of access to reason, as any man with whom I had ever done business; and I must say the same for his successor, Montmorin, one of the most honest and worthy of human beings.

Our commerce, in the Mediterranean, was placed under early alarm, by the capture of two of our vessels and crews by the Barbary cruisers. I was very unwilling that we should acquiesce in the European humiliation, of paying a tribute to those lawless pirates, and endeavored to form an association of the powers subject to habitual depredations from them. I accordingly prepared, and proposed to their Ministers at Paris, for consultation with their governments, articles of a special confederation, in the following form:

"Proposals for concerted operation among the powers at war with the piratical States of Barbary,

1. "It is proposed, that the several powers at war with the piratical States of Barbary, or any two or more of them who shall be willing, shall enter into a convention to carry on their operations against those States, in concert, beginning with the Algerines.

2. "This convention shall remain open to any other powers, who shall, at any future tie, wish to accede to it; the parties reserving the right to prescribe the conditions of such accession, according to the circumstances existing at the time it shall be proposed.

3. "The object of the convention shall be, to compel the piratical States to perpetual peace, without price, and to guarantee that peace to each other.

4. "The operations for obtaining this peace shall be constant cruises on their coast, with a naval force now to be agreed on. It is not proposed that this force shall be so considerable as to be inconvenient to any party. It is believed that half a dozen frigates, with as many Tenders or Xebecs, one half of which shall be in cruise, while the other half is at rest, will suffice.

5. "The force agreed to be necessary, shall be furnished by the parties, in certain quotas, now to be fixed; it being expected, that each will be willing to contribute, in such proportion as circumstances may render reasonable.

6. "As miscarriages often proceed from the want of harmony among officers of different nations, the parties

shall now consider and decide, whether it will not be better to contribute their quotas in money, to be employed in fitting out and keeping on duty, a single fleet of the force agreed on.

7. "The difficulties and delays, too, which will attend the management of these operations, if conducted by the parties themselves separately, distant as their courts may be from one another, and incapable of meeting in consultation, suggest a question, whether it will not be better for them to give full powers, for that purpose, to their Ambassadors, or other Ministers resident at some one court of Europe, who shall form a Committee, or Council, for carrying this convention into effect; wherein, the vote of each member shall be computed in proportion to the quota of his sovereign, and the majority so computed, shall prevail in all questions within the view of this convention. The court of Versailles is proposed, on account of its neighborhood to the Mediterranean, and because all those powers are represented there, who are likely to become parties to this convention.

8. "To save to that Council the embarrassment of personal solicitations for office, and to assure the parties that their contributions will be applied solely to the object for which they are destined, there shall be no establishment of officers for the said Council, such as Commissioners, Secretaries, or any other kind, with either salaries or perquisites, nor any other lucrative appointments but such whose functions are to be exercised on board the said vessels.

9. "Should war arise between any two of the parties to this convention, it shall not extend to this enterprise, nor interrupt it; but as to this they shall be reputed at peace.

10. "When Algiers shall be reduced to peace, the other piratical States, if they refuse to discontinue their piracies, shall become the objects of this convention, either successively or together, as shall seem best.

11. "Where this convention would interfere with treaties actually existing between any of the parties and the States of Barbary, the treaty shall prevail, and such party shall be allowed to withdraw from the operations against the State."

Spain had just concluded a treaty with Algiers, at the expense of three millions of dollars, and did not like to relinquish the benefit of that, until the other party should fail in their observance of it. Portugal, Naples, the two Sicilies, Venice, Malta, Denmark and Sweden, were favorably disposed to such an association; but their representatives at Paris expressed apprehensions that France would interfere, and, either openly or secretly, support the Barbary powers; and they required, that I should ascertain the dispositions of the Count de Vergennes on the subject. I had before taken occasion to inform him of what we were proposing, and, therefore, did not think it proper to insinuate any doubt of the fair conduct of his government; but, stating our propositions, I mentioned the apprehensions entertained by us, that England would interfere in behalf of those piratical governments. "She dares not do it," said he. I pressed it no further. The other Agents were satisfied with this indication of his sentiments, and nothing was now wanting to bring it into direct and formal consideration, but the assent of our government, and their authority to make the formal proposition. I communicated to them the favorable prospect of protecting our commerce from the Barbary depredations, and for such a continuance of time, as, by an exclusion of them from the sea, to change their habits and characters, from a predatory to an agricultural people: toward which, however, it was expected they would contribute a frigate, and its expenses, to be in constant cruise. But they were in no condition to make any such engagement. Their recommendatory powers for obtaining contributions, were so openly neglected by the several States, that they declined an engagement which they were conscious they could not fulfill with punctuality; and so it fell through.

In 1786, while at Paris, I became acquainted with John Ledyard, of Connecticut, a man of genius, of some science, and of fearless courage and enterprise. He had accompanied Captain Cook in his voyage to the Pacific, had distinguished himself on several occasions by an unrivalled intrepidity, and published an account of that voyage, with details unfavorable to Cook's deportment towards the savages, and lessening our regrets at his fate. Ledyard had come to Paris, in the hope of forming a company to engage in the fur trade of the Western coast of America. He was disappointed in this, and, being out of business, and of a roaming, restless character, I suggested to him the enterprise of exploring the Western part of our continent, by passing through St. Petersburg to Kamschatka, and procuring a passage thence in some of the Russian vessels to Nootka Sound, whence he might make his way across the continent to the United States; and I undertook to have the permission of the Empress of Russia solicited. He eagerly embraced the proposition, and M. de Semoulin, the Russian Ambassador, and more particularly Baron Grimm, the special correspondent of the Empress, solicited her permission for him to pass through her dominions, to the Western coast of America. And here I must correct a material error, which I have committed in another place, to the prejudice of the Empress. In writing some notes of the life of Captain Lewis, prefixed to his "Expedition to the Pacific," I stated that the Empress gave the permission asked, and afterwards retracted it. This idea, after a lapse of twenty-six years, had so insinuated itself into my mind, that I committed it to paper, without the least suspicion of error. Yet I find, on recurring to my letters of that date, that the Empress refused permission at once, considering the enterprise as entirely chimerical. But Ledyard would not relinquish it, persuading himself that, by proceeding to St. Petersburg, he could satisfy the Empress of its practicability, and obtain her permission. He went accordingly, but she was absent on a visit to some distant part of her dominions, and he pursued his course to within two hundred miles of Kamschatka, where he was overtaken by an arrest from the Empress, brought back to Poland, and there dismissed. I must therefore, in justice, acquit the Empress of ever having for a moment countenanced, even by the indulgence of an innocent passage through her territories, this interesting enterprise.

The pecuniary distresses of France produced this year a measure of which there had been no example for nearly two centuries, and the consequences of which, good and evil, are not yet calculable. For its remote causes, we must go a little back.

Celebrated writers of France and England had already sketched good principles on the subject of government; yet the American Revolution seems first to have awakened the thinking part of the French nation in general, from the sleep of despotism in which they were sunk. The officers too, who had been to America, were mostly young men, less shackled by habit and prejudice, and more ready to assent to the suggestions of common sense, and feeling of common rights, than others. They came back with new ideas and impressions. The press, notwithstanding its shackles, began to disseminate them; conversation assumed new freedoms; Politics became the theme of all societies, male and female, and a very extensive and zealous party was formed, which acquired the appellation of the Patriotic party, who, sensible of the abusive government under which they lived, sighed for occasions of reforming it. This party comprehended all the honesty of the kingdom, sufficiently at leisure to think, the men of letters, the easy Bourgeois, the young nobility, partly from reflection, partly from mode; for these sentiments became matter of mode, and as such, united most of the young women to the party. Happily for the nation, it happened, at the same moment, that the dissipations of the Queen and court, the abuses of the pension list, and dilapidations in the administration of every branch of the finances, had exhausted the treasures and credit of the nation, insomuch that its most necessary functions were paralyzed. To reform these abuses would have overset the Minister; to impose new taxes by the authority of the King, was known to be impossible, from the determined opposition of the Parliament to their enregistry. No resource remained then, but to appeal to the nation. He advised, therefore, the call of an Assembly of the most distinguished characters of the nation, in the hope that, by promises of various and valuable improvements in the organization and regimen of the government, they would be induced to authorize new taxes, to control the opposition of the Parliament, and to raise the annual revenue to the level of expenditures. An Assembly of Notables therefore, about one hundred and fifty in number, named by the King, convened on the 22d of February. The Minister (Calonne) stated to them, that the annual excess of expenses beyond the revenue, when Louis XVI came to the throne, was thirty-seven millions of livres; that four hundred and forty millions had been borrowed to reestablish the navy; that the American war had cost them fourteen hundred and forty millions (two hundred and fifty-six millions of dollars), and that the interest of these sums, with other increased expenses, had added forty millions more to the annual deficit. (But a subsequent and more candid estimate made it fifty-six millions.) He proffered them a universal redress of grievances, laid open those grievances fully, pointed out sound remedies, and, covering his canvas with objects of this magnitude, the deficit dwindled to a little accessory, scarcely attracting attention. The persons chosen were the most able and independent characters in the kingdom, and their support, if it could be obtained, would be enough for him. They improved the occasion for redressing their grievances, and agreed that the public wants should be relieved; but went into an examination of the causes of them. It was supposed that Calonne was conscious that his accounts could not bear examination; and it was said, and believed, that he asked of the King, to send four members to the Bastile, of whom the Marquis de La Fayette was one, to banish twenty others, and two of his Ministers. The King found it shorter to banish him. His successor went on in full concert with the Assembly. The result was an augmentation of the revenue, a promise of economies in its expenditure, of an annual settlement of the public accounts before a council, which the Comptroller, having been heretofore obliged to settle only with the King in person, of course never settled at all; an acknowledgment that the King could not lay a new tax, a reformation of the Criminal laws, abolition of torture, suppression of corvees, reformation of the gabelles, removal of the interior Custom Houses, free commerce of grain, internal and external, and the establishment of Provincial Assemblies; which, altogether, constituted a great mass of improvement in the condition of the nation. The establishment of the Provisional Assemblies was, in itself, a fundamental improvement. They would be of the choice of the people, one-third renewed every year, in those provinces where there are no States, that is to say, over about three-fourths of the kingdom. They would be partly an Executive themselves, and partly an Executive Council to the Intendant, to whom the Executive power, in his province, had been heretofore entirely delegated. Chosen by the people, they would soften the execution of hard laws, and, having a right of representation to the King, they would censure bad laws, suggest good ones, expose abuses, and their representations, when united, would command respect. To the other advantages, might be added the precedent itself of calling the Assemblee des Notables, which would perhaps grow into habit. The hope was, that the improvements thus promised would be carried into effect; that they would be maintained during the present reign, and that that would be long enough for them to take some root in the constitution, so that they might come to be considered as a part of that, and be protected by time, and the attachment of the nation.

The Count de Vergennes had died a few days before the meeting of the Assembly, and the Count de Montmorin had been named Minister of Foreign Affairs, in his place. Villedeuil succeeded Calonne, as Comptroller General, and Lomenie de Bryenne, Archbishop of Thoulouse, afterwards of Sens, and ultimately Cardinal Lomenie, was named Minister principal, with whom the other Ministers were to transact the business of their departments, heretofore done with the King in person; and the Duke de Nivernois, and M. deMalesherbes, were called to the

Council. On the nomination of the Minister principal, the
Marshals de Segur and de Castries retired from the
departments of War and Marine, unwilling to act
subordinately, or to share the blame of proceedings taken
out of their direction. They were succeeded by the Count
de Brienne, brother of the Prime Minister, and the
Marquis de La Luzerne, brother to him who had been
Minister in the United States.

A dislocated wrist, unsuccessfully set, occasioned advice
from my surgeon, to try the mineral waters of Aix, in
Provence, as a corroborant. I left Paris for that place
therefore, on the 28th of February, and proceeded up the
Seine, through Champagne and Burgundy, and down the
Rhone through the Beaujolais by Lyons, Avignon, Nismes
to Aix; where, finding on trial no benefit from the waters,
I concluded to visit the rice country of Piedmont, to see if
anything might be learned there, to benefit the rivalship
of our Carolina rice with that, and thence to make a tour
of the seaport towns of France, along its Southern and
Western coast, to inform myself, if anything could be
done to favor our commerce with them. From Aix,
therefore, I took my route by Marseilles, Toulon, Hieres,
Nice, across the Col de Tende, by Coni, Turin, Vercelli,
Novara, Milan, Pavia, Novi, Genoa. Thence, returning
along the coast of Savona, Noli, Albenga, Oneglia, Monaco,
Nice, Antibes, Frejus, Aix, Marseilles, Avignon, Nismes,
Montpellier, Frontignan, Cette, Agde, and along the canal
of Languedoc, by Bezieres, Narbonne, Cascassonne,
Castelnaudari, through the Souterrain of St. Feriol, and
back by Castelnaudari, to Toulouse; thence to Montauban,
and down the Garonne by Langon to Bordeaux. Thence
to Rochefort, la Rochelle, Nantes, L'Orient; then back by
Rennes to Nantes, and up the Loire by Angers, Tours,
Amboise, Blois to Orleans, thence direct to Paris, where I

arrived on the 10th of June. Soon after my return from this journey, to wit, about the latter part of July, I received my daughter, Maria, from Virginia, by the way of London, the youngest having died some time before.

The treasonable perfidy of the Prince of Orange, Stadtholder and Captain General of the United Netherlands, in the war which England waged against them, for entering into a treaty of commerce with the United States, is known to all. As their Executive officer, charged with the conduct of the war, he contrived to baffle all the measures of the States General, to dislocate all their military plans and played false into the hands of England against his own country, on every possible occasion, confident in her protection, and in that of the King of Prussia, brother to his Princess. The States General, indignant at this patricidal conduct, applied to France for aid, according to the stipulations of the treaty concluded with her in '85. It was assured to them readily, and in cordial terms, in a letter from the Count de Vergennes, to the Marquis de Verac, Ambassador of France at the Hague, of which the following is an extract:

Extract from the despatch of the Count de Vergennes, to the Marquis de Verac, Ambassador from France, at the Hague, dated March 1, 1786:

"The King will give his aid, as far as may be in his power, towards the success of the affair, and will, on his part, invite the Patriots to communicate to him their views, their plans, and their discontents. You may assure them that the King takes a real interest in themselves as well as their cause, and that they may rely upon his protection. On this they may place the greater dependence, as we do not conceal, that if the Stadtholder resumes his former influence, the English System will soon prevail, and our alliance become a mere affair of the imagination. The Patriots will readily feel, that this position would be incompatible both with the dignity and consideration of his Majesty. But in case the Chief of the Patriots should have to fear a division, they would have time sufficient to reclaim those whom the Anglomaniacs had misled, and to prepare matters in such a manner, that the question when again agitated, might be decided according to their wishes. In such a hypothetical case, the King authorizes you to act in concert with them, to pursue the direction which they may think proper to give you, and to employ every means to augment the number of the partisans of the good cause. It remains for me to speak of the personal security of the Patriots. You may assure them, that under every circumstance, the King will take them under his immediate protection, and you will make known wherever you may judge necessary, that his Majesty will regard as a personal offence every undertaking against their liberty. It is to be presumed that this language, energetically maintained, may have some effect on the audacity of the Anglomaniacs, and that the Prince de Nassau will feel that the runs some risk in provoking the resentment of his Majesty."

This letter was communicated by the Patriots to me, when at Amsterdam, in 1788, and a copy sent by me to Mr. Jay, in my letter to him of March 16, 1788.

The object of the Patriots was, to establish a representative and republican government. The majority of the States General were with them, but the majority of the populace of the towns was with the Prince of Orange; and that populace was played off with great effect, by the triumvirate of . . . Harris, the English Ambassador, afterwards Lord Malmesbury, the Prince of Orange, a stupid man, and the Princess as much a man as either of her colleagues, in audaciousness, in enterprise, and in the thirst of domination. By these, the mobs of the Hague were excited against the members of the States General; their persons were insulted and endangered in the streets; the sanctuary of their houses was violated; and the Prince, whose function and duty it was to repress and punish these violations of order, took no steps for that purpose. The States General, for their own protection, were therefore obliged to place their militia under the command of a Committee. The Prince filled the courts of London and Berlin with complaints at this usurpation of his prerogatives, and, forgetting that he was but the first servant of a Republic, marched his regular troops against the city of Utrecht, where the States were in session. They were repulsed by the militia. His interests now became marshalled with those of the public enemy, and against his own country. The States, therefore, exercising their rights of sovereignty, deprived him of all his powers. The great Frederic had died in August, '86. He had never intended to break with France in support of the Prince of Orange. During the illness of which he died, he had, through the Duke of Brunswick, declared to the Marquis de La Fayette, who was then at Berlin, that he meant not to support the English interest in Holland: that he might assure the government of France, his only wish was, that some honorable place in the Constitution should be reserved for the Stadtholder and his children, and that he would take no part in the quarrel, unless an entire abolition of the Stadtholderate should be attempted. But his place was now occupied by Frederic William, his great nephew, a man of little understanding, much caprice, and very inconsiderate; and the Princess, his sister, although her husband was in arms against the legitimate authorities of the country, attempting to go to Amsterdam, for the purpose of exciting the mobs of that place, and being refused permission to pass a military post on the way, he put the Duke of Brunswick at the head of twenty thousand men, and made demonstrations of marching on Holland. The King of France here upon declared, by his Charge des Affaires in Holland, that if the Prussian troops continued to menace Holland with an invasion, his Majesty, in quality of Ally, was determined to succor that province.   In answer to this, Eden gave official information to Count Montmorin, that England must consider as at an end its convention with France relative to giving notice of its naval armaments, and that she was arming generally. War being now imminent, Eden, since Lord Aukland, questioned me on the effect of our treaty with France, in the case of a war, and what might be our dispositions. I told him frankly, and without hesitation, that our dispositions would be neutral, and that I thought it would be the interest of both these powers that we should be so; because, it would relieve both from all anxiety as to feeding their West India islands; that England, too, by suffering us to remain so, would avoid a heavy land war on our Continent, which might very much cripple her proceedings elsewhere; that our treaty, indeed, obliged us to receive into our ports the armed vessels of France, with their prizes, and to refuse admission to the prizes made on her by her enemies: that there was a clause, also, by which we guaranteed to France her American possessions, which might perhaps force us into the war, if these were attacked. "Then it will be war," said he, "for they will assuredly be attacked." Liston, at Madrid, about the same time, made the same inquiries of Carmichael. The Government of France then declared a determination to form a camp of observation at Givet, commenced arming her marine, and named the Bailli de

Suffrein their Generalissimo on the Ocean. She secretly engaged, also, in negotiations with Russia, Austria, and Spain, to form a quadruple alliance. The Duke of Brunswick having advanced to the confines of Holland, sent some of his officers to Givet, to reconnoitre the state of things there, and report them to him. He said afterwards, that "if there had been only a few tents at that place, he should not have advanced further, for that the King would not, merely for the interest of his sister, engage in a war with France." But, finding that there was not a single company there, he boldly entered the country, took their towns as fast as he presented himself before them, and advanced on Utrecht. The States had appointed the Rhingrave of Salm their Commander-in-Chief; a Prince without talents, without courage, and without principle. He might have held out in Utrecht for a considerable time, but he surrendered the place without firing a gun, literally ran away and hid himself, so that for months it was not known what had become of him. Amsterdam was then attacked, and capitulated. In the meantime, the negotiations for the quadruple alliance were proceeding favorably; but the secrecy with which they were attempted to be conducted, was penetrated by Fraser, Charge d'Affaires of England at St. Petersburg, who instantly notified his court, and gave the alarm to Prussia. The King saw at once what would be his situation, between the jaws of France, Austria, and Russia. In great dismay, he besought the court of London not to abandon him, sent Alvensleben to Paris to explain and soothe; and England through the Duke of Dorset and Eden, renewed her conferences for accommodation. The Archbishop, who shuddered at the idea of war, and preferred a peaceful surrender of right to an armed vindication of it, received them with open arms, entered into cordial conferences, and a declaration, and counter-declaration, were cooked up at Versailles, and sent to London for approbation. They were approved there, reached Paris at one o'clock of the 27th, and were signed that night at Versailles. It was said and believed at Paris, that M. de Montmorin, literally "pleuroit comme un enfant," when obliged to sign this counter-declaration; so distressed was he by the dishonor of sacrificing the Patriots, after assurances so solemn of protection, and absolute encouragement to proceed. The Prince of Orange was reinstated in all his powers, now become regal. A great emigration of the Patriots took place; all were deprived of office, many exiled, and their property confiscated. They were received in France, and subsisted, for some time, on her bounty. Thus fell Holland, by the treachery of her Chief, from her honorable independence, to become a province of England; and so, also, her Stadtholder, from the high station of the first citizen of a free Republic, to be the servile Viceroy of a foreign Sovereign. And this was effected by a mere scene of bullying and demonstration; not one of the parties, France, England, or Prussia, having ever really meant to encounter actual war for the interest of the Prince of Orange. But it had all the effect of a real and decisive war.

Our first essay, in America, to establish a federative government had fallen, on trial, very short of its object. During the war of Independence, while the pressure of an external enemy hooped us together, and their enterprises kept us necessarily on the alert, the spirit of the people, excited by danger, was a supplement to the Confederation, and urged them to zealous exertions, whether claimed by that instrument or not; but, when peace and safety were restored, and every man became engaged in useful and profitable occupation, less attention was paid to the calls of Congress. The fundamental defect of the Confederation was, that congress was not authorized to act immediately on the people, and by its own officers. Their power was only requisitory, and these requisitions were addressed to the several Legislatures, to be by them carried into execution, without other coercion than the moral principle of duty. This allowed, in fact, a negative to every Legislature, on every measure proposed by Congress; a negative so frequently exercised in practice, as to benumb the action of the Federal government, and to render it inefficient in its general objects, and more especially in pecuniary and foreign concerns. The want too, of a separation of the Legislative, Executive, and Judiciary functions, worked disadvantageously in practice. Yet this state of things afforded a happy augury of the future march of our Confederacy, when it was seen that the good sense and good dispositions of the people, as soon as they preceived the incompetence of their first compact, instead of leaving its correction to insurrection and civil war, agreed, with one voice, to elect deputies to a general Convention, who should peaceably meet and agree on such a Constitution as "would ensure peace, justice, liberty, the common defence and general welfare."

This Convention met at Philadelphia on the 25th of May, '87. It sat with closed doors, and kept all its proceedings secret, until its dissolution on the 17th of September, when the results of its labor were published all together. I received a copy, early in November, and read and contemplated its provisions with great satisfaction. As not a member of the Convention, however, nor probably a single citizen of the Union, had approved it in all its parts, so I, too, found articles which I thought objectionable. The absence of express declarations ensuring freedom of religion, freedom of the press, freedom of the person under the uninterrupted protection of the Habeas corpus, and trial by jury in Civil as well as in Criminal cases, excited my jealousy; and the re-eligibility of the President for life, I quite disapproved. I expressed freely, in letters to my friends, and most particularly to Mr. Madison and General Washington, my approbations and objections. How the good should be secured and the ill brought to rights was the difficulty. To refer it back to a new Convention might endanger the loss of the whole. My first idea was, that the nine States first acting, should accept it unconditionally, and thus secure what in it was good, and that the four last should accept on the previous condition, that certain amendments should be agreed to; but a better course was devised, of accepting the whole, and trusting that the good sense and honest intentions of our citizens, would make the alterations which should be deemed necessary. Accordingly, all accepted, six without objection, and seven with recommendations of specified amendments. Those respecting the press, religion, and juries, with several others, of great value, were accordingly made; but the Habeas corpus was left to the discretion of Congress, and the amendment against the re-eligibility of the President was not proposed. My fears of that feature were founded on the importance of the office, on the fierce contentions it might excite among ourselves, if continuable for life, and the dangers of interference, either with money or arms, by foreign nations, to whom the choice of an American President might become interesting. Examples of this abounded in history; in the case of the Roman Emperors, for instance; of the Popes, while of any significance; of the German Emperors; the Kings of Poland, and the Deys of Barbary. I had observed, too, in the feudal history, and in the recent instance, particularly, of the Stadtholder of Holland, how easily offices, or tenures for life, slide into inheritances.

My wish, therefore, was, that the President should be elected for seven years, and be ineligible afterwards. This term I thought sufficient to enable him, with the concurrence of the Legislature, to carry through and establish any system of improvement he should propose for the general good. But the practice adopted, I think, is better, allowing his continuance for eight years, with a liability to be dropped at half way of the term, making that a period of probation. That his continuance should be restrained to seven years was the opinion of the Convention at an earlier stage of its session, when it voted that term, by a majority of eight against two, and by a simple majority that he should be ineligible a second time. This opinion was confirmed by the House so late as July 26, referred to the Committee of detail, reported favorably by them, and changed to the present form by final vote, on the last day but one only of their session. Of this change, three States expressed their disapprobation; New York, by recommending an amendment, that the President should not be eligible a third time, and Virginia and North Carolina that he should not be capable of serving more than eight, in any term of sixteen years; and though this amendment has not been made in form, yet practice seems to have established it. The example of four Presidents voluntarily retiring at the end of their eighth year, and the progress of public opinion, that the principle is salutary, have given it in practice the force of precedent and usage; insomuch, that, should a President consent to be a candidate for a third election, I trust he would be rejected, on this demonstration of ambitious views.

But there was another amendment, of which none of us thought at the time, and in the omission of which, lurks the germ that is to destroy this happy combination of

National powers in the General government, for matters of National concern, and independent powers in the States, for what concerns the States severally. In England, it was a great point gained at the Revolution, that the commissions of the Judges, which had hitherto been during pleasure, should thenceforth be made during good behavior. A Judiciary, dependent on the will of the King, had proved itself the most oppressive of all tools, in the hands of that Magistrate. Nothing, then, could be more salutary, than a change there, to the tenure of good behavior; and the question of good behavior, left to the vote of a simple majority in the two Houses of Parliament. Before the Revolution, we were all good English Whigs, cordial in their free principles, and in their jealousies of their Executive Magistrate. These jealousies are very apparent, in all our state Constitutions; and, in the General government in this instance, we have gone even beyond the English caution, by requiring a vote of two-thirds, in one of the Houses, for removing a Judge; a vote so impossible, where (In the impeachment of Judge Pickering of New Hampshire, a habitual and maniac drunkard, no defence was made. Had there been, the party vote of more than one-third of the Senate would have acquitted him.) any defence is made, before men of ordinary prejudices and passions, that our Judges are effectually independent of the nation. But this ought not to be. I would not, indeed, make them dependent on the Executive authority, as they formerly were in England; but I deem it indispensible to the continuance of this government, that they should be submitted to some practical and impartial control; and that this, to be imparted, must be compounded of a mixture of State and Federal authorities.

It is not enough that honest men are appointed Judges. All know the influence of interest on the mind of man, and how unconsciously his judgment is warped by that influence. To this bias add that of the esprit de corps, of their peculiar maxim and creed, that "it is the office of a good Judge to enlarge his jurisdiction," and the absence of responsibility; and how can we expect impartial decision between the General government, of which they are themselves so eminent a part, and an individual State, from which they have nothing to hope or fear? We have seen, too, that contrary to all correct example, they are in the habit of going out of the question before them, to throw an anchor ahead, and grapple further hold for future advances of power. They are then, in fact, the corps of sappers and miners, steadily working to undermine the independent rights of the States, and to consolidate all power in the hands of that government in which they have so important a freehold estate. But it is not by the consolidation, or concentration of powers, but by their distribution, that good government is effected. Were not this great country already divided into States, that division must be made, that each might do for itself what concerns itself directly, and what it can so much better do than a distant authority. Every State again is divided into counties, each to take care of what lies within its local bounds; each county again into townships or wards, to manage minuter details; and every ward into farms, to be governed each by its individual proprietor. Were we directed from Washington when to sow, and when to reap, we should soon want (?) bread. It is by this partition of cares, descending in gradation from general to particular, that the mass of human affairs may be best managed, for the good and prosperity of all. I repeat, that I do not charge the Judges with willful and ill-intentioned error; but honest error must be arrested, where its toleration leads to public ruin. As, for the safety of society, we commit honest maniacs to Bedlam, so judges should be withdrawn from their bench, whose erroneous biases are leading us to dissolution. It may, indeed, injure them in fame or in fortune; but it saves the Republic, which is the first and supreme law.

Among the debilities of the government of the Confederation, no one was more distinguished or more distressing, than the utter impossibility of obtaining, from the States, the moneys necessary for the payment of debts, or even for the ordinary expenses of the government. Some contributed a little, some less, and some nothing; and the last furnished at length an excuse for the first to do nothing also. Mr. Adams, while residing at the Hague, had a general authority to borrow what sums might be requisite, for ordinary and necessary expenses. Interest on the public debt, and the maintenance of the diplomatic establishment in Europe, had been habitually provided in this way. He was now elected Vice-President of the United States, was soon to return to America, and had referred our bankers to me for future counsel, on our affairs in their hands. But I had no powers, no instructions, no means, and no familiarity with the subject. It had always been exclusively under his management, except as to occasional and partial deposits in the hands of Mr. Grand, banker in Paris, for special and local purposes. These last had been exhausted for some time, and I had fervently pressed the Treasury board to replenish this particular deposit, as Mr. Grand now refused to make further advances. They answered candidly, that no funds could be obtained until the new government should get into action, and have time to make its arrangements. Mr. Adams had received his appointment to the court of London, while engaged at

Paris, with Dr. Franklin and myself, in the negotiations under our joint commissions. He had repaired thence to London, without returning to the Hague, to take leave of that government. He thought it necessary, however, to do so now, before he should leave Europe, and accordingly went there. I learned his departure from London, by a letter from Mrs. Adams, received on the very day on which he would arrive at the Hague. A consultation with him, and some provision for the future, was indispensable, while we could yet avail ourselves of his powers; for when they would be gone, we should be without resource. I was daily dunned by a Company who had formerly made a small loan to the United States, the principal of which was now become due; and our bankers in Amsterdam, had notified me that the interest on our general debt would be expected in June; that if we failed to pay it, it would be deemed an act of bankruptcy, and would effectually destroy the credit of the United States, and all future prospect of obtaining money there; that the loan they had been authorized to open, of which a third only was filled, had now ceased to get forward, and rendered desperate that hope of resource. I saw that there was not a moment to lose, and set out for the Hague on the second morning after receiving the information of Mr. Adams's journey. I went the direct road by Louvres, Senlis, Roye, Pont St. Maxence, Bois le duc, Gournay, Peronne, Cambray, Bouchain, Valenciennes, Mons, Bruxelles, Malines, Antwerp, Mordick, and Rotterdam, to the Hague, where I happily found Mr. Adams. He concurred with me at once in opinion, that something must be done, and that we ought to risk ourselves on doing it without instructions, to save the credit of the United States. We foresaw, that before the new government could be adopted, assembled, establish its financial system, get the money into the Treasury, and place it in Europe, considerable time would elapse; that, therefore, we had better provide at once, for the years '88, '89, and '90, in order to place our government at its ease, and our credit in security, during that trying interval. We set out, therefore, by the way of Leyden, for Amsterdam, where we arrived on the 10th. I had prepared an estimate, showing that

There would be necessary for the year '88, 31,937/10 Florins; '89, 538,540 Florins; '90, 473,540 Florins; Total, 1,544,017/10 Florins.

To meet this, the bankers had in hand 79,268/2/8 Florins; and the unsold bonds would yield 542,800 Florins; Total 622,068/2/8.

Leaving a deficit of 921,949/7/4 Florins. We proposed then to borrow a million, yielding 920,000 Florins.

Which would leave a small deficiency of 1,949/7/4 Florins.

Mr. Adams accordingly executed 1000 bonds, for 1000 florins each, and deposited them in the hands of our bankers, with instructions, however, not to issue them until Congress should ratify the measure. This done, he returned to London, and I set out for Paris; and, as nothing urgent forbade it, I determined to return along the banks of the Rhine, to Strasburg, and thence strike off to Paris. I accordingly left Amsterdam on the 30th of March, and proceeded by Utrecht, Nimeguen, Cleves, Duysberg, Dusseldorf, Cologne, Bonne, Coblentz, Nassau, Hocheim, Frankfort, and made an excursion to Hanau, thence to Mayence, and another excursion to Rudesheim, and Johansberg; then by Oppenheim, Worms, and

Manheim, making an excursion to Heidelberg, then by Spire, Carlsruh, Rastadt and Kelh, to Strasburg, where I arrived April the 16th, and proceeded again on the 18th, by Phalsbourg, Fenestrange, Dieuze, Moyenvie, Nancy, Toul, Ligny, Bar-le-duc, St. Diziers, Vitry, Chalons sur Marne, Epernay, Chateau Thierri, Meaux, to Paris, where I arrived on the 23rd of April; and I had the satisfaction to reflect, that by this journey our credit was secured, the new government was placed at ease for two years to come, and that, as well as myself, relieved from the torment of incessant duns, whose just complaints could not be silenced by any means within our power.

A Consular Convention had been agreed on in '84, between Dr. Franklin and the French government, containing several articles, so entirely inconsistent with the laws of the several States, and the general spirit of our citizens, that Congress withheld their ratification, and sent it back to me, with instructions to get those articles expunged, or modified so as to render them compatible with our laws. The Minister unwillingly released us from these concessions, which, indeed, authorized the exercise of powers very offensive in a free State. After much discussion, the Convention was reformed in a considerable degree, and was signed by the Count Montmorin and myself, on the 14th of November, '88; not, indeed, such as I would have wished, but such as could be obtained with good humor and friendship.

On my return from Holland, I found Paris as I had left it, still in high fermentation. Had the Archbishop, on the close of the Assembly of Notables, immediately carried into operation the measures contemplated, it was believed they would all have been registered by the Parliament; but he was slow, presented his edicts, one after another, and at considerable intervals, which gave time for the feelings excited by the proceedings of the Notables to cool off, new claims to be advanced, and a pressure to arise for a fixed constitution, not subject to changes at the will of the King. Nor should we wonder at this pressure, when we consider the monstrous abuses of power under which this people were ground to powder; when we pass in review the weight of their taxes, and the inequality of their distribution; the oppressions of the tithes, the tailles, the corvees, the gabelles, the farms and the barriers; the shackles on commerce by monopolies; on industry by guilds and corporations; on the freedom of conscience, of thought, and of speech; on the freedom of the press by the Censure; and of the person by Lettres de Cachet; the cruelty of the Criminal code generally; the atrocities of the Rack; the venality of the Judges, and their partialities to the rich; the monopoly of Military honors by the Noblesse; the enormous expenses of the Queen, the Princes and the Court; the prodigalities of pensions; and the riches, luxury, indolence and immorality of the Clergy. Surely under such a mass of misrule and oppression, a people might justly press for a thorough reformation, and might even dismount their rough-shod riders, and leave them to walk on their own legs. The edicts, relative to the corvees and free circulation of grain, were first presented to the Parliament and registered; but those for the impot territorial, and stamp tax, offered some time after, were refused by the Parliament, which proposed a call of the States General, as alone competent to their authorization. Their refusal produced a Bed of justice, and their exile to Troyes. The Advocates, however, refusing to attend them, a suspension in the administration of justice took place. The Parliament held out for awhile, but the ennui of their exile and absence from Paris, began at length to be felt, and some dispositions for compromise to appear. On their consent, therefore, to prolong some of the former taxes, they were recalled from exile, the King met them in session, November 19, '87, promised to call the States General in the year '92, and a majority expressed their assent to register an edict for successive and annual loans from 1788 to '92; but a protest being entered by the Duke of Orleans, and this encouraging others in a disposition to retract, the King ordered peremptorily the registry of the edict, and left the Assembly abruptly. The Parliament immediately protested, that the votes for the enregistry had not been legally taken, and that they gave no sanction to the loans proposed. This was enough to discredit and defeat them. Hereupon issued another edict, for the establishment of a cour pleniere, and the suspension of all the Parliaments in the kingdom. This being opposed, as might be expected, by reclamations from all the Parliaments and Provinces, the King gave way, and by an edict of July 5th, '88, renounced his cour pleniere, and promised the States General for the 1st of May, of the ensuing year; and the Archbishop, finding the times beyond his faculties, accepted the promise of a Cardinal's hat, was removed [September '88] from the Ministry, and M. Necker was called to the department of finance. The innocent rejoicings of the people of Paris on this change provoked the interference of an officer of the city guards, whose order for their dispersion not being obeyed, he charged them with fixed bayonets, killed two or three, and wounded many. This dispersed them for the moment, but they collected the next day in great numbers, burnt ten or twelve guard-houses, killed two or three of the guards, and lost six or eight more of their own number. The city was hereupon put under Martial law, and after awhile the tumult subsided. The effect of this change of ministers, and the promise of the States General at an early day, tranquillized the nation. But two great questions now occurred. 1st. What proportion shall the number of deputies of the Tiers Etat bear to those of the Nobles and Clergy? And 2d, shall they sit in the same or in distinct apartments? M. Necker, desirous of avoiding himself these knotty questions, proposed a second call of the same Notables, and that their advice should be asked on the subject. They met, November 9, '88; and, by five bureaux against one, they recommended the forms of the States General of 1614; wherein the Houses were separate, and voted by orders, not by persons. But the whole nation declaring at once against this, and that the Tiers Etat should be, in numbers, equal to both the other orders, and the Parliament deciding for the same proportion, it was determined so to be, by a declaration of December 27th, '88. A Report of M. Necker, to the King, of about the same date, contained other very important concessions. 1. That the King could neither lay a new tax, nor prolong an old one. 2. It expressed a readiness to agree on the periodical meeting of the States. 3. To consult on the necessary restrictions on Lettres de Cachet; and 4. How far the press might be made free. 5. It admits that the States are to appropriate the public money; and 6. That Ministers shall be responsible for public expenditures. And these concessions came from the very heart of the King. He had not a wish but for the good of the nation; and for that object, no personal sacrifice would ever have cost him a moment's regret; but his mind was weakness itself, his constitution timid, his judgment null, and without sufficient firmness even to stand by the faith of his word. His Queen, too, haughty and bearing no contradiction, had an absolute ascendancy over him; and around her were rallied the King's brother d'Artois, the court generally, and the aristocratic part of his Ministers, particularly Breteuil, Broglio, Vauguyon, Foulon, Luzerne, men whose principles of government were those of the age of Louis XIV. Against this host, the good counsels of Necker, Montmorin, St. Priest, although in unison with the wishes of the King himself, were of little avail. The resolutions of the morning, formed under their advice, would be reversed in the evening, by the influence of the Queen and court. But the hand of heaven weighed heavily indeed on the machinations of this junto; producing collateral incidents, not arising out of the case, yet powerfully co-exciting the nation to force a regeneration of its government, and overwhelming with accumulated difficulties, this liberticide resistance. For, while laboring under the want of money for even ordinary purposes, in a government which required a million of livres a day, and driven to the last ditch by the universal call for liberty, there came on a winter of such severe cold, as was without example in the memory of man, or in the written records of history. The Mercury was at times 50 degrees below the freezing point of Fahrenheit, and 22 degrees below that of Reaumur. All out-door labor was suspended, and the poor, without the wages of labor were, of course, without either bread or fuel. The government found its necessities aggravated by that of procuring immense quantities of firewood, and of keeping great fires at all the cross streets, around which the people gathered in crowds, to avoid perishing with cold. Bread, too, was to be bought, and distributed daily, gratis, until a relaxation of the season should enable the people to work; and the slender stock of bread stuff had for some time threatened famine, and had raised that article to an enormous price. So great, indeed, was the scarcity of bread, that, from the highest to the lowest citizen, the bakers were permitted to deal but a scanty allowance per head, even to those who paid for it; and, in cards of invitation to dine in the richest houses, the guest was notified to bring his own bread. To eke out the existence of the people, every person who had the means, was called on for a weekly subscription, which the Cures collected, and employed in providing messes for the nourishment of the poor, and vied with each other in devising such economical compositions of food, as would subsist the greatest number with the smallest means. This want of bread had been forseen for some time past, and M. de Montmorin had desired me to notify it in America, and that, in addition to the market price, a premium should be given on what should be brought from the United States. Notice was accordingly given, and produced considerable supplies. Subsequent information made the importations from America, during the months of March, April and May, into the Atlantic ports of France, amount to about twenty-one thousand barrels of flour, besides what went to other ports, and in other months; while our supplies to their West Indian islands relieved them also from that drain. This distress for bread continued till July.

Hitherto no acts of popular violence had been produced by the struggle for political reformation. Little riots, on ordinary incidents, had taken place as at other times, in different parts of the kingdom, in which some lives, perhaps a dozen or twenty, had been lost; but in the month of April, a more serious one occurred in Paris, unconnected, indeed, with the Revolutionary principle, but making part of the history of the day. The Fauxbourg St. Antoine is a quarter of the city inhabited entirely by the class of day laborers and journeymen in every line. A rumor was spread among them, that a great paper manufacturer, of the name of Reveillon, had proposed, on some occasion, that their wages should be lowered to fifteen sous a day. Inflamed at once into rage, and without inquiring into its truth, they flew to his house in vast numbers, destroyed everything in it, and in his magazines and work-shops, without secreting, however, a pin's worth to themselves, and were continuing this work of devastation, when the regular troops were called in. Admonitions being disregarded, they were of necessity fired on, and a regular action ensued, in which about one hundred of them were killed, before the rest would disperse. There had rarely passed a year without such a riot, in some part or other of the Kingdom; and this is distinguished only as contemporary with the Revolution, although not produced by it.

The States General were opened on the 5th of May, '89, by speeches from the King, the Garde des Sceaux, Lamoignon, and M. Necker. The last was thought to trip too lightly over the constitutional reformations which were expected. His notices of them in this speech, were not as full as in his previous 'Rapport au Roi.' This was observed, to his disadvantage; but much allowance should have been made for the situation in which he was placed, between his own counsels, and those of the ministers and party of the court. Overruled in his own opinions, compelled to deliver, and to gloss over those of his opponents, and even to keep their secrets, he could not come forward in his own attitude.

The composition of the Assembly, although equivalent, on the whole, to what had been expected, was something different in its elements. It had been supposed, that a superior education would carry into the scale of the Commons a respectable portion of the Noblesse. It did so as to those of Paris, of its vicinity, and of the other considerable cities, whose greater intercourse with enlightened society had liberalized their minds, and prepared them to advance up to the measure of the times. But the Noblesse of the country, which constituted two-thirds of that body, were far in their rear. Residing constantly on their patrimonial feuds, and familiarized, by daily habit, with Seigneurial powers and practice, they had not yet learned to suspect their inconsistence with reason and right. They were willing to submit to equality of taxation, but not to descend from their rank and prerogatives to be incorporated in session with the Tiers Etat. Among the Clergy, on the other hand, it had been apprehended that the higher orders of the Hierarchy, by their wealth and connections, would have carried the elections generally; but it turned out, that in most cases, the lower clergy had obtained the popular majorities. These consisted of the Cures, sons of the peasantry, who had been employed to do all the drudgery of parochial services for ten, twenty, or thirty Louis a year; while their superiors were consuming their princely revenues in palaces of luxury and indolence.

The objects for which this body was convened, being of the first order of importance, I felt it very interesting to understand the views of the parties of which it was composed, and especially the ideas prevalent as to the organization contemplated for their government. I went, therefore, daily from Paris to Versailles, and attended their debates, generally till the hour of adjournment. Those of the Noblesse were impassioned and tempestuous. They had some able men on both sides, actuated by equal zeal. The debates of the Commons were temperate, rational, and inflexibly firm. As preliminary to all other business, the awful questions came on, shall the States sit in one, or in distinct apartments? And shall they vote by heads or houses? The opposition was soon found to consist of the Episcopal order among the clergy, and two-thirds of the Noblesse; while the Tiers Etat were, to a man, united and determined. After various propositions of compromise had failed, the Commons undertook to cut the Gordian knot. The Abbe Sieyes, the most logical head of the nation, (author of the pamphlet "Qu'est ce que le Tiers Etat?" which had electrified that country, as Paine's Common Sense did us,) after an impressive speech on the 10th of June, moved that a last invitation should be sent to the Noblesse and Clergy, to attend in the hall of the States, collectively or individually, for the verification of powers, to which the Commons would proceed immediately, either in their presence or absence. This verification being finished, a motion was made, on the 15th, that they should constitute themselves a National Assembly; which was decided on the 17th, by a majority of four-fifths. During the debates on this question, about twenty of the Cures had joined them, and a proposition was made, in the chamber of the Clergy, that their whole body should join. This was rejected, at first, by a small majority only; but, being afterwards somewhat modified, it was decided affirmatively, by a majority of eleven. While this was under debate, and unknown to the court, to wit, on the 19th, a council was held in the afternoon, at Marly, wherein it was proposed that the King should interpose, by a declaration of his sentiments, in a *seance royale.* A form of declaration was proposed by Necker, which, while it censured, in general, the proceedings, both of the Nobles and Commons, announced the King's views, such as substantially to coincide with the Commons. It was agreed to in Council, the *seance* was fixed for the 22d, the meetings of the States were till then to be suspended, and everything, in the meantime, kept secret. The members, the next morning (the 20th) repairing to their house, as usual, found the doors shut and guarded, a proclamtion posted up for a *seance royale* on the 22d, and a suspension of their meetings in the meantime. Concluding that their dissolution was now to take place, they repaired to a building called the "Jeu de paume" (or Tennis court) and there bound themselves by oath to each other, never to separate, of their own accord, till they had settled a constitution for the nation, on a solid basis, and, if separated by force, that they would reassemble in some other place. The next day they met in the church of St. Louis, and were joined by a majority of the clergy. The heads of the Aristocracy saw that all was lost without some bold exertion. The King was still at Marly. Nobody was permitted to approach him but their friends. He was assailed by falsehoods in all shapes. He was made to believe that the Commons were about to absolve the army from their oath of fidelity to him, and to raise their pay. The court party were now all rage and desperation. They procured a committee to be held, consisting of the King and his Ministers, to which Monsieur and the Count d'Artois should be admitted. At this committee, the latter attacked M. Necker personally, arraigned his declaration, and proposed one which some of his prompters had put into his hands. M. Necker was brow-beaten and intimidated, and the King shaken. He detemined that the two plans should be deliberated on the next day, and the *seance royale* put off a day longer. This encouraged a fiercer attack on M. Necker the next day. His draught of a declaration was entirely broken up, and that of the Count d' Artois inserted into it. Himself and Montmorin offered their resignation, which was refused; the Count d' Artois saying to M. Necker, "No, sir, you must be kept as the hostage; we hold you responsible for all the ill which shall happen." This change of plan was immediately whispered without doors. The Noblesse were in triumph; the people in consternation. I was quite alarmed at this state of things. The soldiery had not yet indicated which

side they should take, and that which they should support
would be sure to prevail.   I considered a successful
reformation of government in France, as insuring a
general reformation through Europe, and the resurrection,
to a new life, of their people, now ground to dust by the
abuses of the governing powers.   I was much acquainted
with the leading patriots of the Assembly.   Being from a
country which had successfully passed through a similar
reformation, they were disposed to my acquaintance, and
had confidence in me.   I urged, most strenuously, an
immediate compromise; to secure what the government
was now ready to yield, and trust to future occasions for
what might still be wanting.   It was well understood that
the King would grant, at this time, 1. Freedom of the
person by Habeas corpus: 2. Freedom of conscience: 3.
Freedom of the press: 4. Trial by jury: 5. A representative
Legislature: 6. Annual meetings: 7. The origination of
laws: 8. The exclusive right of taxation and appropriation:
and 9. The responsibility of Ministers; and with the
exercise of these powers they could obtain, in future,
whatever might be further necessary to improve and
preserve their constitution.   They thought otherwise,
however, and events have proved their lamentable error.
For, after thirty years of war, foreign and domestic, the
loss of millions of lives, the prostration of private
happiness, and the foreign subjugation of their own
country for a time, they have obtained no more, nor even
that securely.   They were unconscious of (who could
foresee?) the melancholy sequel of their well-meant
perseverance; that their physical force would be usurped
by a first tyrant to trample on the independence, and even
the existence, of other nations: that this would afford a
fatal example for the atrocious conspiracy of Kings
against their people; would generate their unholy and
homicide alliance to make common cause among

themselves, and to crush, by the power of the whole, the efforts of any part to moderate their abuses and oppressions.

When the King passed, the next day, through the lane formed from the Chateau to the "Hotel des Etats," there was a dead silence. He was about an hour in the House, delivering his speech and declaration. On his coming out, a feeble cry of "vive le Roi" was raised by some children, but the people remained silent and sullen. In the close of his speech, he had ordered that the members should follow him, and resume their deliberations the next day. The Noblesse followed him, and so did the Clergy, except about thirty, who, with the Tiers, remained in the room, and entered into deliberation. They protested against what the King had done, adhered to all their former proceedings, and resolved the inviolability of their own persons. An officer came, to order them out of the room in the King's name. "Tell those who sent you," said Mirabeau, "that we shall not move hence but at our own will, or the point of the bayonet." In the afternoon, the people, uneasy, began to assemble in great numbers in the courts, and vicinities of the palace. This produced alarm. The Queen sent for M. Necker. He was conducted, amidst the shouts and acclamations of the multitude, who filled all the apartments of the palace. He was few minutes only with the Queen, and what passed between them did not transpire. The King went out to ride. He passed through the crowd to his carriage, and into it, without being in the least noticed. As M. Necker followed him, universal acclamations were raised of "vive Monsieur Necker, vive le sauveur de la France opprimee." He was conducted back to his house with the same demonstrations of affection and anxiety. About two hundred deputies of the Tiers, catching the enthusiasm of the moment, went to his house, and extorted from him a promise that he would not resign. On the 25th, forty-eight of the Nobles joined the Tiers, and among them the Duke of Orleans. There were then with them one hundred and sixty-four members of the Clergy, although the minority of that body still sat apart, and called themselves the Chamber of the Clergy. On the 26th, the Archbishop of Paris joined the Tiers, as did some others of the Clergy and of the Noblesse.

These proceedings had thrown the people into violent ferment. It gained the soldiery, first of the French guards, extended to those of every other denomination, except the Swiss, and even to the body-guards of the King. They began to quit their barracks, to assemble in squads, to declare they would defend the life of the King, but would not be the murderers of their fellow-citizens. They called themselves the soldiers *of the nation*, and left now no doubt on which side they would be, in case of rupture. Similar accounts came in from the troops in other parts of the kingdom, giving good reason to believe they would side with their fathers and brothers, rather than with their officers. The operation of this medicine at Versailles was as sudden as it was powerful. The alarm there was so complete, that in the afternoon of the 27th, the King wrote, with his own hand, letters to the Presidents of the Clergy and Nobles, engaging them immediately to join the Tiers. These two bodies were debating, and hesitating, when notes from the Count d'Artois decided their compliance. They went in a body, and took their seats with the Tiers, and thus rendered the union of the orders in one chamber complete.

The Assembly now entered on the business of their mission, and first proceeded to arrange the order in which they would take up the heads of their constitution, as follows:

First, and as Preliminary to the whole, a general Declaration of the Rights of Man. Then, specifically, the Principles of the Monarchy; Rights of the Nation; Rights of the King; Rights of the Citizens; Organization and Rights of the National Assembly; Forms necessary for the enactment of Laws; Organization and Functions of the Provisional and Municipal Assemblies; Duties and Limits of the Judiciary power; Functions and Duties of the Military power.

A Declaration of the Rights of Man, as the preliminary of their work, was accordingly prepared and proposed by the Marquis de La Fayette.

But the quiet of their march was soon disturbed by information that troops, and particularly the foreign troops, were advancing on Paris from various quarters. The King had probably been advised to this, on the pretext of preserving peace in Paris. But his advisers were believed to have other things in contemplation. The Marshal de Broglio was appointed to their command, a high-flying aristocrat, cool and capable of everything. Some of the French guards were soon arrested, under other pretexts, but really, on account of their dispositions in favor of the National cause. The people of Paris forced their prison, liberated them, and sent a deputation to the Assembly to solicit a pardon. The Assembly recommended peace and order to the people of Paris, the prisoners to the King, and asked from him the removal of the troops. His answer was negative and dry, saying they might remove themselves, if they pleased, to Noyons or Soissons. In the meantime, these troops, to the number of twenty or thirty thousand, had arrived, and were posted in, and between Paris and Versailles. The bridges and passes were guarded. At three o'clock in the afternoon of the 11 of July, the Count de La Luzerne was sent to notify M. Necker of his dismission, and to enjoin him to retire instantly, without saying a word of it to anybody. He went home, dined, and proposed to his wife a visit to a friend, but went in fact to his country house at St. Ouen, and at midnight set out for Brussels. This was not known till the next day (the 12th,) when the whole Ministry was changed, except Villedeuil, of the domestic department, and Barenton Garde des Sceaux. The changes were as follows:

The Baron de Breteuil, President of the Council of Finance; de la Galaisiere, Comptroller General, in the room of M. Necker; the Marshal de Broglio, Minister of War, and Foulon under him, in the room of Puy-Segur; the Duke de la Vauguyon, Minister of Foreign Affairs, instead of the Count de Montmorin; de La Porte, Minister of Marine, in place of the Count de La Luzerne; St. Priest was also removed from the Council. Luzerne and Puy-Segur had been strongly of the Aristocratic party in the Council, but they were not considered equal to the work now to be done. The King was now completely in the hands of men, the principal among whom had been noted, through their lives, for the Turkish despotism of their characters, and who were associated around the King, as proper instruments for what was to be executed. The news of this change began to be known at Paris, about one or two o'clock. In the afternoon, a body of about one hundred German cavalry were advanced, and drawn up in the Place Louis XV, and about two hundred Swiss posted at a little distance in their rear. This drew people to the spot, who thus accidentally found themselves in front of the troops, merely at first as spectators; but, as their numbers increased, their indignation rose. They retired a few steps, and posted themselves on and behind large piles of stones, large and small, collected in that place for a bridge, which was to be built adjacent to it. In this position, happening to be in my carriage on a visit, I passed through the lane they had formed, without interruption. But the moment after I had passed, the people attacked the cavalry with stones. They charged, but the advantageous position of the people, and the showers of stones, obliged the horse to retire, and quit the field altogether, leaving one of their number on the ground, and the Swiss in the rear not moving to their aid. This was the signal for universal insurrection, and this body of cavalry, to avoid being massacred, retired towards Versailles. The people now armed themselves with such weapons as they could find in armorer's shops, and private houses, and with bludgeons; and were roaming all night, through all parts of the city, without any decided object. The next day (the 13th) the Assembly pressed on the King to send away the troops, to permit the Bourgeoisie of Paris to arm for the preservation of order in the city, and offered to send a deputation from their body to tranquillize them; but their propositions were refused. A committee of magistrates and electors of the city were appointed by those bodies, to take upon them its government. The people, now openly joined by the French guards, forced the prison of St. Lazare, released all the prisoners, and took a great store of corn, which they carried to the corn-market. Here they got some arms, and the French guards began to form and train them. The city-committee determined to raise forty-eight thousand Bourgeoise, or rather to restrain their numbers to forty-eight thousand. On the 14th, they sent one of their members (Monsieur de Corny) to the Hotel des Invalides, to ask arms for their Garde Bourgeoise. He was followed by, and he found there, a great collection of people. The Governor of the Invalids came out, and represented the impossibility of his delivering arms, without the orders of those from whom he received them. De Corny advised the people then to retire, and retired himself; but the people took possession of the arms. It was remarkable, that not only the Invalids themselves made no opposition, but that a body of five thousand foreign troops, within four hundred yards, never stirred. M. de Corny, and five others, were then sent to ask arms of M. de Launay, Governor of the Bastile. They found a great collection of people already before the place, and they immediately planted a flag of truce, which was answered by a like flag hoisted on the parapet. The deputation prevailed on the people to fall back a little, advanced themselves to make their demand of the Governor, and in that instant, a discharge from the Bastile killed four persons of those nearest to the deputies. The deputies retired. I happened to be at the house of M. de Corny, when he returned to it, and received from him a narrative of these transactions. On the retirement of the deputies, the people rushed forward, and almost in an instant, were in possession of a fortification of infinite strength, defended by one hundred men, which in other times had stood several regular sieges, and had never been taken. How they forced their entrance has never been explained. They took all the arms, discharged the prisoners, and such of the garrison as were not killed in the first moment of fury; carried the Governor and Lieutenant Governor, to the Place de Greve, (the place of public execution,) cut off their heads, and sent them through the city, in triumph, to the Palais royal. About the same instant, a treacherous correspondence having been discovered in M. de Flesselles, Prevot des Marchands, they seized him in the Hotel de Ville, where he was in the execution of his office, and cut off his head. These events, carried imperfectly to Versailles, were the subject of two successive deputations from the Assembly to the King, to both of which he gave dry and hard answers; for nobody had as yet been permitted to inform him, truly and fully, of what had passed at Paris. But at night, the Duke de Liancourt forced his way into the King's bedchamber, and obliged him to hear a full and animated detail of the disasters of the day in Paris. He went to bed fearfully impressed. The decapitation of de Launay worked powerfully through the night on the whole Aristocratic party; insomuch, that in the morning, those of the greatest influence on the Count d'Artois, represented to him the absolute necessity that the King should give up everything to the Assembly. This according with the dispositions of the King, he went about eleven o'clock, accompanied only by his brothers, to the Assembly, and there read to them a speech, in which he asked their interposition to reestablish order. Although couched in terms of some caution, yet the manner in which it was delivered, made it evident that it was meant as a surrender at discretion. He returned to the Chateau on foot, accompanied by the Assembly. They sent off a deputation to quiet Paris, at the head of which was the Marquis de La Fayette, who had, the same morning, been named Commandant en chef of the Milice Bourgeoise; and Monsieur Bailly, former President of the States General, was called for as Prevot des Marchands. The demolition of the Bastile was now ordered and begun. A body of the Swiss guards, of the regiment of Ventimille, and the city horse guards joined the people. The alarm at Versailles increased. The foreign troops were ordered off instantly. Every Minister resigned. The King confirmed Bailly as Prevot des Marchands, wrote to M. Necker, to recall him, sent his letter open to the

Assembly, to be forwarded by them, and invited them to go with him to Paris the next day, to satisfy the city of his dispositions; and that night, and the next morning, the Count d'Artois, and M. de Montesson, a deputy connected with him, Madame de Polignac, Madame de Guiche, and the Count de Vaudreuil, favorites of the Queen, the Abbe de Vermont her confessor, the Prince of Conde, and Duke of Bourbon fled. The King came to Paris, leaving the Queen in consternation for his return. Omitting the less important figures of the procession, the King's carriage was in the centre; on each side of it, the Assembly, in two ranks a foot; at their head the Marquis de La Fayette, as Commander-in-chief, on horseback, and Bourgeois guards before and behind. About sixty thousand citizens, of all forms and conditions, armed with the conquest of the Bastile and Invalids, as far as they would go, the rest with pistols, swords, pikes, pruning-hooks, scythes, etc., lined all the streets through which the procession passed, and with the crowds of people in the streets, doors, and windows, saluted them everywhere with the cries of "vive la nation," but not a single "vive le Roi" was heard. The King stopped at the Hotel de Ville. There M. Bailly presented, and put into his hat, the popular cockade, and addressed him. The King being unprepared, and unable to answer, Bailly went to him, gathered from him some scraps of sentences, and made out an answer, which he delivered to the audience, as from the King. On their return, the popular cries were "vive le Roi et la nation." He was conducted by a garde Bourgeoise to his palace at Versailles, and thus concluded an "amende honorable," as no sovereign ever made, and no people ever received.

And here, again, was lost another precious occasion of sparing to France the crimes and cruelties through which she has since passed, and to Europe, and finally America, the evils which flowed on them also from this mortal source. The King was now become a passive machine in the hands of the National Assembly, and had he been left to himself, he would have willingly acquiesced in whatever they should devise as best for the nation. A wise constitution would have been formed, heredity in his line, himself placed at its head,with powers so large as to enable him to do all the good of his station, and so limited, as to restrain him from its abuse. This he would have faithfully administered, and more than this, I do not believe, he ever wished. But he had a Queen of absolute sway over his weak mind and timid virtue, and of a character the reverse of his in all points. This angel, as gaudily painted in the rhapsodies of Burke, with some smartness of fancy, but no sound sense, was proud, disdainful of restraint, indignant at all obstacles to her will, eager in the pursuit of pleasure, and firm enough to hold to her desires, or perish in their wreck. Her inordinate gambling and dissipations, with those of the Count d'Artois, and others of her *clique*, had been a sensible item in the exhaustion of the treasury, which called into action the reforming hand of the nation; and her opposition to it, her inflexible perverseness, and dauntless spirit, led herself to the Guillotine, drew the King on with her, and plunged the world into crimes and calamities which will forever stain the pages of modern history. I have ever believed, that had there been no Queen, there would have been no revolution. No force would have been provoked, nor exercised. The King would have gone hand in hand with the wisdom of his sounder counsellors, who, guided by the increased lights of the age, wished only, with the same pace, to advance the principles of their social constitution. The deed which closed the mortal course of these sovereigns, I shall neither approve nor condemn. I am not prepared to say, that the first magistrate of a nation cannot commit treason against his country, or is unamenable to its punishment; nor yet, that where there is no written law, no regulated tribunal, there is not a law in our hearts, and a power in our hands, given for righteous employment in maintaining right, and redressing wrong. Of those who judged the King, many thought him wilfully criminal; many, that his existence would keep the nation in perpetual conflict with the horde of Kings who would war against a generation which might come home to themselves, and that it were better that one should die than all. I should not have voted with this portion of the legislature. I should have shut up the Queen in a convent, putting harm out of her power and placed the King in his station, investing him with limited powers, which, I verily believe, he would have honestly exercised, according to the measure of his understanding. In this way, no void would have been created, courting the usurpation of a military adventurer, nor occasion given for those enormities which demoralized the nations of the world, and destroyed, and is yet to destroy, millions and millions of its inhabitants. There are three epochs in history, signalized by the total extinction of national morality. The first was of the successors of Alexander, not omitting himself: The next, the successors of the first Caesar: The third, our own age. This was begun by the partition of Poland, followed by that of the treaty of Pilnitz; next the conflagration of Copenhagen; then the enormities of Bonaparte, partitioning the earth at his will, and devastating it with fire and sword; now the conspiracy of Kings, the successors of Bonaparte, blasphemously calling themselves the Holy Alliance, and treading in the footsteps of their incarcerated leader; not yet, indeed, usurping the government of other nations, avowedly and in detail, but controlling by their armies the forms in which they will permit them to be governed; and reserving, *in petto*, the order and extent of the usurpations further meditated. But I will return from a digression, anticipated, too, in time, into which I have been led by reflection on the criminal passions which refused to the world a favorable occasion of saving it from the afflictions it has since suffered.

M. Necker had reached Basle before he was overtaken by the letter of the King, inviting him back to resume the office he had recently left. He returned immediately, and all the other Ministers having resigned, a new administration was named, to wit: St. Priest and Montmorin were restored; the Archbishop of Bordeaux was appointed Garde des Sceaux, La Tour du Pin, Minster of War; La Luzerne, Minister of Marine. This last was believed to have beem effected by the friendship of Montmorin; for although differing in politics, they continued firm in friendship, and Luzerne, although not an able man, was thought an honest one. And the Prince of Bauvau was taken into the Council.

Seven Princes of the blood Royal, six ex-Ministers, and many of the high Noblesse, having fled, and the present Ministers, except Luzerne, being all of the popular party, all the functionaries of government moved, for the present, in perfect harmony.

In the evening of August the 4th, and on the motion of the Viscount de Noailles, brother in law of La Fayette, the Assembly abolished all the titles of rank, all the abusive privileges of feudalism, the tithes and casuals of the Clergy, all Provincial privileges, and, in fine, the Feudal regimen generally. To the suppression of tithes, the Abbe Sieyes was vehemently opposed; but his learned and logical arguments were unheeded, and his estimation lessened by a contrast of his egoism (for he was beneficed on them), with the generous abandonment of rights by the other members of the Assembly. Many days were employed in putting into the form of laws, the numerous demolitions of ancient abuses; which done, they proceeded to the preliminary work of a Declaration of Rights. There being much concord of sentiment on the elements of this instrument, it was liberally framed, and passed with a very general approbation. They then appointed a Committee for the "reduction of a projet" of a constitution, at the head of which was the Archbishop of Bordeaux. I received from him, as chairman of the Committee, a letter of July 20th, requesting me to attend and assist at their deliberations; but I excused myself, on the obvious considerations, that my mission was to the King as Chief Magistrate of the nation, that my duties were limited to the concerns of my own country, and forbade me to intermeddle with the internal transactions of that, in which I had been received under a specific character only. Their plan of a constitution was discussed in sections, and so reported from time to time, as agreed to by the Committee. The first respected the general frame of the government; and that this should be formed into three departments, Executive, Legislative and Judiciary, was generally agreed. But when they proceeded to subordinate developments, many and various shades of opinion came into conflict, and schism, strongly marked, broke the Patriots into fragments of very discordant principles. The first question, Whether there should be a King? met with no open opposition; and it was readily agreed, that the government of France should be monarchical and hereditary. Shall the King have a negative on the laws? shall that negative be absolute, or suspensive only? Shall there be two Chambers of

Legislation, or one only? If two, shall one of them be hereditary? or for life? or for a fixed term? and named by the King? or elected by the people? These questions found strong differences of opinion, and produced repulsive combinations among the Patriots. The Aristocracy was cemented by a common principle, of preserving the ancient regime, or whatever should be nearest to it. Making this their polar star, they moved in phalanx, gave preponderance on every question to the minorities of the Patriots, and always to those who advocated the least change. The features of the new constitution were thus assuming a fearful aspect, and great alarm was produced among the honest Patriots by these dissensions in their ranks. In this uneasy state of things, I received one day a note from the Marquis de La Fayette, informing me that he should bring a party of six or eight friends to ask a dinner of me the next day. I assured him of their welcome. When they arrived, they were La Fayette himself, Duport, Barnave, Alexander la Meth, Blacon, Mounier, Maubourg, and Dagout. These were leading Patriots, of honest but differing opinions, sensible of the necessity of effecting a coalition by mutual sacrifices, knowing each other, and not afraid, therefore, to unbosom themselves mutually. This last was a material principle in the selection. With this view, the Marquis had invited the conference, and had fixed the time and place inadvertently, as to the embarrassment under which it might place me. The cloth being removed, and wine set on the table, after the American manner, the Marquis introduced the objects of the conference, by summarily reminding them of the state of things in the Assembly, the course which the principles of the Constitution were taking, and the inevitable result, unless checked by more concord among the Patriots themselves. He observed, that although he also had his opinion, he was ready to sacrifice it to that of his brethren of the same cause; but that a common opinion must now be formed, or the Aristocracy would carry everything, and that, whatever they should now agree on, he, at the head of the National force, would maintain. The discussions began at the hour of four, and were continued till ten o'clock in the evening; during which time, I was a silent witness to a coolness and candor of argument, unusual in the conflicts of political opinion; to a logical reasoning, and chaste eloquence, disfigured by no gaudy tinsel of rhetoric or declamation, and truly worthy of being placed in parallel with the finest dialogues of antiquity, as handed to us by Xenophon, by Plato and Cicero. The result was, that the King should have a suspensive veto on the laws, that the legislature should be composed of a single body only, and that to be chosen by the people. This Concordate decided the fate of the constitution. The Patriots all rallied to the principles thus settled, carried every question agreeably to them, and reduced the Aristocracy to insignificance and impotence. But duties of exculpation were now incumbent on me. I waited on Count Montmorin the next morning, and explained to him, with truth and candor, how it had happened that my house had been made the scene of conferences of such a character. He told me, he already knew everything which had passed, that so far from taking umbrage at the use made of my house on that occasion, he earnestly wished I would habitually assist at such conferences, being sure I should be useful in moderating the warmer spirits, and promoting a wholesome and practicable reformation only. I told him, I knew too well the duties I owed to the King, to the nation, and to my own country, to take any part in councils concerning their internal government, and that I should persevere, with care, in the character of a neutral and passive spectator, with wishes only, and very sincere ones, that those measures might prevail which would be for the greatest good of the nation.

I have no doubts, indeed, that this conference was previously known and approved by this honest Minister, who was in confidence and communication with the Patriots, and wished for a reasonable reform of the Constitution.

Here I discontinue my relation of the French Revolution. The minuteness with which I have so far given its details, is disproportioned to the general scale of my narrative. But I have thought it justified by the interest which the whole world must take in this Revolution. As yet, we are but in the first chapter of its history. The appeal to the rights of man, which had been made in the United States, was taken up by France, first of the European nations. From her, the spirit has spread over those of the South. The tyrants of the North have allied indeed against it; but it is irresistible. Their opposition will only multiply its millions of human victims; their own satellites will catch it, and the condition of man through the civilized world, will be finally and greatly ameliorated. This is a wonderful instance of great events from small causes. So inscrutable is the arrangement of causes and consequences in this world, that a two-penny duty on tea, unjustly imposed in a sequestered part of it, changes the condition of all its inhabitants. I have been more minute in relating the early transactions of this regeneration, because I was in circumstances peculiarly favorable for a knowledge of the truth. Possessing the confidence and intimacy of the leading Patriots, and more than all, of the Marquis Fayette, their head and Atlas, who had no secrets from me, I learned with correctness the views and proceedings of that party; while my intercourse with the diplomatic missionaries of Europe at Paris, all of them with the court, and eager in prying into its councils and proceedings, gave me a knowledge of these also. My information was always, and immediately committed to writing, in letters to Mr. Jay, and often to my friends, and a recurrence to these letters now insures me against errors of memory.

These opportunities of information ceased at this period, with my retirement from this interesting scene of action. I had been more than a year soliciting leave to go home, with a view to place my daughters in the society and care of their friends, and to return for a short time to my station at Paris. But the metamorphosis though which our government was then passing from its Chrysalid to its Organic form suspended its action in a great degree; and it was not till the last of August, that I received the permission I had asked. And here, I cannot leave this great and good country, without expressing my sense of its pre-eminence of character among the nations of the earth. A more benevolent people I have never known, nor greater warmth and devotedness in their select friendships. Their kindness and accommodation to strangers is unparalleled, and the hospitality of Paris is beyond anything I had conceived to be practicable in a large city. Their eminence, too, in science, the communicative dispositions of their scientific men, the politeness of the general manners, the ease and vivacity of their conversation, give a charm to their society, to be found no where else. In a comparison of this, with other countries, we have the proof of primacy, which was given to Themistocles, after the battle of Salamis. Every general voted to himself the first reward of valor, and the second to Themistocles. So, ask the travelled inhabitant of any nation, in what country on earth would you rather live? Certainly, in my own, where are all my friends, my relations, and the earliest and sweetest affections and recollections of my life. Which would be your second choice? France.

On the 26th of September I left Paris for Havre, where I was detained by contrary winds until the 8th of October. On that day, and the 9th, I crossed over to Cowes, where I had engaged the Clermont, Capt. Colley, to touch for me. She did so; but here again we were detained by contrary winds, until the 22d, when we embarked, and landed at Norfolk on the 23d of November. On my way home, I passed some days at Eppington, in Chesterfield, the residence of my friend and connection, Mr. Eppes; and, while there, I received a letter from the President, General Washington, by express, covering an appointment to be Secretary of State. I received it with real regret. My wish had been to return to Paris, where I had left my household establishment, as if there myself, and to see the end of the Revolution, which I then thought would be certainly and happily closed in less than a year. I then meant to return home, to withdraw from political life, into which I had been impressed by the circumstances of the times, to sink into the bosom of my family and friends, and devote myself to studies more congenial to my mind. In my answer of December 15th, I expressed these dispositions candidly to the President, and my preference of a return to Paris; but assured him, that if it was believed I could be more useful in the administration of the government, I would sacrifice my own inclinations without hesitation, and repair to that destination; this I left to his decision. I arrived at Monticello on the 23d of December, where I received a second letter from the President, expressing his continued wish that I should take my station there, but leaving me still at liberty to continue in my former office, if I could not reconcile myself to that now proposed. This silenced my reluctance, and I accepted the new appointment.

In the interval of my stay at home, my eldest daughter had been happily married to the eldest son of the Tuckahoe branch of Randolphs, a young gentleman of genius, science, and honorable mind, who afterwards filled a dignified station in the General Government, and the most dignified in his own State. I left Monticello on the first of March, 1790, for New York. At Philadelphia I called on the venerable and beloved Franklin. He was then on the bed of sickness from which he never rose. My recent return from a country in which he had left so many friends, and the perilous convulsions to which they had been exposed, revived all his anxieties to know what part they had taken, what had been their course, and what their fate. He went over all in succession, with a rapidity and animation almost too much for his strength. When all his inquiries were satisfied, and a pause took place, I told him I had learned with much pleasure that, since his return to America, he had been occupied in preparing for the world the history of his own life. I cannot say much of that, said he; but I will give you a sample of what I shall leave; and he directed his little grandson (William Bache) who was standing by the bedside, to hand him a paper from the table, to which he pointed. He did so; and the Doctor putting it into my hands, desired me to take it and read it at my leisure. It was about a quire of folio paper, written in a large and running hand, very like his own. I looked into it slightly, then shut it, and said I would accept his permission to read it, and would carefully return it. He said, "no, keep it." Not certain of his meaning, I again looked into it, folded it for my pocket, and said again, I would certainly return it. "No," said he, "keep it." I put it into my pocket, and shortly after took leave of him. He died on the 17th of the ensuing month of April; and as I understood that he had bequeathed all his papers to his grandson, William Temple Franklin, I immediately wrote to Mr. Franklin, to inform him I possessed this paper, which I should consider as his property, and would deliver to his order. He came on immediately to New York, called on me for it, and I delivered it to him. As he put it into his pocket, he said carelessly, he had either the original, or another copy of it, I do not recollect which. This last expression struck my attention forcibly, and for the first time suggested to me the thought that Dr. Franklin had meant it as a confidential deposit in my hands, and that I had done wrong in parting from it. I have not yet seen the collection he published of Dr. Franklin's works, and,therefore, know not if this is among them. I have been told it is not. It contained a narrative of the negotiations between Dr. Franklin and the British Ministry, when he was endeavoring to prevent the contest of arms which followed. The negotiation was brought about by the intervention of Lord Howe and his sister, who, I believe, was called Lady Howe, but I may misremember her title. Lord Howe seems to have been friendly to America, and exceedingly anxious to prevent a rupture. His intimacy with Dr. Franklin, and his position with the Ministry, induced him to undertake a mediation between them; in which his sister seemed to have been associated. They carried from one to the other, backwards and forwards, the several propositions and answers which passed, and seconded with their own intercessions, the importance of mutual sacrifices, to preserve the peace and connection of the two countries. I remember that Lord North's answers were dry, unyielding, in the spirit of unconditional submission, and betrayed an absolute

indifference to the occurrence of a rupture; and he said to
the mediators distinctly, at last, that "a rebellion was not
to be deprecated on the part of Great Britain; that the
confiscations it would produce would provide for many of
their friends." This expression was reported by the
mediators to Dr. Franklin, and indicated so cool and
calculated a purpose in the Ministry, as to render
compromise hopeless, and the negotiation was
discontinued. If this is not among the papers published,
we ask, what has become of it? I delivered it with my
own hands, into those of Temple Franklin. It certainly
established views so atrocious in the British government,
that its suppression would, to them, be worth a great price.
But could the grandson of Dr. Franklin be, in such degree,
an accomplice in the parricide of the memory of his
immortal grandfather? The suspension for more than
twenty years of the general publication, bequeathed and
confided to him, produced, for awhile, hard suspicions
against him; and if, at last, all are not published, a part of
these suspicions may remain with some.

I arrived at New York on the 21st of March, where
Congress was in session.

THE JEFFERSON BIBLE

I have made a wee-little book from the Gospels which I call the Philosophy of Jesus. It is a paradigma of his doctrines, made by cutting the texts out of the book and arranging them on the pages of a blank book, in a certain order of time or subject. A more beautiful or precious morsel of ethics I have never seen. It is a document in proof that I am a REAL CHRISTIAN, that is to say, a disciple of the doctrines of Jesus, very different from the Platonists, who call ME infidel and THEMSELVES Christians and preachers of the Gospel, while they draw all their characteristic dogmas from what its author never said nor saw. They have compounded from the heathen mysteries a system beyond the comprehension of man, of which the great reformer of the vicious ethics and deism of the Jews, were he to return on earth, would not recognize one feature.

THE LIFE AND MORALS
OF JESUS OF NAZARETH

I. Joseph and Mary go to Bethlehem,
Where Jesus is Born.

And it came to pass in those days, that there went out a decree from Caesar Augustus, that all the world should be taxed. ^{2} (And this taxing was first made when Cyrenius was governor of Syria.) ^{3} And all went to be taxed, every one into his own city. ^{4} And Joseph also went up from Galilee, out of the city of Nazareth, into Judaea, unto the city of David, which is called Bethlehem, (because he was of the house and lineage of David,) ^{5} To be taxed with Mary his espoused wife, being great with child. ^{6} And so it was, that, while they were there, the days were accomplished that she should be delivered. ^{7} And she brought forth her firstborn son, and wrapped him in swaddling clothes, and laid him in a manger; because there was no room for them in the inn.

II. He is Circumcised and Named
and they Return to Nazareth.

And when eight days were accomplished for the circumcising of the child, his name was called JESUS. ^{2} And when they had performed all things according to the law of the Lord, they returned into Galilee, to their own city Nazareth.

III. At Twelve Years of Age He Accompanies his Parents
to Jerusalem and Returns.

And the child grew, and waxed strong in spirit, filled with wisdom: and the grace of God was upon him. ^{2} And when he was twelve years old, they went up to Jerusalem after the custom of the feast. [3] And when they had fulfilled the days, as they returned, the child Jesus tarried behind in Jerusalem; and Joseph and his mother knew not of it. [4] But they, supposing him to have been in the company, went a day's journey; and they sought him among their kinsfolk and acquaintance. [5] And when they found him not, they turned back again to Jerusalem, seeking him. [6] And it came to pass, that after three days they found him in the temple, sitting in the midst of the doctors, both hearing them, and asking them questions. [7] And all that heard him were astonished at his understanding and answers. [8] And when they saw him, they were amazed: and his mother said unto him, Son, why hast thou thus dealt with us? behold, they father and I have sought thee sorrowing. [9] And he went down with them, and came to Nazareth, and was subject unto them: but his mother kept all these sayings in her heart. [10] And Jesus increased in wisdom and stature, and in favour with God and man.

IV. John Baptizes in Jordan.

Now in the fifteenth year of the reign of Tiberius Caesar, Pontius Pilate being governor of Judaea, and Herod being tetrarch of Galilee, and his brother Philip tetrarch of Ituraea and of the region of Trachonitis, and Lysanias the tetrarch of Abilene, [2] Annas and Caiaphas being the high priests, the word of God came unto John the son of Zacharias in the wilderness. [3] John did baptize in the wilderness, and preach the baptism of repentance for the remission of sins. [4] And the same John had his raiment of camel's hair, and a leathern girdle about his loins; and his meat was locusts and wild honey. [5] Then went out to him Jerusalem, and all Judaea, and all the region round about Jordan; 6 And were baptized of him in Jordan, confessing their sins.

V. Jesus is Baptized at 30 Years of Age.

Then cometh Jesus from Galilee to Jordan unto John, to be baptized of him. 2 And Jesus himself began to be about thirty years of age, being (as was supposed) the son of Joseph, which was the son of Heli.

VI. Drives the Traders Out of the Temple.

After this he went down to Capernaum, he, and his mother, and his brethren, and his disciples: and they continued there not many days. 2 And the Jews' passover was at hand, and Jesus went up to Jerusalem; 3 And found in the temple those that sold oxen and sheep and doves, and the changers of money sitting; 4 And when he had made a scourge of small cords, he drove them all out of the temple, and the sheep, and the oxen; and poured out the changers' money, and overthrew the tables; 5 And said unto them that sold doves, Take these things hence; make not my Father's house an house of merchandise.

VII. He Baptizes, but Retires into Galilee on the Death of John.

After these things came Jesus and his disciples into the land of Judaea; and there he tarried with them, and baptized. 2 Now when Jesus had heard that John was cast into prison, he departed into Galilee; 3 For Herod himself had sent forth and laid hold upon John, and bound him in prison for Herodias' sake, his brother Philip's wife: for he had married her. 4 For John had said unto Herod, It is not lawful for thee to have thy brother's wife. [5] Therefore Herodias had a quarrel against him, and would have killed him; but she could not: [6] For Herod feared John, knowing that he was a just man and an holy, and observed him; and when he heard him, he did many things, and heard him gladly. [7] And when a convenient day was come, that Herod on his birthday made a supper to his lords, high captains, and chief estates of Galilee; [8] And when the daughter of the said Herodias came in, and danced, and pleased Herod and them that sat with him, the king said unto the damsel, Ask of me whatsoever thou wilt, and I will give it thee. [9] And he sware unto her, Whatsoever thou shalt ask of me, I will give it thee, unto the half of my kingdom. [10] And she went forth, and said unto her mother, What shall I ask? And she said, The head of John the Baptist. [11] And she came in straightway with haste unto the king, and asked, saying, I will that thou give me by and by in a charger the head of John the Baptist. [12] And the king was exceeding sorry; yet for his oath's sake, and for their sakes which sat with him, he would not reject her. [13] And immediately the king sent an executioner, and commanded his head to be brought: and he went and beheaded him in the prison, [14] And brought his head in a charger, and gave it to the damsel: and the damsel gave it to her mother.

VIII. He Teaches in the Synagogue.

And they went into Capernaum; and straightway on the sabbath day he entered into the synagogue, and taught. [2] And they were astonished at his doctrine: for he taught them as one that had authority, and not as the scribes.

IX. Explains the Sabbath.

At that time Jesus went on the sabbath day through the corn; and his disciples were an hungred, and began to pluck the ears of corn, and to eat. 2 But when the Pharisees saw it, they said unto him, Behold, the disciples do that which is not lawful to do upon the sabbath day. 3 But he said unto them, Have ye not read what David did, when he was an hungred, and they that were with him; 4 How he entered into the house of God, and did eat the shew-bread, which was not lawful for him to eat, neither for them which were with him, but only for the priests? 5 Or have ye not read in the law, how that on the sabbath days the priests in the temple profane the sabbath, and are blameless? 6 And when he was departed thence, he went into their synagogue: 7 And, behold, there was a man which had his hand withered. And they asked him, saying, Is it lawful to heal on the sabbath days? that they might accuse him. 8 And he said unto them, What man shall there be among you, that shall have one sheep, and if it fall into a pit on the sabbath day, will he not lay hold on it, and lift it out? 9 How much them is a man better than a sheep? Wherefore it is lawful to do well on the sabbath days. 10 And he said unto them, The sabbath was made for man, and not man for the sabbath. 11 Then the Pharisees went out, and held a council against him, how they might destroy them. 12 But when Jesus knew it, he withdrew himself from thence; and great multitudes followed him; and he healed them all.

X. Call of His Disciples.

And it came to pass in those days, that he went out into a mountain to pray, and continued all night in prayer to God. 2 And when it was day, he called unto him his disciples: and of them he chose twelve, whom also he named apostles; ³ Simon, (whom he also named Peter,) and Andrew his brother, James and John, Philip and Bartholomew, ⁴ Matthew and Thomas, James the son of Alphaeus, and Simon called Zelotes, ⁵ And Judas the brother of James, and Judas Iscariot, which also was the traitor. ⁶ And he came down with them, and stood in the plain, and the company of his disciples, and a great multitude of people out of all Judaea and Jerusalem, and from the sea coast of Tyre and Sidon, which came to hear him, and to be healed of their diseases.

XI. The Sermon on the Mount.

And seeing the multitudes, he went up into a mountain: and when he was set, his disciples came unto him: ² And he opened his mouth, and taught them, saying, ³ Blessed are the poor in spirit: for theirs is the kingdom of heaven. ⁴ Blessed are they that mourn: for they shall be comforted. ⁵ Blessed are the meek: for they shall inherit the earth. ⁶ Blessed are they which do hunger and thirst after righteousness: for they shall be filled. ⁷ Blessed are the merciful: for they shall obtain mercy. ⁸ Blessed are the pure in heart: for they shall see God. ⁹ Blessed are the peacemakers; for they shall be called the children of God. ¹⁰ Blessed are they which are persecuted for righteousness' sake: for theirs is the kingdom of heaven. ¹¹ Blessed are ye, when men shall revile you, and persecute you, and shall say all manner of evil against you falsely, for my sake. ¹² Rejoice, and be exceeding glad: for great is your reward in heaven: for so persecuted they the prophets which were before you. ¹³ But woe unto you that are rich! for ye have received your consolation. ¹⁴ Woe unto you that are full! for ye shall hunger. Woe unto you that laugh now! for ye shall mourn and weep. ¹⁵ Woe unto you, when all men shall speak well of you!

for so did their fathers to the false prophets. [16] Ye are the salt of the earth: but if the salt have lost his savour, wherewith shall it be salted? it is thenceforth good for nothing, but to be cast out, and to be trodden under foot of men. [17] Ye are the light of the world. A city that is set on an hill cannot be hid. [18] Neither do men light a candle, and put it under a bushel, but on a candlestick; and it giveth light unto all that are in the house. [19] Let your light so shine before men, that they may see your good works, and glorify your Father which is in heaven. [20] Think not that I am come to destroy the law, or the prophets: I am not come to destroy, but to fulfil. [21] For verily I say unto you, Till heaven and earth pass, one jot or one tittle shall in no wise pass from the law, till all be fulfilled. [22] Whosoever therefore shall break one of these least commandments, and shall teach men so, he shall be called the least in the kingdom of heaven: but whosoever shall do and teach *them*, the same shall be called great in the kingdom of heaven. [23] For I say unto you, That except your righteousness shall exceed the righteousness of the scribes and Pharisees, ye shall in no case enter into the kingdom of heaven. [24] Ye have heard that it was said by them of old time, Thou shalt not kill; and whosoever shall kill shall be in danger of the judgment: [25] But I say unto you, That whosoever is angry with his brother without a cause shall be in danger of the judgment: and whosoever shall say to his brother, Raca, shall be in danger of the council; but whosoever shall say, Thou fool, shall be in danger of hell fire. [26] Therefore if thou bring thy gift to the altar, and there rememberest that thy brother hath ought against thee; [27] Leave there thy gift before the altar, and go thy way; first be reconciled to thy brother, and then come and offer thy gift. [28] Agree with thine adversary quickly, whiles thou are in the way with him; lest at any time the adversary deliver thee to the judge, and the judge deliver thee to the officer, and thou be cast into prison. 29 Verily I say unto thee, Thou shalt by no means come out thence, till thou hast paid the uttermost farthing. 30 Ye have heard that it was said by them of old time, Thou shalt not commit adultery: 31 But I say unto you, That whosoever looketh on a woman to lust after her hath committed adultery with her already in his heart. 32 And if thy right eye offend thee, pluck it out, and cast it from thee: for it is profitable for thee that one of the members should perish, and not that thy whole body should be cast into hell. 33 And if thy right hand offend thee, cut it off, and cast it from thee: for it is profitable for thee that one of thy members should perish, and not that thy whole body should be cast into hell. 34 It hath been said, Whosoever shall put away his wife, let him give her a writing of divorcement: 35 But I say unto you, That whosoever shall put away his wife, saving for the cause of fornication, causeth her to commit adultery: and whosoever shall marry her that is divorced committeth adultery. 36 Again, ye have heard that it hath been said by them of old time, Thou shalt not forswear thyself, but shalt perform unto the Lord thine oaths: 37 But I say unto you, Swear not at all; neither by heaven; for it is God's throne: 38 Nor by the earth; for it is his footstool: neither by Jerusalem; for it is the city of the great King. 39 Neither shalt thou swear by thy head, because thou canst not make one hair white or black. 40 But let your communication be, Yea, yea; Nay, nay: for whatsoever is more than these cometh of evil. 41 Ye have heard that it hath been said, An eye for an eye, and a tooth for a tooth: 42 But I say unto you, That ye resist not evil: but whosoever shall smite thee on thy right cheek, turn to him the other also. ^{43} And if any man will sue thee at the law, and take away thy coat, let him have thy cloak also. ^{44} And whosoever shall compel thee to go a mile, go with him twain. ^{45} Give to him that asketh thee, and from him that would borrow of thee turn not thou away. ^{46} Ye have heard that it hath been said, Thou shalt love thy neighbour, and hate thine enemy. ^{47} But I say unto you, Love your enemies, bless them that curse you, do good to them that hate you, and pray for them which despitefully use you, and persecute you; ^{48} That ye may be the children of your Father which is in heaven: for he maketh his sun to rise on the evil and on the good, and sendeth rain on the just and on the unjust. ^{49} For if ye love them which love you, what reward have ye? do not even the publicans the same? ^{50} And if ye salute your brethren only, what do ye more than others? do not even the publicans so? ^{51} And if ye lend to them of whom ye hope to receive, what thank have ye? for sinners also lend to sinners, to receive as much again. ^{52} But love ye your enemies, and do good, and lend, hoping for nothing again; and your reward shall be great, and ye shall be the children of the Highest: for he is kind unto the unthankful and to the evil. ^{53} Be ye therefore merciful, as your Father also is merciful. ^{54} Take heed that ye do not your alms before men, to be seen of them: otherwise ye have no reward of your Father which is in heaven. ^{55} Therefore when thou doest thine alms, do not sound a trumpet before thee, as the hypocrites do in the synagogues and in the streets, that they may have glory of men. Verily I say unto you, They have their reward. ^{56} But when thou doest alms, let not thy left hand know what thy right hand doeth: ^{57} That thine alms may be in secret: and thy Father which seeth in secret himself shall reward thee openly. 58 And when thou prayest, thou shalt not be as the hypocrites are: for they love to pray standing in the synagogues and in the corners of the streets, that they may be seen of men. Verily I say unto you, They have their reward. 59 But thou, when thou prayest, enter into thy closet, and when thou hast shut thy door, pray to thy Father which is in secret; and thy Father which seeth in secret shall reward thee openly. 60 But when ye pray, use not vain repetitions, as the heathen do: for they think that they shall be heard for their much speaking. 61 Be not ye therefore like unto them: for your Father knoweth what things ye have need of, before ye ask him. 62 After this manner therefore pray ye: Our Father which are in heaven, Hallowed be thy name. 63 Thy kingdom come. Thy will be done in earth, as it is in heaven. 64 Give us this day our daily bread. 65 And forgive us our debts, as we forgive our debtors. 66 And lead us not into temptation, but deliver us from evil: For thine is the kingdom, and the power, and the glory, for ever. Amen. 67 For if ye forgive men their trespasses, your heavenly Father will also forgive you: 68 But if ye forgive not men their trespasses, neither will your Father forgive your trespasses. 69 Moreover when ye fast, be not, as the hypocrites, of a sad countenance: for they disfigure their faces, that they may appear unto men to fast. Verily I say unto you, They have their reward. 70 But thou, when thou fastest, anoint thine head, and wash thy face; 71 That thou appear not unto men to fast, but unto thy Father which is in secret: and thy Father, which seeth in secret, shall reward thee openly. 72 Lay not up for yourselves treasures upon earth, where moth and rust doth corrupt, and where thieves break through and steal: 73 But lay up for yourselves treasures in heaven, where neither moth nor rust doth corrupt, and where thieves do not break through nor steal. 74 For where your treasure is, there will your heart be also. 75 The light of the body is the eye: if therefore thine eye be single, thy whole body shall be full of light. 76 But if thine eye be evil, thy whole body shall be full of darkness. If therefore the light that is in thee be darkness, how great is that darkness! 77 No man can serve two masters: for either he will hate the one, and love the other; or else he will hold to the one, and despise the other. Ye cannot serve God and mammon. 78 Therefore I say unto you, Take no thought for your life, what ye shall eat, or what ye shall drink; nor yet for your body, what ye shall put on. Is not the life more than the meat, and the body than raiment? 79 Behold the fowls of the air: for they sow not, neither do they reap, nor gather into barns; yet your heavenly Father feedeth them. Are ye not much better than they? 80 Which of you by taking thought can add one cubit unto his stature? 81 And why take ye thought for raiment? Consider the lilies of the field, how they grow; they toil not, neither do they spin: 82 And yet I say unto you, That even Solomon in all his glory was not arrayed like one of these. 83 Wherefore, if God so clothe the grass of the field, which today is, and tomorrow is cast into the oven, shall he not much more clothe you, O ye of little faith? 84 Therefore take no thought, saying, What shall we eat? or, What shall we drink? or, Wherewithal shall we be clothed? 85 (For after all these things do the Gentiles seek:) for your heavenly Father knoweth that ye have need of all these things. 86 But seek ye first the kingdom of God, and his righteousness; and all these things shall be added unto you. 87 Take therefore no thought for the morrow: for the morrow shall take thought for the things of itself. Sufficient unto the day is the evil thereof. 88 Judge not, that ye be not judged.

89 For with what judgment ye judge, ye shall be judged: and with what measure ye mete, it shall be measured to you again. 90 Give, and it shall be given unto you; good measure, pressed down, and shaken together, and running over, shall men give into your bosom. For with the same measure that ye mete withal it shall be measured to you again. 91 And why beholdest thou the mote that is in thy brother's eye, but considerest not the beam that is in thine own eye? 92 Or how wilt thou say to thy brother, Let me pull out the mote out of thine eye; and, behold, a beam is in thine own eye? 93 Thou hypocrite, first cast out the beam out of thine own eye; and then shalt thou see clearly to cast out the mote out of thy brother's eye. 94 Give not that which is holy unto the dogs, neither cast ye your pearls before swine, lest they trample them under their feet, and turn again and rend you. 95 Ask, and it shall be given you; seek, and ye shall find; knock, and it shall be opened unto you: 96 For every one that asketh receiveth; and he that seeketh findeth; and to him that knocketh it shall be opened. 97 Or what man is there of you, whom if his son ask bread, will he give him a stone? 98 Or if he ask a fish, will he give him a serpent? 99 If ye then, being evil, know how to give good gifts unto your children, how much more shall your Father which is in heaven give good things to them that ask him? 100 Therefore all things whatsoever ye would that men should do to you, do ye even so to them: for this is the law and the prophets. 101 Enter ye in at the strait gate; for wide is the gate, and broad is the way, that leadeth to destruction, and many there be which go in thereat: 102 Because strait is the gate, and narrow is the way, which leadeth unto life, and few there be that find it. 103 Beware of false prophets, which come to you in sheep's clothing, but inwardly they are ravening wolves.

104 Ye shall know them by their fruits. Do men gather grapes of thorns, or figs of thistles? 105 Even so every good tree bringeth forth good fruit; but a corrupt tree bringeth forth evil fruit. 106 A good tree cannot bring forth evil fruit, neither can a corrupt tree bring forth good fruit. 107 Every tree that bringeth not forth good fruit is hewn down, and cast into the fire. 108 Wherefore by their fruits ye shall know them. 109 A good man out of the good treasure of the heart bringeth forth good things: and an evil man out of the evil treasure bringeth forth evil things. 110 But I say unto you, That every idle word that men shall speak, they shall give account thereof in the day of judgment. 111 For by thy words thou shalt be justified, and by thy words thou shalt be condemned. 112 Therefore whosoever heareth these sayings of mine, and doeth them, I will liken him unto a wise man, which built his house upon a rock: 113 And the rain descended, and the floods came, and the winds blew, and beat upon that house; and it fell not: for it was founded upon a rock. 114 And every one that heareth these sayings of mine, and doeth them not, shall be likened unto a foolish man, which built his house upon the sand: 115 And the rain descended, and the floods came, and the winds blew and beat upon that house; and it fell: and great was the fall of it. 116 And it came to pass, when Jesus had ended these sayings, the people were astonished at his doctrine: 117 For he taught them as one having authority, and not as the scribes.

XII. Exhorts.

When he was come down from the mountain, great multitudes followed him. 2 And he marvelled because of their unbelief. And he went round about the villages, teaching. ³ Come unto me, all ye that labour and are heavy laden, and I will give you rest. ⁴ Take my yoke upon you, and learn of me; for I am meek and lowly in heart: and ye shall find rest unto your souls. ⁵ For my yoke is easy, and my burden is light.

XIII. A Woman Annointeth Him.

And one of the Pharisees desired him that he would eat with him. And he went into the Pharisee's house, and sat down to meat. ² And, behold, a woman in the city, which was a sinner, when she knew that Jesus sat at meat in the Pharisee's house, brought an alabaster box of ointment, ³ And stood at his feet behind him weeping, and began to wash his feet with tears, and did wipe them with the hairs of her head, and kissed his feet, and anointed them with the ointment. ⁴ Now when the Pharisee which had bidden him saw it, he spake within himself, saying, This man, if he were a prophet, would have known who and what manner of woman this is that toucheth him: for she is a sinner. ⁵ And Jesus answering said unto him, Simon, I have somewhat to say unto thee. And he saith, Master, say on. ⁶ There was a certain creditor which had two debtors: the one owed five hundred pence, and the other fifty. ⁷ And when they had nothing to pay, he frankly forgave them both. Tell me therefore, which of them will love him most? ⁸ Simon answered and said, I suppose that he to whom he forgave most. And he said unto him, Thou has rightly judged. ⁹ And he turned to the woman, and said unto Simon, Seest thou this woman? I entered into thine house, thou gavest me no water for my feet: but she hath washed my feet with tears, and wiped them with the hairs of her head. ¹⁰ Thou gavest me no kiss: but this woman since the time I came in hath not ceased to kiss my feet. ¹¹ My head with oil thou didst not anoint:

but this woman hath anointed my feet with ointment. 12 Wherefore I say unto thee, Her sins, which are many, are forgiven; for she loved much: but to whom little is forgiven, the same loveth little. 13 And he said unto her, Thy sins are forgiven. 14 And they that sat at meat with him began to say within themselves, Who is this that forgiveth sins also? 15 And he said to the woman, Thy faith hath saved thee; go in peace.

XIV. Precepts.

There came then his brethren and his mother, and, standing without, sent unto him, calling him. 2 And the multitude sat about him, and they said unto him, Behold, thy mother and thy brethren without seek for thee. 3 And he answered them, saying, Who is my mother, or my brethren? 4 And he looked round about on them which sat about him, and said, Behold my mother and my brethren! 5 For whosoever shall do the will of God, the same is my brother, and my sister, and mother. 6 In the mean time, when there were gathered together an innumerable multitude of people, insomuch that they trode one upon another, he began to say unto his disciples first of all, Beware ye of the leaven of the Pharisees, which is hypocrisy. 7 For there is nothing covered, that shall not be revealed; neither hid, that shall not be known. 8 Therefore whatsoever ye have spoken in darkness shall be heard in the light; and that which ye have spoken in the ear in closets shall be proclaimed upon the housetops. 9 And I say unto you my friends, Be not afraid of them that kill the body, and after that have no more that they can do. 10 But I will forewarn you whom ye shall fear: Fear him, which after he hath killed hath power to cast into hell; yea, I say unto you, Fear him. 11 Are not five sparrows sold for two farthings, and not one of them is forgotten before God? ^{12} But even the very hairs of your head are all numbered. Fear not therefore; ye are of more value than many sparrows. ^{13} And one of the company said unto him, Master, speak to my brother, that he divide the inheritance with me. ^{14} And he said unto him, Man, who made me a judge or a divider over you? ^{15} And he said unto them, Take heed, and beware of covetousness: for a man's life consisteth not in the abundance of the things which he possesseth.

XV. Parable of the Rich Man.

And he spake a parable unto them, saying, The ground of a certain rich man brought forth plentifully: ^{2} And he thought within himself, saying, What shall I do, because I have no room where to bestow my fruits? ^{3} And he said, This will I do: I will pull down my barns, and build greater; and there will I bestow all my fruits and my goods. ^{4} And I will say to my soul, Soul, thou hast much goods laid up for many years; take thine ease, eat, drink, and be merry. ^{5} But God said unto him, Thou fool, this night thy soul shall be required of thee: then whose shall those things be, which thou hast provided? ^{6} So is he that layeth up treasure for himself, and is not rich toward God.

XVI. Precepts.

And he said unto his disciples, Therefore I say unto you, Take no thought for your life, what ye shall eat; neither for the body, what ye shall put on. ^{2} The life is more than meat, and the body is more than raiment. ^{3} Consider the ravens: for they neither sow nor reap; which neither have storehouse nor barn; and God feedeth them: how much more are ye better than the fowls? ^{4} And which of you with taking thought can add to his stature one cubit?

5 If ye then be not able to do that thing which is least, why take ye thought for the rest? 6 Consider the lilies how they grow; they toil not, they spin not; and yet I say unto you, that Solomon in all his glory was not arrayed like one of these. 7 If then God so clothe the grass, which is today in the field, and tomorrow is cast into the oven; how much more will he clothe you, O ye of little faith? 8 And seek not ye what ye shall eat, or what ye shall drink, neither be ye of doubtful mind. 9 For all these things do the nations of the world seek after: and your Father knoweth that ye have need of these things. 10 But rather seek ye the kingdom of God; and all these things shall be added unto you. 11 Fear not, little flock; for it is your Father's good pleasure to give you the kingdom. 12 Sell that ye have, and give alms; provide yourselves bags which wax not old, a treasure in the heavens that faileth not, where no thief approacheth, neither moth corrupteth. 13 For where your treasure is, there will your heart be also. 14 Let your loins be girded about, and your lights burning; 15 And ye yourselves like unto men that wait for their lord, when he will return from the wedding; that when he cometh and knocketh, they may open unto him immediately. 16 Blessed are those servants, whom the Lord when he cometh shall find watching; verily I say unto you, that he shall gird himself, and make them to sit down to meat, and will come forth and serve them. 17 And if he shall come in the second watch, or come in the third watch, and find them so, blessed are those servants. 18 And this know, that if the goodman of the house had known what hour the thief would come, he would have watched, and not have suffered his house to be broken through. 19 Be ye therefore ready also: for the Son of man cometh at an hour when ye think not. 20 Then Peter said unto him, Lord, speakest thou this

parable unto us, or even to all? ²¹ And the Lord said, Who then is that faithful and wise steward, whom his lord shall make ruler over his household, to give them their portion of meat in due season? ²² Blessed is that servant, whom his lord when he cometh shall find so doing. ²³ Of a truth, I say unto you, that he will make him ruler over all that he hath. ²⁴ But and if that servant say in his heart, My lord delayeth his coming; and shall begin to beat the menservants and maidens, and to eat and drink, and to be drunken; ²⁵ The lord of that servant will come in a day when he looketh not for him, and at an hour when he is not aware, and will cut him in sunder, and will appoint him his portion with the unbelievers. ²⁶ And that servant, which knew his lord's will, and prepared not himself, neither did according to his will, shall be beaten with many stripes. ²⁷ But he that knew not, and did commit things worthy of stripes, shall be beaten with few stripes. For unto whomsoever much is given, of him shall be much required: and to whom men have committed much, of him they will ask the more. ²⁸ And he said also to the people, When ye see a cloud rise out of the west, straightway ye say, There cometh a shower; and so it is. ²⁹ And when ye see the south wind blow, ye say, There will be heat; and it cometh to pass. ³⁰ Ye hypocrites, ye can discern the face of the sky and of the earth; but how is it that ye do not discern this time? ³¹ Yea, and why even of yourselves judge ye not what is right? ³² When thou goest with thine adversary to the magistrate, as thou art in the way, give diligence that thou mayest be delivered from him; lest he hale thee to the judge, and the judge deliver thee to the officer, and the officer cast thee into prison. ³³ I tell thee, thou shalt not depart thence, till thou hast paid the very last mite. ³⁴ There were present at that season some that told him of the

Galileans, whose blood Pilate had mingled with their sacrifices. [35] And Jesus answering said unto them, Suppose ye that these Galileans were sinners above all the Galileans, because they suffered such things? [36] I tell you, Nay: but, except ye repent, ye shall all likewise perish. [37] Or those eighteen, upon whom the tower in Siloam fell, and slew them, think ye that they were sinners above all men that dwelt in Jerusalem? [38] I tell you, Nay: but, except ye repent, ye shall all likewise perish.

XVII. Parable of the Fig Tree.

He spake also this parable; A certain man had a fig tree planted in his vineyard; and he came and sought fruit thereon, and found none. [2] Then said he unto the dresser of his vineyard, Behold, these three years I come seeking fruit on this fig tree, and find none: cut it down; why cumbereth it the ground? [3] And he answering said unto him, Lord, let it alone this year also, till I shall dig about it, and dung it: [4] And if it bear fruit, well: and if not, then after that thou shalt cut it down.

XVIII. Precepts.

And as he spake a certain Pharisee besought him to dine with him: and he went in, and sat down to meat. [2] And when the Pharisee saw it, he marvelled that he had not first washed before dinner. [3] And the Lord said unto him, Now do ye Pharisees make clean the outside of the cup and the platter; but your inward part is full of ravening and wickedness. [4] Ye fools, did not he that made that which is without make that which is within also? [5] But rather give alms of such things as ye have; and, behold, all things are clean unto you. [6] But woe unto you, Pharisees! for ye tithe mint and rue and all manner of herbs, and pass over judgment and the love of God: these ought ye to have done, and not to leave the other undone. 7 Woe unto you, Pharisees! for ye love the uppermost seats in the synagogues, and greetings in the markets. 8 Woe unto you, scribes and Pharisees, hypocrites! for ye are as graves which appear not, and the men that walk over them are not aware of them. 9 Then answered one of the lawyers, and said unto him, Master, thus saying thou reproachest us also. 10 And he said, Woe unto you also, ye lawyers! for ye lade men with burdens grievous to be borne, and ye yourselves touch not the burdens with one of your fingers. 11 Woe unto you, lawyers! for ye have taken away the key of knowledge: ye entered not in yourselves, and them that were entering in ye hindered. 12 And as he said these things unto them, the scribes and the Pharisees began to urge him vehemently, and to provoke him to speak of many things: 13 Laying wait for him, and seeking to catch something out of his mouth, that they might accuse him.

XIX. Parable of the Sower.

The same day went Jesus out of the house, and sat by the sea side. 2 And great multitudes were gathered together unto him, so that he went into a ship, and sat; and the whole multitude stood on the shore. 3 And he spoke many things unto them in parables, saying, Behold, a sower went forth to sow; 4 And when he sowed, some seeds fell by the way side, and the fowls came and devoured them up: 5 Some fell upon stony places, where they had not much earth: and forthwith they sprung up, because they had no deepness of earth: 6 And when the sun was up, they were scorched; and because they had no root, they withered away. 7 And some fell among thorns;

and the thorns sprung up, and choked them: 8 But other fell into good ground, and brought forth fruit, some an hundredfold, some sixtyfold, some thirtyfold. 9 Who hath ears to hear, let him hear. 10 And when he was alone, they that were about him with the twelve asked of him the parable. 11 Hear ye therefore the parable of the sower. 12 When any one heareth the word of the kingdom, and understandeth it not, then cometh the wicked one, and catcheth away that which was sown in his heart. This is he which received seed by the way side. 13 But he that received the seed into stony places, the same is he that heareth the word, and anon with joy receiveth it; 14 Yet hath he not root in himself, but dureth for a while; for when tribulation or persecution ariseth because of the word, by and by he is offended. 15 He also that received seed among the thorns is he that heareth the word; and the care of this world, and the deceitfulness of riches choke the word, and he becometh unfruitful. 16 But he that received seed into the good ground is he that heareth the word, and understandeth it; which also beareth fruit, and bringeth forth, some an hundredfold, some sixty, some thirty.

XX. Precepts.

And he said unto them, Is a candle brought to be put under a bushel, or under a bed? and not to be set on a candlestick? 2 For there is nothing hid, which shall not be manifested; neither was any thing kept secret, but that it should come abroad. 3 If any man have ears to hear, let him hear.

XXI. Parable of the Tares.

Another parable put he forth unto them, saying, The kingdom of heaven is likened unto a man which sowed good seed in his field. ² But while men slept, his enemy came and sowed tares among the wheat, and went his way. ³ But when the blade was sprung up, and brought forth fruit, then appeared the tares also. ⁴ So the servants of the householder came and said unto him, Sir, didst not thou sow good seed in thy field? from whence then hath it tares? ⁵ He said unto them, An enemy hath done this. The servants said unto him, Wilt thou then that we go and gather them up? ⁶ But he said, Nay; lest while ye gather up the tares, ye root up also the wheat with them. ⁷ Let both grow together until the harvest: and in the time of harvest I will say to the reapers, Gather ye together first the tares, and bind them in bundles to burn them: but gather the wheat into my barn. ⁸ Then Jesus sent the multitude away, and went into the house: and his disciples came unto him, saying, Declare unto us the parable of the tares of the field. ⁹ He answered and said unto them, He that soweth the good seed is the Son of man; ¹⁰ The field is the world; the good seed are the children of the kingdom; but the tares are the children of the wicked *one*; ¹¹ The enemy that sowed them is the devil; the harvest is the end of the world; and the reapers are the angels. ¹² As therefore the tares are gathered and burned in the fire; so shall it be in the end of this world. ¹³ The Son of man shall send forth his angels, and they shall gather out of his kingdom all things that offend, and them which do iniquity. ¹⁴ And shall cast them into a furnace of fire: there shall be wailing and gnashing of teeth. ¹⁵ Then shall the righteous shine forth as the sun in the kingdom of their Father. Who hath ears to hear, let him hear. ¹⁶ Again, the kingdom of heaven is like unto treasure hid in a field; the which when a man hath found, he hideth, and for joy thereof goeth and selleth all that he hath, and buyeth that field. ^{17} Again, the kingdom of heaven is like unto a merchant man, seeking goodly pearls: ^{18} Who, when he had found one pearl of great price, went and sold all that he had, and bought it. ^{19} Again, the kingdom of heaven is like unto a net, that was cast into the sea, and gathered of every kind: ^{20} Which, when it was full, they drew to shore, and sat down, and gathered the good into vessels, but cast the bad away. ^{21} So shall it be at the end of the world: the angels shall come forth, and sever the wicked from among the just, ^{22} And shall cast them into the furnace of fire: there shall be wailing and gnashing of teeth. ^{23} Jesus saith unto them, Have ye understood all these things? They say unto him, Yea, Lord. ^{24} Then said he unto them, Therefore every scribe which is instructed unto the kingdom of heaven is like unto a man that is an householder, which bringeth forth out of his treasure things new and old.

XXII. Precepts.

And he said, So is the kingdom of God, as if a man should cast seed into the ground; ^{2} And should sleep, and rise night and day, and the seed should spring and grow up, he knoweth not how. ^{3} For the earth bringeth forth fruit of herself; first the blade, then the ear, after that the full corn in the ear. ^{4} But when the fruit is brought forth, immediately he putteth in the sickle, because the harvest is come. ^{5} And he said, Whereunto shall we liken the kingdom of God? or with what comparison shall we compare it? ^{6} It is like a grain of mustard seed, which, when it is sown in the earth, is less than all the seeds that be in the earth: ^{7} But when it is sown, it groweth up, and becometh greater than all herbs, and shooteth out great branches; so that the fowls of the air may lodge under the shadow of it. 8 And with many such parables spake he the word unto them, as they were able to hear it. 9 But without a parable spake he not unto them; and when they were alone, he expounded all things to his disciples. 10 And it came to pass, that, as they went in the way, a certain man said unto him, Lord, I will follow thee whithersoever thou goest. 11 And Jesus said unto him, Foxes have holes, and birds of the air have nests; but the Son of man hath not where to lay his head. 12 And he said unto another, Follow me. But he said, Lord, suffer me first to go and bury my father. 13 Jesus said unto him, Let the dead bury their dead: but go thou and preach the kingdom of God. 14 And another also said, Lord, I will follow thee; but let me first go bid them farewell, which are at home at my house. 15 And Jesus said unto him, No man, having put his hand to the plough and looking back, is fit for the kingdom of God. 16 And after these things he went forth, and saw a publican named Levi, sitting at the receipt of custom: and he said unto him, Follow me. 17 And he left all, rose up, and followed him. 18 And Levi made him a great feast in his own house; and it came to pass, that, as Jesus sat at meat in his house, many publicans and sinners sat also together with Jesus and his disciples: for there were many, and they followed them. 19 And when the scribes and Pharisees saw him eat with publicans and sinners, they said unto his disciples, How is it that he eateth and drinketh with publicans and sinners? 20 When Jesus heard it, he saith unto them, They that are whole have no need of the physician, but they that are sick: I came not to call the righteous, but sinners to repentance.

XXIII. Parable of New Wine in Old Bottles.

And he spake also a parable unto them; No man putteth a piece of a new garment upon an old; if otherwise, then both the new maketh a rent, and the piece that was taken out of the new agreeth not with the old. ² And no man putteth new wine into old bottles; else the new wine will burst the bottles, and be spilled and the bottles shall perish. ³ But new wine must be put into new bottles; and both are preserved. ⁴ No man also having drunk old wine straightway desireth new: for he saith, The old is better.

XXIV. A Prophet Hath no Honor in his Own Country.

And it came to pass, that when Jesus had finished these parables, he departed thence. ² And when he was come into his own country, he taught them in their synagogue, insomuch that they were astonished and said, Whence hath this man this wisdom, and these mighty works? ³ Is not this the carpenter's son? is not his mother called Mary? and his brethren James, and Joses, and Simon, and Judas? ⁴ And his sisters, are they not all with us? Whence then hath this man all these things? ⁵ And they were offended in him. But Jesus said unto them, A prophet is not without honour, save in his own country, and in his own house.

XXV. Mission Instructions, Return of Apostles.

But when he saw the multitudes, he was moved with compassion on them, because they fainted and were scattered abroad, as sheep having no shepherd. ² And he called unto him the twelve, and began to send them forth by two and two; and gave them power over unclean spirits; ³ These twelve Jesus sent forth, and commanded them, saying, Go not into the way of the Gentiles, and into any city of the Samaritans enter ye not: 4 But go rather to the lost sheep of the house of Israel. 5 Provide neither gold, nor silver, nor brass in your purses, 6 Nor scrip for your journey, neither two coats, neither shoes, nor yet staves: for the workman is worthy of his meat. 7 And into whatsoever city or town ye shall enter, enquire who in it is worthy; and there abide till ye go thence. 8 And when you come into an house, salute it. 9 And if the house be worthy, let your peace come upon it: but if it be not worthy, let your peace return to you. 10 And whosoever shall not receive you, nor hear your words, when ye depart out of that house or city, shake off the dust of your feet. 11 Verily I say unto you, It shall be more tolerable for the land of Sodom and Gomorrah in the day of judgment, than for that city. 12 Behold, I send you forth as sheep in the midst of wolves: be ye therefore wise as serpents, and harmless as doves. 13 But beware of men: for they will deliver your up to the councils, and they will scourge you in their synagogues; 14 And ye shall be brought before governors and kings for my sake, for a testimony against them and the Gentiles. 15 But when they persecute you in this city, flee ye into another: for verily I say unto you, Ye shall not have gone over the cities of Israel, till the Son of man be come. 16 Fear them not therefore: for there is nothing covered, that shall not be revealed; and hid, that shall not be known. 17 What I tell you in darkness, that speak ye in light: and what ye her in the ear, that preach ye upon the housetops. 18 And fear not them which kill the body, but are not able to kill the soul: but rather fear him which is able to destroy both soul and body in hell. 19 Are not two sparrows sold for a farthing? and one of them shall not fall on the ground without your Father. 20 But the very hairs of your head are all numbered. 21 Fear ye not therefore, ye are of more value than many sparrows. 22 And they went out, and preached that men should repent. 23 And the apostles gathered themselves together unto Jesus, and told him all things, both what they had done, and what they had taught.

XXVI. Precepts.

After these things Jesus walked in Galilee: for he would not walk in Jewry, because the Jews sought to kill him. 2 Then came together unto him the Pharisees, and certain of the scribes, which came from Jerusalem. 3 And when they saw some of his disciples eat bread with defiled, that is to say, with unwashen, hands, they found fault. 4 For the Pharisees, and all the Jews, except they wash their hands oft, eat not, holding the tradition of the elders. 5 And when they come from the market, except they wash, they eat not. And many other things there be, which they have received to hold, *as* the washing of cups and pots, brazen vessels, and of tables. 6 Then the Pharisees and scribes asked him, Why walk not thy disciples according to the tradition of the elders, but eat bread with unwashen hands? 7 And when he had called all the people unto him, he said unto them, Hearken unto me every one of you, and understand: 8 There is nothing from without a man, that entering into him can defile him: but the things which come out of him, those are they that defile the man. 9 If any man have ears to hear let him hear. 10 And when he was entered into the house from the people, his disciples asked him concerning the parable. 11 And he saith unto them, Are ye so without understanding also? Do ye not perceive, that whatsoever thing from without entereth into the man, it cannot defile him; 12 Because it entereth not into his heart, but into the belly, and goeth out into the draught, purging all meats? 13 And he said, That which cometh out of the man, that defileth the man. 14 For from within, out of the heart of men, proceed evil thoughts, adulteries, fornications, murders, 15 Thefts, covetousness, wickedness, deceit, lasciviousness, an evil eye, blasphemy, pride, foolishness: 16 All these evil things come from within, and defile the man. 17 And from thence he arose, and went into the borders of Tyre and Sidon, and entered into an house, and would have no man know it: but he could not be hid. 18 At the same time came the disciples unto Jesus, saying, Who is the greatest in the kingdom of heaven? 19 And Jesus called a little child unto him, and set him in the midst of them, 20 And said, Verily I say unto you, Except ye be converted, and become as little children, ye shall not enter into the kingdom of heaven. 21 Whosoever therefore shall humble himself as this little child, the same is greatest in the kingdom of heaven. 22 Woe unto the world because of offences! for it must needs be that offences come; but wo to that man by whom the offence cometh! 23 Wherefore if thy hand or thy foot offend thee, cut them off, and cast them from thee: it is better for thee to enter into life halt or maimed, rather than having two hands or two feet to be cast into everlasting fire. 24 And if thine eye offend thee, pluck it out, and cast it from thee: it is better for thee to enter into life with one eye, rather than having two eyes to be cast into hell fire. 25 How think ye? if a man have an hundred sheep, and one of them be gone astray, doth he not leave the ninety and nine, and goeth into the mountains, and seeketh that which is gone astray? 26 And if so be that he find it, verily I say unto you, he rejoiceth more of that sheep, than of the ninety and nine which went not astray. 27 Even so it is not the will of your Father which is in heaven, that one of these little ones should perish. 28 Moreover if thy brother shall trespass against thee, go and tell him his fault between thee and him alone: if he shall hear thee, thou hast gained thy brother. 29 But if he will not hear thee, then take with thee one or two more, that in the mouth of two or three witnesses every word may be established. 30 And if he shall neglect to hear them, tell it unto the church: but if he neglect to hear the church, let him be unto thee as an heathen man and a publican. 31 Then came Peter to him, and said, Lord, how oft shall my brother sin against me, and I forgive him? till seven times? 32 Jesus saith unto him, I say not unto thee, Until seven times: but, Until seventy times seven.

XXVII. Parable of the Wicked Servant.

Therefore is the kingdom of heaven likened unto a certain king, which would take account of his servants. 2 And when he had begun to reckon, one was brought unto him, which owed him ten thousand talents. 3 But forasmuch as he had not to pay, his lord commanded him to be sold, and his wife, and children, and all that he had, and payment to be made. 4 The servant therefore fell down, and worshipped him, saying, Lord, have patience with me, and I will pay thee all. 5 The the lord of that servant was moved with compassion, and loosed him, and forgave him the debt. 6 But the same servant went out, and found one of his fellow-servants, which owed him an hundred pence: and he laid hands on him, and took him by the throat, saying, Pay me that thou owest. 7 And his fellow-servant fell down at his feet, and besought him,

saying, Have patience with me, and I will pay thee all.
[8] And he would not: but went and cast him into prison,
till he should pay the debt. [9] So when his fellow-servants
saw what was done, they were very sorry, and came and
told unto their lord all that was done. [10] Then his lord,
after that he had called him, said unto him, O thou wicked
servant, I forgave thee all that debt, because thou desiredst
me; [11] Shouldest not thou also have had compassion on
thy fellow-servant, even as I had pity on thee? [12] And his
lord was wroth, and delivered him to the tormentors, till
he should pay all that was due unto him. [13] So likewise
shall my heavenly Father do also unto you, if ye from
your hearts forgive not every one his brother their
trespasses.

XXVIII. Mission of the Seventy.

After these things the Lord appointed other seventy also,
and sent them two and two before his face into every city
and place, whither he himself would come. [2] Therefore
said he unto them, The harvest truly *is* great, but the
labourers are few: pray ye therefore the Lord of the
harvest, that he would send forth labourers into his
harvest. [3] Go your ways: behold, I send you forth as
lambs among wolves. [4] Carry neither purse, nor scrip, nor
shoes: and salute no man by the way. [5] And into
whatsoever house ye enter, first say, Peace *be* to this
house. [6] And if the son of peace be there, your peace
shall rest upon it: if not, it shall turn to you again. [7] And
in the same house remain, eating and drinking such things
as they give: for the labourer is worthy of his hire. Go
not from house to house. [8] And into whatsoever city ye
enter, and they receive you, eat such things as are set
before you: [9] But into whatsoever city ye enter, and they
receive you not, go your ways out into the streets of the

same, and say, [10] Even the very dust of your city, which cleaveth on us, we do wipe off against you: notwithstanding be ye sure of this, that the kingdom of God is come nigh unto you. [11] But I say unto you, that it shall be more tolerable in that day for Sodom, than for that city.

XXIX. The Feast of the Tabernacles.

Now the Jews' feast of tabernacles was at hand. [2] His brethren therefore said unto him, Depart hence, and go into Judea, that thy disciples also may see the works that thou doest. [3] For there is no man that doeth any thing in secret and he himself seeketh to be known openly. If thou do these things, shew thyself to the world. [4] For neither did his brethren believe in him. [5] Then Jesus said unto them, My time is not yet come: but your time is always ready. [6] The world cannot hate you; but me it hateth, because I testify of it, that the works thereof are evil. [7] Go ye up unto this feast: I go not up yet unto this feast; for my time is not yet full come. [8] When he had said these words unto them, he abode still in Galilee. [9] But when his brethren were gone up, then went he also up unto the feast, not openly, but as it were in secret. [10] Then the Jews sought him at the feast, and said, Where is he? [11] And there was much murmuring among the people concerning him: for some said, He is a good man: others said, Nay; but he deceiveth the people. [12] Howbeit no man spake openly of him for fear of the Jews. [13] Now about the midst of the feast Jesus went up into the temple, and taught. [14] And the Jews marveled, saying, How knoweth this man letters, having never learned? [15] Jesus answered them, and said, My doctrine is not mine, but his that sent me. [16] Did not Moses give you the law, and yet none of you keepeth the

law?   Why go ye about to kill me?   ¹⁷ The people
answered and said, Thou hast a devil: who goeth about to
kill thee?   ¹⁸ Jesus answered and said unto them, I have
done one work, and ye all marvel.   ¹⁹ Moses therefore
gave unto you circumcision; (not because it is of Moses,
but of the fathers;) and ye on the sabbath day circumcise
a man.   ²⁰ If a man on the sabbath day receive
circumcision, that the law of Moses should not be broken;
are ye angry at me, because I have made a man every whit
whole on the sabbath day?   ²¹ Judge not according to the
appearance, but judge righteous judgment.   ²² Then said
some of them of Jerusalem, Is not this he, whom they seek
to kill?   ²³ But, lo, he speaketh boldly, and they say
nothing unto him. Do the rulers know indeed that this
the very Christ?   ²⁴ The Pharisees heard that the people
murmured such   things concerning   him; and   the
Pharisees and the   chief priests   sent officers   to take
him.   ²⁵ So there was   a division   among the   people
because of him.   ²⁶ And   some of them would have
taken him; but no man laid hands on him.   ²⁷ Then
came the officers to the chief priests and Pharisees; and
they said   unto them,   Why have ye not   brought him?
²⁸ The officers   answered, Never man spake like this
man.   ²⁹ Then answered them the Pharisees, Are ye
also deceived?   ³⁰ Have any of the rulers or of the
Pharisees believed   on him?   ³¹ But this people who
knoweth not   the law   are cursed.   ³² Nicodemus saith
unto them, (he that came to Jesus by night, being one of
them,) ³³ Doth our law judge any man, before it hear
him, and know what he doeth?   ³⁴ They answered and
said unto him, Art thou also of Galilee? Search, and look:
for out of Galilee ariseth no prophet. ³⁵ And every man
went unto his own house.

XXX. The Woman Taken in Adultery.

Jesus went unto the mount of Olives. 2 And early in the morning he came again into the temple, and all the people came unto him; and he sat down, and taught them. 3 And the scribes and Pharisees brought unto him a woman taken in adultery; and when they had set her in the midst, 4 They say unto him, Master, this woman was taken in adultery, in the very act. 5 Now Moses in the law commanded us, that such should be stoned; but what sayest thou? 6 This they said, tempting him, that they might have to accuse him. But Jesus stooped down, and with his finger wrote on the ground, as though he heard them not. 7 So when they continued asking him, he lifted up himself, and said unto them, He that is without sin among you, let him first cast a stone at her. 8 And again he stooped down, and wrote on the ground. 9 And they which heard it, being convicted by their own conscience, went out one by one beginning at the eldest, even unto the last: and Jesus was left alone, and the woman standing in the midst. 10 When Jesus had lifted up himself, and saw none but the woman, he said unto her, Woman, where are those thine accusers? hath no man condemned thee? 11 She said, No man, Lord. And Jesus said unto her, Neither do I condemn thee; go, and sin no more.

XXXI. To be Born Blind No Proof of Sin.

And as Jesus passed by, he saw a man which was blind from his birth. 2 And his disciples asked him, saying, Master, who did sin, this man, or his parents, that he was born blind? 3 Jesus answered, Neither hath this man sinned, nor his parents: but that the works of God should be made manifest in him.

XXXII. The Good Shepherd.

Verily, verily, I say unto you, He that entereth not by the door into the sheepfold, but climbeth up some other way, the same is a thief and robber. 2 But he that entereth in by the door is the shepherd of the sheep. 3 To him the porter openeth; and the sheep hear his voice: and he calleth his own sheep by name, and leadeth them out. 4 And when he putteth forth his own sheep, he goeth before them, and the sheep follow him; for they know his voice. 5 And a stranger will they not follow, but will flee from him: for they know not the voice of strangers. 6 I am the good shepherd: the good shepherd giveth his life for the sheep. 7 But he that is an hireling, and not the shepherd, whose own the sheep are not, seeth the wolf coming, and leaveth the sheep, and fleeth: and the wolf catcheth them, and scattereth the sheep. 8 The hireling fleeth, because he is an hireling, and careth not for the sheep. 9 I am the good shepherd, and know my sheep, and am known of mine. 10 And other sheep I have, which are not of this fold: them also I must bring, and they shall hear my voice; and there shall be one fold, and one shepherd.

XXXIII. Love God and Thy Neighbor; Parable of the Samaritan.

And, behold, a certain lawyer stood up, and tempted him, saying, Master, what shall I do to inherit eternal life? 2 He said unto him, What is written in the law? how readest thou? 3 And he answering said, Thou shalt love the Lord thy God with all thy heart, and with all thy soul, and with all thy strength, and with all thy mind; and thy neighbour as thyself. 4 And he said unto him, Thou hast answered right: this do, and thou shalt live. 5 But he, willing to justify himself, said unto Jesus, And who is my neighbour? 6 And Jesus answering said, A certain man went down from Jerusalem to Jericho, and fell among thieves, which stripped him of his raiment, and wounded him, and departed, leaving him half dead. 7 And by chance there came down a certain priest that way: and when he saw him he passed by on the other side. 8 And likewise a Levite, when he was at the place, came and looked on him, and passed by on the other side. 9 But a certain Samaritan, as he journeyed, came where he was: and when he saw him, he had compassion on him, 10 And went to him, and bound up his wounds, pouring in oil and wine, and set him on his own beast, and brought him to an inn, and took care of him. 11 And on the morrow when he departed, he took out two pence, and gave them to the host, and said unto him, Take care of him; and whatsoever thou spendest more, when I come again, I will repay thee. 12 Which now of these three, thinkest thou, was neighbour unto him that fell among the thieves? 13 And he said, He that shewed mercy on him. Then said Jesus unto him, Go, and do thou likewise.

XXXIV. Form of Prayer.

And it came to pass, as he was praying in a certain place, when he ceased, one of his disciples said unto him, Lord, teach us to pray, as John also taught his disciples. 2 And he said unto them, When ye pray, say, Our Father which art in heaven, Hallowed by thy name. Thy kingdom come. Thy will be done, as in heaven, so in earth. 3 Give us day by day our daily bread. 4 And forgive us our sins; for we also forgive every one that is indebted to us. And lead us not into temptation; but deliver us from evil. 5 And he said unto them, Which of you shall have a friend, and shall go unto him at midnight, and say unto him, Friend, lend me three loaves; ⁶ For a friend of mine in his journey is come to me, and I have nothing to set before him? ⁷ And he from within shall answer and say, Trouble me not: the door is now shut; and my children are with me in bed; I cannot rise and give thee. ⁸ I say unto you, Though he will not rise and give him because he is his friend, yet because of his importunity he will rise and give him as many as he needeth. ⁹ And I say unto you, Ask, and it shall be given you; seek, and ye shall find; knock, and it shall be opened unto you. ¹⁰ For every one that asketh receiveth; and he that seeketh findeth; and to him that knocketh it shall be opened. ¹¹ If a son shall ask bread of any of you that is a father, will he give him a stone? or if he ask a fish, will he for a fish give him a serpent? ¹² Or if he shall ask an egg, will he offer him a scorpion? ¹³ If ye then, being evil, know how to give good gifts unto your children: how much more shall your heavenly Father give the Holy Spirit to them that ask him?

XXXV. The Sabbath.

And it came to pass, as he went into the house of one of the chief Pharisees to eat bread on the sabbath day, that they watched him. ² And, behold, there was a certain man before him which had the dropsy. ³ And Jesus answering spake unto the lawyers and Pharisees, saying, Is it lawful to heal on the sabbath day? ⁴ And they held their peace. And he took him, and healed him, and let him go; ⁵ And answered them, saying, Which of you shall have an ass or an ox fallen into a pit, and will not straightway pull him out on the sabbath day? ⁶ And they could not answer him again to these things.

XXXVI. The Bidden to a Feast.

And he put forth a parable to those which were bidden, when he marked how they chose out the chief rooms; saying unto them, 2 When thou art bidden of any man to a wedding, sit not down in the highest room; lest a more honourable man than thou be bidden of him; 3 And he that bade thee and him come and say to thee, Give this man place; and thou begin with shame to take the lowest room. 4 But when thou art bidden, go and sit down in the lowest room; that when he that bade thee cometh, he may say unto thee, Friend, go up higher: then shalt thou have worship in the presence of them that sit at meat with thee. 5 For whosoever exalteth himself shall be abased; and he that humbleth himself shall be exalted. 6 Then he said he also to him that bade him, When thou makest a dinner or a supper, call not thy friends, nor thy brethren, neither thy kinsmen, nor thy rich neighbours; lest they also bid thee again, and a recompense be made thee. 7 But when thou makest a feast, call the poor, the maimed, the lame, the blind: 8 And thou shalt be blessed; for they cannot recompense thee: for thou shalt be recompensed at the resurrection of the just. 9 And when one of them that sat at meat with him heard these things, he said unto him, Blessed is he that shall eat bread in the kingdom of God. 10 Then said he unto him, A certain man made a great supper, and bade many: 11 And sent his servant at supper time to say to them that were bidden, Come; for all things are now ready. 12 And they all with one consent began to make excuse. The first said unto him, I have bought a piece of ground, and I must needs go and see it: I pray thee have me excused. 13 And another said, I have bought five yoke of oxen, and I go to prove them: I pray thee have me excused. 14 And another said, I have married a wife, and therefore I cannot come. 15 So that servant came, and shewed his lord these things. Then the master of the house being angry said to his servant, Go out quickly into the streets and lanes of the city, and bring in hither the poor, and the maimed, and the halt, and the blind. [16] And the servant said, Lord it is done as thou hast commanded, and yet there is room. [17] And the lord said unto the servant, Go out into the highways and hedges, and compel them to come in, that my house may be filled. [18] For I say unto you, That none of those men which were bidden shall taste of my supper.

XXXVII. Precepts.

For which of you, intending to build a tower, sitteth not down first, and counteth the cost, whether he have sufficient to finish it? [2] Lest haply, after he hath laid the foundation, and is not able to finish it, all that behold it begin to mock him, [3] Saying, This man began to build, and was not able to finish. [4] Or what king, going to make war against another king, sitteth not down first, and consulteth whether he be able with ten thousand to meet him that cometh against him with twenty thousand? [5] Or else, while the other is yet a great way off, he sendeth an ambassage, and desireth conditions of peace.

XXXVIII. Parables of the Lost Sheep and Prodigal Son.

Then drew near unto him all the publicans and sinners for to hear him. [2] And the Pharisees and scribes murmured, saying, This man receiveth sinners, and eateth with them. [3] And he spake this parable unto them, saying, [4] What man of you, having an hundred sheep, if he lose one of them, doth not leave the ninety and nine in the wilderness, and go after that which is lost, until he find it? [5] And when he hath found it, he layeth it on his shoulders, rejoicing. 6 And when he cometh home, he calleth together his friends and neighbours, saying unto them, Rejoice with me; for I have found my sheep which was lost. 7 I say unto you, likewise joy shall be in heaven over one sinner that repenteth, more than over ninety and nine just persons, which need no repentance. 8 Either what woman having ten pieces of silver, if she lose one piece, doth not light a candle, and sweep the house, and seek diligently till she find it? 9 And when she hath found it, she calleth her friends and her neighbors together, saying, Rejoice with me; for I have found the piece which I had lost. 10 Likewise, I say unto you, there is joy in the presence of the angels of God over one sinner that repenteth. 11 And he said, A certain man had two sons: 12 And the younger of them said to his father, Father, give me the portion of goods that falleth to me. And he divided unto them his living. 13 And not many days after the younger son gathered all together and took his journey into a far country, and there wasted his substance with riotous living. 14 And when he had spent all, there arose a mighty famine in that land; and he began to be in want. 15 And he went and joined himself to a citizen of that country; and he sent him into his fields to feed swine. 16 And he would fain have filled his belly with the husks that the swine did eat: and no man gave unto him. 17 And when he came to himself, he said, How many hired servants of my father's have bread enough and to spare, and I perish with hunger! 18 I will arise and go to my father, and will say unto him, Father, I have sinned against heaven, and before thee, 19 And am no more worthy to be called thy son: make me as one of thy hired servants. 20 And he arose, and came to his father. But when he was yet a great way off, his father saw him, and had compassion, and ran, and fell on his neck, and kissed him. 20 And the son said unto him, Father, I have sinned against heaven, and in thy sight, and am no more 21 worthy to be called thy son. 22 But the father said to his servants, Bring forth the best robe, and put it on him; and put a ring on his hand, and shoes on his feet: 23 And bring hither the fatted calf, and kill it; and let us eat, and be merry: 24 For this my son was dead, and is alive again; he was lost, and is found. And they began to be merry. 25 Now his elder son was in the field; and as he came and drew nigh to the house, he heard music and dancing. 26 And he called one of the servants, and asked what these things meant. 27 And he said unto him, Thy brother is come; and thy father hath killed the fatted calf, because he hath received him safe and sound. 28 And he was angry, and would not go in: therefore came his father out, and intreated him. 29 And he answering said to his father, Lo, these many years do I serve thee, neither transgressed I at any time thy commandment: and yet thou never gavest me a kid, that I might make merry with my friends: 30 But as soon as this thy son was come, which hath devoured thy living with harlots, thou hast killed for him the fatted calf. 31 And he said unto him, Son, thou art ever with me, and all that I have is thine. 32 It was meet that we should make merry, and be glad; for this thy brother was dead, and is alive again; and was lost, and is found.

XXXIX. Parable of the Unjust Steward.

And he said also unto his disciples, There was a certain rich man, which had a steward; and the same was accused unto him that he had wasted his goods. 2 And he called him, and said unto him, How is it that I hear this of thee? give an account of thy stewardship; for thou mayest be no longer steward. 3 Then the steward said within himself,

What shall I do? for my lord taketh away from me the stewardship: I cannot dig; to beg I am ashamed. 4 I am resolved what to do, that, when I am put out of the stewardship, they may receive me into their houses. 5 So he called every one of his lord's debtors unto him, and said unto the first, How much owest thou unto my lord? 6 And he said, An hundred measures of oil. And he said unto him, Take thy bill, and sit down quickly, and write fifty. 7 Then said he to another, And how much owest thou? And he said, An hundred measures of wheat. And he said unto him, Take thy bill, and write fourscore. 8 And the lord commended the unjust steward, because he had done wisely; for the children of this world are in their generation wiser than the children of light. 9 And I say unto you, Make to yourselves friends of the mammon of unrighteousness; that, when ye fail, they may receive you into everlasting habitations. 10 He that is faithful in that which is least is faithful also in much: and he that is unjust in the least is unjust also in much. 11 If therefore ye have not been faithful in the unrighteous mammon, who will commit to your trust the true riches? 12 And if ye have not been faithful in that which is another man's, who shall give you that which is your own? 13 No servant can serve two masters: for either he will hate the one, and love the other; or else he will hold to the one, and despise the other. Ye cannot serve God and mammon. 14 And the Pharisees also, who were covetous, heard all these things: and they derided him. 15 And he said unto them, Ye are they which justify yourselves before men; but God knoweth your hearts: for that which is highly esteemed among men is abomination in the sight of God.

XL. Parable of Lazarus.

There was a certain rich man, which was clothed in purple and fine linen and fared sumptuously every day: 2 And there was a certain beggar named Lazarus, which was laid at his gate, full of sores, 3 And desiring to be fed with the crumbs which fell from the rich man's table: moreover the dogs came and licked his sores. 4 And it came to pass, that the beggar died, and was carried by the angels into Abraham's bosom: the rich man also died, and was buried; 5 And in hell he lift up his eyes, being in torments and seeth Abraham afar off, and Lazarus in his bosom. 6 And he cried and said, Father Abraham, have mercy on me, and send Lazarus, that he may dip the tip of his finger in water, and cool my tongue; for I am tormented in this flame. 7 But Abraham said, Son, remember that thou in thy lifetime receivedst thy good things, and likewise Lazarus evil things: but now he is comforted, and thou art tormented. 8 And beside all this, between us and you there is a great gulf fixed: so that they which would pass from hence to you cannot; neither can they pass to us, that would come from thence. 9 Then he said, I pray thee therefore, father, that thou wouldest send him to my father's house: 10 For I have five brethren; that he may testify unto them, lest they also come into this place of torment. 11 Abraham saith unto him, they have Moses and the prophets; let them hear them. 12 And he said, Nay, father Abraham: but if one went unto them from the dead, they will repent. 13 And he said unto him, If they hear not Moses and the prophets, neither will they be persuaded, though one rose from the dead.

XLI. Precepts to be Always Ready.

Then said he unto the disciples, it is impossible but that offences will come: but woe unto him, through whom they come! 2 It were better for him that a millstone were hanged about his neck, and he cast into the sea, than that he should offend one of these little ones. 3 Take heed to yourselves: If thy brother trespass against thee, rebuke him; and if he repent, forgive him. 4 And if he trespass against thee seven times in a day, and seven times in a day turn again to thee, saying, I repent; thou shalt forgive him. 5 But which of you, having a servant plowing or feeding cattle, will say unto him by and by, when he is come from the field, Go and sit down to meat? 6 And will not rather say unto him, Make ready wherewith I may sup, and gird thyself, and serve me, till I have eaten and drunken; and afterward thou shalt eat and drink? 7 Doth he thank that servant because he did the things that were commanded him? I trow not. 8 So likewise ye, when ye shall have done all those things which are commanded you, say, We are unprofitable servants: we have done that which was our duty to do. 9 And when he was demanded of the Pharisees, when the kingdom of God should come, he answered them and said, The Kingdom of God cometh not with observation. 10 And as it was in the days of Noe, so shall it be also in the days of the Son of man. 11 They did eat, they drank, they married wives, they were given in marriage, until the day that Noe entered into the ark, and the flood came, and destroyed them all. 12 Likewise also as it was in the days of Lot; they did eat, they drank, they bought, they sold, they planted, they builded; 13 But the same day that Lot went out of Sodom it rained fire and brimstone from heaven, and destroyed them all. 14 Even thus shall it be in the day when the Son of man is revealed. 15 In that day, he which shall be upon the housetop, and his staff in the house, let him not come down to take it away: and he that is in the field, let him likewise not return back. 16 Remember Lot's wife. 17 Whosoever shall seek to save his life shall lose it; and whosoever shall lose his life shall preserve it. 18 I tell you, in that night there shall be two men in one bed; the one shall be taken, and the other shall be left. 19 Two women shall be grinding together; the one shall be taken, and the other left. 20 Two men shall be in the field; the one shall be taken, and the other left.

XLII. Parables of the Widow and Judge, the Pharisee and Publican.

And he spake a parable unto them to this end, that men ought always to pray, and not to faint; 2 Saying, There was in a city a judge, which feared not God, neither regarded man: 3 And there was a widow in that city; and she came unto him, saying, Avenge me of mine adversary. 4 And he would not for a while: but afterward he said within himself, Though I fear not God, nor regard man, 5 Yet because this widow troubleth me, I will avenge her, lest by her continual coming she weary me. 6 And the Lord said, Her what the unjust judge saith. 7 And shall not God avenge his own elect, which cry day and night unto him, though he bear long with them? 8 I tell you that he will avenge them speedily. Nevertheless when the Son of man cometh, shall he find faith on the earth? 9 And he spake this parable unto certain which trusted in themselves that they were righteous, and despised others: 10 Two men went up into the temple to pray; the one a Pharisee, and the other a publican. 11 The Pharisee stood and prayed thus with himself, God, I thank thee that I am not as other men are, extortioners, unjust, adulterers, or even as this publican. ^{12} I fast twice in the week, I give tithes of all that I possess. ^{13} And the publican, standing afar off, would not lift up so much as his eyes unto heaven, but smote upon his breast, saying, God be merciful to me a sinner. ^{14} I tell you, this man went down to his house justified rather than the other: for every one that exalteth himself shall be abased; and he that humbleth himself shall be exalted.

XLIII. Precepts.

Now it came to pass, as they went, that he entered into a certain village: and a certain woman named Martha received him into her house. ^{2} And she had a sister called Mary, which also sat at Jesus' feet, and heard his word. ^{3} But Martha was cumbered about much serving, and came to him, and said, Lord, dost thou not care that my sister hath left me to serve alone? bid her therefore that she help me. ^{4} And Jesus answered and said unto her, Martha, Martha, thou art careful and troubled about many things: ^{5} But one thing is needful: and Mary hath chosen that good part, which shall not be taken away from her. ^{6} And it came to pass, that when Jesus had finished these sayings, he departed from Galilee, and came into the coasts of Judea beyond Jordan; ^{7} And great multitudes followed him; and he healed them there. ^{8} The Pharisees also came unto him, tempting him, and saying unto him, Is it lawful for a man to put away his wife for every cause? ^{9} And he answered and said unto them, Have ye not read, that he which made them at the beginning made them male and female, ^{10} And said, For this cause shall a man leave father and mother, and shall cleave to his wife: and they twain shall be one flesh? ^{11} Wherefore they are no more twain, but one flesh. What therefore God hath joined together, let not man put asunder. ^{12} They say unto him, Why did Moses then command to give a writing of divorcement, and to put her away? 13 He saith unto them, Moses because of the hardness of your hearts suffered you to put away your wives: but from the beginning it was not so. 14 And I say unto you, Whosoever shall put away his wife, except it be for fornication, and shall marry another, commiteth adultery: and whoso marrieth her which is put away doth commit adultery. 15 His disciples say unto him, If the case of the man be so with his wife, it is not good to marry. 16 But he said unto them, All men cannot receive this saying, save they to whom it is given. 17 For there are some eunuchs, which were so born from their mother's womb: and there are some eunuchs, which were made eunuchs of men; and there be eunuchs, which have made themselves eunuchs for the kingdom of heaven's sake. He that is able to receive it, let him receive it. 18 Then were there brought unto him little children, that he should put his hands on them, and pray: and the disciples rebuked them. 19 But Jesus said, Suffer little children, and forbid them not, to come unto me: for of such is the kingdom of heaven. 20 And he laid his hands on them, and departed thence. 21 And, behold, one came and said unto him, Good Master, what good thing shall I do, that I may have eternal life? 22 And he said unto him, Why callest thou me good? there is none good but one, that is, God: but if thou wilt enter into life, keep the commandments. 23 He saith unto him, Which? Jesus said, Thou shalt do no murder, Thou shalt not commit adultery, Thou shalt not steal, Thou shalt not bear false witness, 24 Honour thy father and thy mother: and, Thou shalt love thy neighbour as thyself. 25 The young man saith unto him, All these things have I kept from my youth up: what lack I yet? 26 Jesus said unto him, If thou wilt be perfect, go and sell that thou hast, and give to the poor, and thou shalt have treasure in heaven: and come and follow me. 27 But when the young man heard that saying, he went away sorrowful: for he had great possessions. 28 Then said Jesus unto his disciples, Verily I say unto you, That a rich man shall hardly enter into the kingdom of heaven. 29 And again I say unto you, It is easier for a camel to go through the eye of a needle, than for a rich man to enter into the kingdom of God. 30 When his disciples heard it, they were exceedingly amazed, saying, Who then can be saved? 31 But Jesus beheld them, and said unto them, With men this is impossible; but with God all things are possible.

XLIV. Parable of the Labourers in the Vineyard.

For the kingdom of heaven is like unto a man that is an householder, which went out early in the morning to hire labourers into his vineyard. 2 And when he had agreed with the labourers for a penny a day, he sent them into his vineyard. 3 And he went out about the third hour, and saw others standing idle in the marketplace, 4 And said unto them: Go ye also into the vineyard, and whatsoever is right I will give you. And they went their way. 5 Again he went out about the sixth and ninth hour, and did likewise. 6 And about the eleventh hour he went out, and found others standing idle, and saith unto them, Why stand ye here all the day idle? 7 They say unto him, Because no man hath hired us. He saith unto them, Go ye also into the vineyard; and whatsoever is right, that shall ye receive. 8 So when even was come, the lord of the vineyard saith unto his steward, Call the labourers, and give them their hire, beginning from the last unto the first. 9 And when they came that were hired about the eleventh hour, they received every man a penny. 10 But when the first came, they supposed that they should have received more; and they likewise received every man a penny. 11 And when they had received it, they murmured against the goodman of the house, 12 Saying, These last have wrought but one hour, and thou hast made them equal unto us, which have borne the burden and heat of the day. 13 But he answered one of them, and said, Friend, I do thee no wrong; didst thou not agree with me for a penny? 14 Take that thine is and go thy way: I will give unto this last, even as unto thee. 15 Is it not lawful for me to do what I will with mine own? Is thine eye evil, because I am good? 16 So the last shall be first, and the first last: for many be called, but few chosen.

XLV. Zacchaeus, and the Parable of the Talents.

And Jesus entered and passed through Jericho. 2 And, behold, there was a man named Zacchaeus, which was the chief among the publicans, and he was rich. 3 And he sought to see Jesus who he was; and could not for the press, because he was little of stature. 4 And he ran before, and climbed up into a sycamore tree to see him: for he was to pass that way. 5 And when Jesus came to the place, he looked up, and saw him, and said unto him, Zacchaeus, make haste, and come down; for today I must abide at thy house. 6 And he made haste, and came down, and received him joyfully. 7 And when he saw it, they all murmured, saying, That he was gone to be guest with a man that is a sinner. 8 And Zacchaeus stood, and said unto the Lord; Behold, Lord, the half of my goods I give to the poor; and if I have taken anything from any man by false accusation, I restore him fourfold. 9 And Jesus said unto him, This day is salvation come to this house, forsomuch as he also is a son of Abraham. 10 For the Son of man is come to seek and to save that which was lost.

11 And as they heard these things, he added and spake a parable, because he was nigh to Jerusalem, and because they thought that the kingdom of God should immediately appear. 12 He said therefore, A certain nobleman went into a far country to receive for himself a kingdom, and to return. 13 And he called his ten servants, and delivered them ten pounds, and said unto them, Occupy till I come. 14 But his citizens hated him, and sent a message after him, saying, We will not have this man to reign over us. 15 And it came to pass, that when he was returned, having received the kingdom, then he commanded these servants to be called unto him, to whom he had given the money, that he might know how much every man had gained by trading. 16 Then came the first, saying, Lord, thy pound hath gained ten pounds. 17 And he said unto him, Well, thou good servant: because thou hast been faithful in a very little, have thou authority over ten cities. 18 And the second came, saying, Lord, thy pound hath gained five pounds. 19 And he said likewise to him, Be thou also over five cities. 20 And another came, saying, Lord, behold, here is thy pound, which I have kept laid up in a napkin: 21 For I feared thee, because thou art an austere man: thou takest up that thou layedst not down, and reapest that thou didst not sow. 22 And he saith unto him, Out of thine own mouth will I judge thee, thou wicked servant. Thou knewest that I was an austere man, taking up that I laid not down, and reaping that I did not sow: 23 Wherefore then gavest not thou my money into the bank, that at my coming I might have required mine own with usury? 24 And he said unto them that stood by, Take from him the pound, and give it to him that hath ten pounds. 25 (And they said unto him, Lord, he hath ten pounds.) 26 For I say unto you, That

unto every one which hath shall be given; and from him that hath not, even that he hath shall be taken away from him. 27 But those mine enemies which would not that I should reign over them, bring hither, and slay them before me. 28 And when he had thus spoken, he went before, ascending up to Jerusalem.

XLVI. Goes to Jerusalem and Bethany.

And when they drew nigh unto Jerusalem, and were come to Bethphage, unto the mount of Olives, then sent Jesus two disciples, 2 Saying unto them, Go into the village over against you, and straightway ye shall find an ass tied, and a colt with her: loose them, and bring them unto me. 3 And if any man say ought unto you, ye shall say, The Lord hath need of them; and straightway he will send them. 4 And the disciples went, and did as Jesus commanded them, 5 And brought the ass, and the colt, and put on them their clothes, and they set him thereon. 6 And a very great multitude spread their garments in the way; others cut down branches from the trees, and strawed them in the way. 7 And when he was come into Jerusalem, all the city was moved, saying, Who is this? 8 The Pharisees therefore said among themselves, Perceive ye how ye prevail nothing? behold, the world is gone after him. 9 And there were certain Greeks among them that came up to worship at the feast: 10 The same came therefore to Philip, which was of Bethsaida of Galilee, and desired him, saying, Sir, we would see Jesus. 11 Philip cometh and telleth Andrew: and again Andrew and Philip tell Jesus. 12 And Jesus answered them, saying, The hour is come, that the Son of man should be glorified. 13 Verily, verily, I say unto you, Except a corn of wheat fall into the ground and die, it abideth alone: but if it die, it bringeth forth much fruit. 14 And he left them, and went out of the city into Bethany; and he lodged there.

XLVII. The Traders Cast Out from the Temple.

And on the morrow, when they were come from Bethany, he was hungry: ² And they came to Jerusalem: and Jesus went into the temple, and began to cast out them that sold and bought in the temple, and overthrew the tables of the money changers, and the seats of them that sold doves; ³ And would not suffer that any man should carry any vessel through the temple. ⁴ And he taught, saying unto them, is it not written, My house shall be called of all nations the house of prayer? but ye have made it a den of thieves. ⁵ And the scribes and chief priests heard it, and sought how they might destroy him: for they feared him, because all the people was astonished at his doctrine. ⁶ And when even was come, he went out of the city.

XLVIII. Parable of the Two Sons.

And they came again to Jerusalem: and as he was walking in the temple, there came to him the chief priests, and the scribes, and the elders, ² And they answered Jesus and said, We cannot tell. And he said unto them, Neither tell I you by what authority I do these things. ³ But what think ye? A certain man had two sons; and he came to the first, and said, Son, go work today in my vineyard. ⁴ He answered and said, I will not: but afterward he repented, and went. ⁵ And he came to the second, and said likewise. And he answered and said I go, sir: and went not. ⁶ Whether of them twain did the will of his father? They say unto him, The first. Jesus saith unto them,

Verily I say unto you, That the publicans and the harlots go into the kingdom of God before you.

XLIX. Parable of the Vineyard and Husbandmen.

Hear another parable: There was a certain householder, which planted a vineyard, and hedged it round about, and digged a wine-press in it, and built a tower, and let it out to husbandmen, and went into a far country: 2 And at the season he sent to the husbandmen a servant, that he might receive from the husbandmen of the fruit of the vineyard. 3 And they caught him, and beat him, and sent him away empty. 4 And again he sent unto them another servant; and at him they cast stones, and wounded him in the head, and sent him away shamefully handled. 5 And again he sent another; and him they killed, and many others; beating some, and killing some. 6 Having yet therefore one son, his well-beloved, he sent him also last unto them, saying, They will reverence my son. 7 But those husbandmen said among themselves, This is the heir; come, let us kill him, and the inheritance shall be ours. 8 And they took him, and killed him and cast him out of the vineyard. 9 What shall therefore the lord of the vineyard do? he will come and destroy the husbandmen, and will give the vineyard unto others. 10 And when the chief priests and Pharisees had heard his parables, they perceived that he spake of them. 11 But when they sought to lay hands on him, they feared the multitude, because they took him for a prophet.

L. Parable of the King and the Wedding.

And Jesus answered and spake unto them again by parables, and said, 2 The kingdom of heaven is like unto a certain king, which made a marriage for his son; 3 And sent forth his servants to call them that were bidden to the wedding; and they would not come. 4 Again, he sent forth other servants, saying, Tell them which are bidden, Behold, I have prepared my dinner; my oxen and my fatlings are killed, and all things are ready: come unto the marriage. 5 But they made light of it, and went their ways, one to his farm, another to his merchandise: 6 And the remnant took his servants, The Wedding is ready, but they which were bidden were not worthy. 9 Go ye therefore into the highways, and as many as ye shall find, bid to the marriage. 10 So those servants went out into the highways, and gathered together all as many as they found, both bad and good; and the wedding was furnished with guests. 11 And when the king came in to see the guests, he saw there a man which had not on a wedding garment: 12 And he saith unto him, Friend, how camest thou in hither not having a wedding garment? And he was speechless. 13 Then the king said to the servants, Bind him hand and foot, and take him away and cast him into outer darkness: there shall be weeping and gnashing of teeth. 14 For many are called, but few are chosen.

LI. Tribute, Marriage, Resurrection.

Then went the Pharisees, and took counsel how they might entangle him in his talk. 2 And they sent out unto him their disciples with the Herodians, saying, Master, we know that thou are true, and teachest the way of God in truth, neither carest thou for any man: for thou regardest not the person of men. 3 Tell us therefore, What thinkest thou? Is it lawful to give tribute unto Caesar, or not? 4 But Jesus perceived their wickedness, and said, Why tempt ye me, ye hypocrites? 5 Shew me the tribute money. And they brought unto him a penny. 6 And he saith unto them, Whose is this image and superscription?

7 They say unto him, Caesar's. Then saith he unto them,
Render therefore unto Caesar the things which are
Caesar's; and unto God the things that are God's. 8 When
they had heard these words, they marvelled, and left him
and went their way. 9 The same day came to him the
Sadducees, which say that there is no resurrection, and
asked him, 10 Saying, Master, Moses said, If a man die,
having no children, his brother shall marry his wife, and
raise up seed unto his brother. 11 Now there were with
us seven brethren: and the first, when he had married a
wife, deceased, and, having no issue, left his wife unto his
brother: 12 Likewise the second also, and the third, unto
the seventh. 13 And last of all the woman died also.
14 Therefore in the resurrection whose wife shall she be
of the seven? for they all had her. 15 Jesus answered and
said unto them, Ye do err, not knowing the scriptures, nor
the power of God. 16 For in the resurrection they neither
marry, nor are given in marriage, but are as the angels of
God in heaven. 17 But as touching the resurrection of the
dead, have ye not read that which was spoken unto you by
God, saying, 18 I am the God of Abraham, and the God of
Isaac and the God of Jacob? God is not the God of the
dead, but of the living. 19 And when the multitude heard
this, they were astonished at his doctrine.

LII. The Two Commandments.

And one of the scribes came, and having heard them
reasoning together, and perceiving that he had answered
them well, asked him, Which is the first commandment of
all? 2 And Jesus answered him, The first of all the
commandments is, Hear, O Israel; The Lord our God is
one Lord: 3 And thou shalt love the Lord thy God with
all thy heart, and with all thy soul, and with all thy mind,
and with all thy strength: this is the first commandment.

4 And the second is like, namely this, Thou shalt love thy neighbour as thyself. There is none other commandment greater than these. 5 On these two commandments hang all the law and the prophets. 6 And the scribe said unto him, Well, Master, thou hast said the truth: for there is one God; and there is none other but he: 7 And to love him with all the heart, and with all the understanding, and with all the soul, and with all the strength, and to love his neighbour as himself, is more than all whole burnt offerings and sacrifices.

LIII. Precepts, Pride, Hypocrisy, Swearing.

Then spake Jesus to the multitude, and to his disciples, 2 Saying, The scribes and the Pharisees sit in Moses' seat: 3 All therefore whatsoever they bid you observe, that observe and do; but do not ye after their works: for they say, and do not. 4 For they bind heavy burdens and grievous to be borne, and lay them on men's shoulders; but they themselves will not move them with one of their fingers. 5 But all their works they do for to be seen of men: they make broad their phylacteries, and enlarge the borders of their garments, 6 And love the uppermost rooms at feasts, and the chief seats in the synagogues, 7 And greetings in the markets, and to be called of men, Rabbi, Rabbi. 8 But be not ye called Rabbi: for one is your Master, even Christ; and all ye are brethren. 9 And call no man your father upon the earth; for one is your Father, which is in heaven. 10 Neither be ye called masters: for one is your Master, even Christ. 11 But he that is greatest among you shall be your servant. 12 And whosoever shall exalt himself shall be abased; and he that shall humble himself shall be exalted. 13 But woe unto you, scribes and Pharisees, hypocrites! for ye shut up the kingdom of heaven against men: for ye neither go in yourselves, neither suffer ye them that are entering to go in. ^{14} Woe unto you, scribes and Pharisees, hypocrites! for ye devour widows' houses, and for a pretence make long prayer: therefore ye shall receive the greater damnation. ^{15} Woe unto you, scribes and Pharisees, hypocrites! for ye compass sea and land to make one proselyte, and when he is made, ye make him twofold more the child of hell than yourselves. ^{16} Woe unto you, ye blind guides, which say, Whosoever shall swear by the temple, it is nothing; but whosoever shall swear by the gold of the temple, he is a debtor! ^{17} Ye fools and blind: for whether is greater, the gold, or the temple that sanctifieth the gold? ^{18} And, Whosoever shall swear by the altar, it is nothing; but whosoever sweareth by the gift that is upon it, he is guilty. ^{19} Ye fools and blind: for whether is greater, the gift, or the altar that sanctifieth the gift? ^{20} Whoso therefore shall swear by the altar, sweareth by it, and by all things thereon. ^{21} And whoso shall swear by the temple, sweareth by it, and by him that dwelleth therein. ^{22} And he that shall swear by heaven, sweareth by the throne of God, and by him that sitteth thereon. ^{23} Woe unto you, scribes and Pharisees, hypocrites! for ye pay tithe of mint and anise and cummin, and have omitted the weightier matters of the law, judgment, mercy, and faith: these ought ye to have done, and not to leave the other undone. ^{24} Ye blind guides, which strain at a gnat, and swallow a camel. ^{25} Woe unto you, scribes and Pharisees, hypocrites! for ye make clean the outside of the cup and of the platter, but within they are full of extortion and excess. ^{26} Thou blind Pharisee, cleanse first that which is within the cup and platter, that the outside of them may be clean also. ^{27} Woe unto you, scribes and Pharisees, hypocrites! for ye are like unto whited sepulchres, which indeed appear beautiful outward, but are within full of dead men's bones, and of all uncleanness. 28 Even so ye also outwardly appear righteous unto men, but within ye are full of hypocrisy and iniquity. 29 Woe unto you, scribes and Pharisees, hypocrites! because ye build the tombs of the prophets, and garnish the sepulchres of the righteous, 30 And say, If we had been in the days of our fathers, we would not have been partakers with them in the blood of the prophets. 31 Wherefore ye be witnesses unto yourselves, that ye are the children of them which killed the prophets. 32 Fill ye up then the measure of your fathers. 33 Ye serpents, ye generation of vipers, how can ye escape the damnation of hell?

LIV. The Widow's Mite.

And Jesus sat over against the treasury, and beheld how the people cast money into the treasury: and many that were rich cast in much. 2 And there came a certain poor widow, and she threw in two mites, which make a farthing. 3 And he called unto him his disciples, and saith unto them, Verily I say unto you, That this poor widow hath cast more in, than all they which have cast into the treasury: 4 For all they did cast in of their abundance; but she of her want did cast in all that she had, even all her living.

LV. Jerusalem and the Day of Judgment.

And Jesus went out, and departed from the temple: and his disciples came to him for to shew him the buildings of the temple. 2 And Jesus said unto them, See ye not all these things? verily I say unto you, There shall not be left here one stone upon another, that shall not be thrown down. 3 Then let them which be in Judea flee into the mountains: 4 Let him which is on the housetop not come down to take any thing out of his house: 5 Neither let him which is in the field return back to take his clothes. 6 And woe unto them that are with child, and to them that give suck in those days! 7 But pray ye that your flight be not in the winter, neither on the sabbath day: 8 For then shall be great tribulation, such as was not since the beginning of the world to this time, no, nor ever shall be. 9 Now learn a parable of the fig tree; When his branch is yet tender, and putteth forth leaves, ye know that summer is nigh: 10 So likewise ye, when ye shall see all these things, know that it is near even at the doors. 11 But of that day and hour knoweth no man, no, not the angels of heaven, but my Father only. 12 But as the days of Noe were, so shall also the coming of the Son of man be. 13 For as in the days that were before the flood they were eating and drinking, marrying and giving in marriage until the day that Noe entered into the ark, 14 And knew not until the flood came, and took them all away; so shall also the coming of the Son of man be. 15 Then shall two be in the field; the one shall be taken, and the other left. 16 Two women shall be grinding at the mill; the one shall be taken, and the other left. 17 Watch therefore: for ye know not what hour your Lord doth come. 18 But know this, that if the goodman of the house had known in what watch the thief would come, he would have watched, and would not have suffered his house to be broken up. 19 Therefore be ye also ready: for in such an hour as ye think not the Son of man cometh.

LVI. The Faithful and Wise Servant.

Who then is a faithful and wise servant, whom his lord hath made ruler over his household, to give them meat in due season? 2 Blessed is that servant, whom his lord when he cometh shall find so doing. 3 Verily I say unto you, That he shall make him ruler over all his goods. 4 But and if that evil servant shall say in his heart, My lord delayeth his coming; 5 And shall begin to smite his fellow-servants, and to eat and drink with the drunken; 6 The lord of that servant shall come in a day when he looketh not for him, and in an hour that he is not aware of, 7 And shall cut him asunder, and appoint him his portion with the hypocrites: there shall be weeping and gnashing of teeth.

LVII. Parable of the Ten Virgins.

Then shall the kingdom of heaven be likened unto ten virgins, which took their lamps, and went forth to meet the bridegroom. 2 And five of them were wise, and five were foolish. 3 They that were foolish took their lamps, and took no oil with them: 4 But the wise took oil in their vessels with their lamps. 5 While the bridegroom tarried, they all slumbered and slept. 6 And at midnight there was a cry made, Behold, the bridegroom cometh; go ye out to meet him. 7 Then all those virgins arose, and trimmed their lamps. 8 And the foolish said unto the wise, Give us of your oil; for our lamps are gone out. 9 But the wise answered, saying, Not so; lest there be not enough for us and you: but go ye rather to them that sell, and buy for yourselves. 10 And while they went to buy, the bridegroom came; and they that were ready went in with him to the marriage: and the door was shut. 11 Afterward came also the other virgins, saying, Lord, Lord, open to us. 12 But he answered and said, Verily I say unto you, I know you not. 13 Watch, therefore, for ye know neither the day nor the hour wherein the Son of man cometh.

LVIII. Parable of the Talents.

For the kingdom of heaven is as a man travelling into a far country, who called his own servants, and delivered unto them his goods. 2 And unto one he gave five talents, to another two, and to another one; to every man according to his several ability; and straightway took his journey. 3 Then he that had received the five talents went and traded with the same, and made them other five talents. 4 And likewise he that had received two, he also gained other two. 5 But he that had received one went and digged in the earth, and hid his lord's money. 6 After a long time the lord of those servants cometh, and reckoneth with them. 7 And so he that had received five talents came and brought other five talents, saying, Lord, thou deliveredst unto me five talents; behold, I have gained beside them five talents more. 8 His lord said unto him, Well done, thou good and faithful servant: thou hast been faithful over a few things, I will make thee ruler over many things: enter thou into the joy of thy lord. 9 He also that had received two talents came and said, Lord, thou deliveredst unto me two talents: behold, I have gained two other talents beside them. 10 His lord said unto him, Well done, good and faithful servant; thou hast been faithful over a few things, I will make thee ruler over many things; enter thou into the joy of thy lord. 11 Then he which had received the one talent came and said, Lord, I knew thee that thou art an hard man, reaping where thou hast not sown, and gathering where thou hast not strawed: 12 And I was afraid, and went and hid thy talent in the earth: lo, there thou hast that is thine. 13 His lord answered and said unto him, Thou wicked and slothful servant, thou knewest that I reap where I sowed not, and gather where I have not stawed: 14 Thou oughtest therefore to have put my money to the exchangers, and then at my coming I should have received mine own with usury. ^{15} Take therefore the talent from him, and give it unto him which hath ten talents. ^{16} For unto every one that hath shall be given, and he shall have abundance: but from him that hath not shall be taken away even that which he hath. ^{17} And cast ye the unprofitable servant into outer darkness: there shall be weeping and gnashing of teeth.

LIX. The Day of Judgment.

And take heed to yourselves, lest at any time your hearts be overcharged with surfeiting, and drunkenness, and cares of this life, and so that day come upon you unawares. ^{2} For as a snare shall it come on all them that dwell on the face of the whole earth. ^{3} Watch ye therefore, and pray always, that ye may be accounted worthy to escape all these things that shall come to pass, and to stand before the Son of man. ^{4} When the Son of man shall come in his glory, and all the holy angels with him, then shall he sit upon the throne of his glory: ^{5} And before him shall be gathered all nations: and he shall separate them one from another, as a shepherd divideth his sheep from the goats: ^{6} And he shall set the sheep on his right hand, but the goats on the left. ^{7} Then shall the King say unto them on his right hand, Come, ye blessed of my Father, inherit the kingdom prepared for you from the foundation of the world: ^{8} For I was an hungred, and ye gave me meat: I was thirsty, and ye gave me drink: I was a stranger, and ye took me in: ^{9} Naked, and ye clothed me: I was sick, and ye visited me: I was in prison, and ye came unto me. ^{10} Then shall the righteous answer him, saying, Lord, when saw we thee an hungred, and fed thee? or thirsty, and gave thee drink? ^{11} When saw we thee a stranger, and took thee in? or naked, and clothed thee? ¹² Or when saw we thee sick, or in prison, and came unto thee? ¹³ And the King shall answer and say unto them, Verily I say unto you, Inasmuch as ye have done it unto one of the least of these my brethren, ye have done it unto me. ¹⁴ Then shall he say also unto them on the left hand, Depart from me, ye cursed, into everlasting fire, prepared for the devil and his angels: ¹⁵ For I was an hungred, and ye gave me no meat: I was thirsty, and ye gave me no drink: ¹⁶ I was a stranger, and ye took me not in: naked, and ye clothed me not: sick, and in prison, and ye visited me not. ¹⁷ Then shall they also answer him, saying, Lord, when saw we thee an hungred, or athirst, or a stranger, or naked, or sick, or in prison, and did not minister unto thee? ¹⁸ Then shall he answer them, saying, Verily, I say unto you, Inasmuch as ye did it not to one of the least of these, ye did it not to me. ¹⁹ And these shall go away into everlasting punishment: but the righteous into life eternal.

LX. A Woman Anointeth Him.

After two days was the feast of the passover, and of unleavened bread: and the chief priests and the scribes sought how they might take him by craft, and put him to death. ² But they said, Not on the feast day, lest there be an uproar of the people. ³ And being in Bethany in the house of Simon the leper, as he sat at meat, there came a woman having an alabaster box of ointment of spikenard very precious; and she brake the box, and poured it on his head. ⁴ And there were some that had indignation within themselves, and said, Why was this waste of the ointment made? ⁵ For it might have been sold for more than three hundred pence, and have been given to the poor. And they murmured against her. ⁶ And Jesus said, Let her alone; why trouble ye her? she hath wrought a good work on me. 7 For ye have the poor with you always, and whensoever ye will ye may do them good: but me ye have not always. 8 She hath done what she could: she is come aforehand to anoint my body to the burying.

LXI. Judas Undertakes to Point Out Jesus.

Then one of the twelve, called Judas Iscariot, went unto the chief priests, 2 And said unto them, What will ye give me, and I will deliver him unto you? And they covenanted with him for thirty pieces of silver. 3 And from that time he sought opportunity to betray him.

LXII. Precepts to His Disciples, Washes their Feet, Trouble of Mind and Prayer.

Now the first day of the feast of unleavened bread the disciples came to Jesus, saying unto him, Where wilt thou that we prepare for thee to eat the passover? 2 And he said, Go into the city to such a man, and say unto him, The Master saith, My time is at hand; I will keep the passover at thy house with my disciples. 3 And the disciples did as Jesus had appointed them; and they made ready the passover. 4 Now when the even was come, he sat down with the twelve. 5 And there was also a strife among them, which of them should be accounted the greatest. 6 And he said unto them, The kings of the Gentiles exercised lordship over them; and they that exercise authority upon them are called benefactors. 7 But ye shall not be so: but he that is greatest among you, let him be as the younger; and he that is chief, as he that doth serve. 8 For whether is greater, he that sitteth at meat, or he that serveth? is not he that sitteth at meat? but I am among you as he that serveth.
9 And supper being ended, the devil having now put into

the heart of Judas Iscariot, Simon's son, to betray him;
10 He riseth from super, and laid aside his garments; and took a towel, and girded himself. 11 After that he poureth water into a bason, and began to wash the disciples' feet, and to wipe them with the towel wherewith he was girded. 12 Then cometh he to Simon Peter; and Peter saith unto him, Lord, dost thou wash my feet? 13 Jesus answered and said unto him, What I do thou knowest not now; but thou shalt know hereafter. 14 Peter saith unto him, Thou shalt never wash my feet. Jesus answered him, If I wash thee not, thou hast no part with me. 15 Simon Peter saith unto him, Lord, not my feet only, but also my hands and my head. 16 Jesus saith to Him, He that is washed needeth not save to wash his feet, but is clean every whit: and ye are clean, but not all. 17 For he knew who should betray him; therefore said he, Ye are not all clean. 18 So after he had washed their feet, and had taken his garments, and was set down again, he said unto them, Know ye what I have done to you? 19 Ye call me Master and Lord: and ye say well; for so I am. 20 If I then, your Lord and Master, have washed your feet; ye also ought to wash one another's feet. 21 For I have given you an example, that ye should do as I have done to you. 22 Verily, verily, I say unto you, The servant is not greater than his lord; neither he that is sent greater than he that sent him. 23 If ye know these things, happy are ye if ye do them. 24 When Jesus had thus said, he was troubled in spirit, and testified, and said, Verily, verily, I say unto you, that one of you shall betray me. 25 Then the disciples looked one on another, doubting of whom he spake. 26 Now there was leaning on Jesus' bosom one of his disciples whom Jesus loved. 27 Simon Peter therefore beckoned to him, that he should ask who it should be of

whom he spake. 28 He then lying on Jesus' breast saith unto him, Lord, who is it? 29 Jesus answered, He it is, to whom I shall give a sop, when I have dipped it. And when he had dipped the sop, he gave it to Judas Iscariot, the son of Simon. 30 Therefore, when he was gone out, Jesus said, Now is the Son of man glorified, and God is glorified in him. 31 A new commandment I give unto you, That ye love one another; as I have loved you, that ye also love one another. 32 By this shall all men know that ye are my disciples, if ye have love one to another. 33 Then said Jesus unto them, All ye shall be offended because of me this night: for it is written, I will smite the shepherd, and the sheep of the flock shall be scattered abroad. 34 Peter answered and said unto him, Though all men shall be offended because of thee, yet will I never be offended. 35 And he said unto him, Lord, I am ready to go with thee, both into prison, and to death. 36 And he said, I tell thee, Peter, the cock shall not crow this day, before that thou shalt thrice deny that thou knowest me. 37 Peter said unto him, Though I should die with thee, yet will I not deny thee. Likewise also said all the disciples. 38 Then cometh Jesus with them unto a place called Gethsemane, and said unto the disciples, Sit ye here, while I go and pray yonder. 39 And he took with him Peter and the two sons of Zebedee, and began to be sorrowful and very heavy. 40 Then saith he unto them, My soul is exceeding sorrowful, even unto death: tarry ye here, and watch with me. 41 And he went a little farther, and fell on his face, and prayed, saying, O my Father, if it be possible, let this cup pass from me: nevertheless not as I will, but as thou wilt. 42 And he cometh unto the disciples, and findeth them asleep, and saith unto Peter, What, could ye not watch with me one hour? 43 Watch and pray, that ye enter not into temptation: the spirit indeed is willing, but the flesh is weak. [44] He went away again the second time, and prayed, saying, O my Father, if this cup may not pass away from me, except I drink it, thy will be done. [45] And he came and found them asleep again: for their eyes were heavy. [46] And he left them, and went away again, and prayed the third time, saying the same words. [47] Then cometh he to his disciples, and saith unto them, Sleep on now, and take your rest: behold, the hour is at hand, and the Son of man is betrayed into the hands of sinners.

LXIII. Judas Conducts the Officers to Jesus.

When Jesus had spoken these words, he went forth with his disciples over the brook Cedron, where was a garden, into the which he entered, and his disciples. [2] And Judas also, which betrayed him, knew the place: for Jesus ofttimes resorted thither with his disciples. [3] Judas then, having received a band of men and officers from the chief priests and Pharisees, cometh thither with lanterns and torches and weapons. [4] Now he that betrayed him gave them a sign, saying, Whomsoever I shall kiss, that same is he: hold him fast. [5] And forthwith he came to Jesus, and said, Hail, master; and kissed him. [6] And Jesus said unto him, Friend, wherefore art thou come? Then came they, and laid hands on Jesus, and took him.

LXIV. He is Arrested and Carried Before Caiaphas, the High Priest and is Condemned.

Jesus therefore, knowing all things that should come upon him, went forth, and said unto them, Whom seek ye? [2] They answered him, Jesus of Nazareth. Jesus saith unto them, I am he. And Judas also, which betrayed him, stood with them. 3 As soon then as he had said unto them, I am he, they went backward, and fell to the ground. 4 Then asked he them again, Whom seek ye? And they said, Jesus of Nazareth. 5 Jesus answered, I have told you that I am he; if therefore ye seek me, let these go their way: 6 And Jesus said unto him, Friend, wherefore art thou come? Then came they, and laid hands on Jesus, and took him. 7 And, behold, one of them which were with Jesus stretched out his hand, and drew his sword, and struck a servant of the high priest's, and smote off his ear. 8 Then said Jesus unto him, Put up again thy sword into his place: for all they that take the sword shall perish with the sword. 9 In that same hour said Jesus to the multitudes, Are ye come out as against a thief with swords and staves for to take me? I sat daily with you teaching in the temple, and ye laid no hold on me. 10 But all this was done, that the scriptures of the prophets might be fulfilled. Then all the disciples forsook him, and fled. 11 And there followed him a certain young man, having a linen cloth cast about his naked body; and the young men laid hold on him: 12 And he left the linen cloth, and fled from them naked. 13 And they that had laid hold on Jesus led him away to Caiaphas the high priest, where the scribes and the elders were assembled. 14 And Simon Peter followed Jesus, and so did another disciple: that disciple was known unto the high priest, and went in with Jesus into the palace of the high priest. 15 But Peter stood at the door without. Then went out that other disciple, which was known unto the high priest, and spake unto her that kept the door, and brought in Peter. 16 Then saith the damsel that kept the door, unto Peter, Art not thou also one of this man's disciples? He saith, I am not. 17 And the servants and officers stood there, who had made a fire of coals; for it was cold: and they warmed themselves: and Peter stood with them, and warmed himself. 18 And Simon Peter stood and warmed himself. They said therefore unto him, Art not thou also one of his disciples? He denied it, and said, I am not. 19 One of the servants of the high priest, being his kinsman whose ear Peter cut off, saith, Did not I see thee in the garden with him? 20 Peter then denied again: and immediately the cock crew. 21 And Peter remembered the word of Jesus, which said unto him, Before the cock crow, thou shalt deny me thrice. And he went out, and wept bitterly. 22 The high priest then asked Jesus of his disciples, and of his doctrine. 23 Jesus answered him, I spake openly to the world; I ever taught in the synagogue, and in the temple, whither the Jews always resort; and in secret have I said nothing. 24 Why askest thou me? ask them which heard me, what I have said unto them: behold, they know what I said. 25 And when he had thus spoken, one of the officers which stood by struck Jesus with the palm of his hand, saying, Answerest thou the high priest so? 26 Jesus answered him, If I have spoken evil, bear witness of the evil; but if well, why smitest thou me? 27 And the chief priests and all the council sought for witness against Jesus to put him to death; and found none. 28 For many bare false witness against him, but their witness agreed not together. 29 And there arose certain, and bare false witness against him, saying, 30 We heard him say, I will destroy this temple that is made with hands, and within three days I will build another made without hands. 31 But neither so did their witness agree together. 32 And the high priest stood up in the midst, and asked Jesus, saying, Answerest thou nothing? what is it which these witness against thee? 33 But he held his peace, and answered nothing. Again the high priest asked him, and said unto him, Art thou the Christ, the Son of the Blessed? 34 Art thou the Christ? tell us. And he said unto them, If I tell you, ye will not believe: 35 And if I also ask you, ye will not answer me, nor let me go. 36 Then said they all, Art thou then the Son of God? And he said unto them, Ye say that I am. 37 Then the high priest rent his clothes, and saith, What need we any further witnesses? 38 Ye have heard the blasphemy: what think ye? And they all condemned him to be guilty of death. 39 And some began to spit on him, and to cover his face, and to buffet him, and to say unto him, Prophesy: and the servants did strike him with the palms of their hands.

LXV. Is then Carried to Pilate.

Then led they Jesus from Caiaphas unto the hall of judgment: and it was early; and they themselves went not into the judgment hall, lest they should be defiled; but that they might eat the passover. 2 Pilate then went out unto them, and said, What accusation bring ye against this man? 3 They answered and said unto him, If he were not a malefactor, we would not have delivered him up unto thee. 4 Then said Pilate unto them, Take ye him, and judge him according to your law. The Jews therefore said unto him, it is not lawful for us to put any man to death. 5 Then Pilate entered into the judgment hall again, and called Jesus, and said unto him, Art thou the King of the Jews? 6 Jesus answered him, Sayest thou this thing of thyself, or did others tell it thee of me? 7 Pilate answered, Am I a Jew? Thine own nation and the chief priests have delivered thee unto me: what hast thou done? 8 Jesus answered, My kingdom is not of this world; if my kingdom were of this world, then would my servants fight, that I should not be delivered to the Jews: but now is my kingdom not from hence. ^{9} Pilate therefore said unto him, Art thou a king then? Jesus answered, Thou sayest that I am a king. To this end was I born, and for this cause came I into the world, that I should bear witness unto the truth. Every one that is of the truth heareth my voice. ^{10} Pilate saith unto him, What is truth? And when he had said this, he went out again unto the Jews, and saith unto them, I find in him no fault at all. ^{11} And they were the more fierce, saying, He stirreth up the people, teaching throughout all Jewry, beginning from Galilee to this place. ^{12} Then said Pilate unto him, Hearest thou not how many things they witness against thee?

LXVI. Who Sends Him to Herod.

When Pilate heard of Galilee, he asked whether the man were a Galilean. ^{2} And as soon as he knew that he belonged unto Herod's jurisdiction, he sent him to Herod, who himself also was at Jerusalem at that time. ^{3} And when Herod saw Jesus, he was exceeding glad: for he was desirous to see him of a long season, because he had heard many things of him; and he hoped to have seen some miracle done by him. ^{4} Then he questioned with him in many words; but he answered him nothing. ^{5} And the chief priests and scribes stood and vehemently accused him. ^{6} And Herod with his men of war set him at naught, and mocked him, and arrayed him in a gorgeous robe, and sent him again to Pilate. ^{7} And the same day Pilate and Herod were made friends together: for before they were at enmity between themselves.

LXVII. Receives Him Back, Scourges and Delivers Him to Execution.

And Pilate, when he had called together the chief priests and the rulers and the people, 2 Said unto them, Ye have brought this man unto me, as one that perverteth the people: and, behold, I, having examined him before you, have found no fault in this man touching those things whereof ye accuse him: 3 No, nor yet Herod: for I sent you to him; and, lo, nothing worthy of death is done unto him. 4 I will therefore chastise him, and release him. 5 Now at that feast the governor was wont to release unto the people a prisoner, whom they would. 6 And they had then a notable prisoner, called Barabbas. 7 Therefore when they were gathered together, Pilate said unto them, Whom will ye that I release unto you? Barabbas, or Jesus which is called Christ? 8 For he knew that for envy they had delivered him. 9 When he was set down on the judgment seat, his wife sent unto him, saying, Have thou nothing to do with that just man: for I have suffered many things this day in a dream because of him. 10 But the chief priests and elders persuaded the multitude that they should ask Barabbas, and destroy Jesus. 11 The governor answered and said unto them, Whether of the twain will ye that I release unto you? They said, Barabbas. 12 Pilate saith unto them, What shall I then with Jesus which is called Christ? They all say unto him, Let him be crucified. 13 And the governor said, Why, what evil hath he done? But they cried out the more, saying, Let him be crucified. 14 Then released he Barabbas unto them: and when he had scourged Jesus, he delivered him to be crucified.

LXVIII. His Crucifixion, Death, and Burial.

Then the soldiers of the governor took Jesus into the common hall, and gathered unto him the whole band of soldiers. 2 And when they had platted a crown of thorns, they put it upon his head, and a reed in his right hand: and they bowed the knee before him, and mocked him, saying, Hail, King of the Jews! 3 And they spit upon him, and took the reed and smote him on the head. 4 And after that they had mocked him, they took the robe off from him, and put his own raiment on him, and led him away to crucify him. 5 Then Judas, which had betrayed him, when he saw that he was condemned, repented himself, and brought again the thirty pieces of silver to the chief priests and elders, 6 Saying, I have sinned in that I have betrayed the innocent blood. And they said, What is that to us? see thou to that. 7 And he cast down the pieces of silver in the temple, and departed, and went and hanged himself. 8 And the chief priests took the silver pieces, and said, It is not lawful for to put them into the treasury, because it is the price of blood. 9 And they took counsel, and bought with them the potter's field, to bury strangers in. 10 Wherefore that field was called, The field of blood, unto this day. 11 And as they led him away, they laid hold upon one Simon, a Cyrenian, coming out of the country, and on him they laid the cross, that he might bear it after Jesus. 12 And there followed him a great company of people, and of women, which also bewailed and lamented him. 13 But Jesus turning unto them said, Daughters of Jerusalem, weep not for me, but weep for yourselves, and for your children. 14 For, behold, the days are coming, in the which they shall say, Blessed are the barren, and the wombs that never bare, and the paps which never gave suck. 15 Then shall they begin to say to the mountains, Fall on us; and to the hills,

Cover us. 16 For if they do these things in a green tree, what shall be done in the dry? 17 And there were also two other, malefactors, led with him to be put to death. 18 And he bearing his cross went forth into a place called the place of a skull, which is called in the Hebrew, Golgotha: 19 Where they crucified him, and two other with him, on either side one, and Jesus in the midst. 20 And Pilate wrote a title, and put it on the cross. And the writing was, JESUS OF NAZARETH THE KING OF THE JEWS. 21 This title then read many of the Jews: for the place where Jesus was crucified was nigh to the city: and it was written in Hebrew, and Greek, and Latin. 22 Then said the chief priests of the Jews to Pilate, Write not, The King of the Jews; but that he said, I am King of the Jews. 23 Pilate answered, What I have written I have written. 24 Then the soldiers, when they had crucified Jesus, took his garments, and made four parts, to every soldier a part; and also his coat: now the coat was without seam, woven from the top throughout. 25 They said therefore among themselves, Let us not rend it, but cast lots for it, whose it shall be: that the scripture might be fulfilled, which saith, They parted my raiment among them, and for my vesture they did cast lots. These things therefore the soldiers did. 26 And they that passed by reviled him, wagging their heads, 27 And saying, Thou that destroyest the temple, and buildest it in three days, save thyself. If thou be the Son of God, come down from the cross. 28 Likewise also the chief priests mocking him, with the scribes and elders, said, 29 He saved others; himself he cannot save. If he be the King of Israel, let him now come down from the cross, and we will believe him. 30 He trusted in God; let him deliver him now, if he will have him: for he said, I am the Son of God. 31 And one of the malefactors which were hanged railed on him, saying, If thou be Christ, save thyself and us. [32] But the other answering rebuked him, saying, Dost not thou fear God, seeing thou art in the same condemnation? [33] And we indeed justly; for we receive the due reward of our deeds: but this man hath done nothing amiss. [34] Then said Jesus, Father, forgive them; for they know not what they do. And they parted his raiment, and cast lots. [35] Now there stood by the cross of Jesus his mother, and his mother's sister, Mary the wife of Cleophas, and Mary Magdalene. [36] When Jesus therefore saw his mother, and the disciple standing by, whom he loved, he saith unto his mother, Woman, behold thy son! [37] Then saith he to the disciple, Behold thy mother! And from that hour that disciple took her unto his own home. [38] And about the ninth hour Jesus cried with a loud voice, saying, Eli, Eli, lama sabachthani? that is to say, My God, my God, why hast thou forsaken me? [39] Some of them that stood there, when they heard that, said, This man calleth for Elias. [40] And straightway one of them ran, and took a spunge, and filled it with vinegar, and put it on a reed, and gave him to drink. [41] The rest said, Let be, let us see whether Elias will come to save him. [42] Jesus, when he had cried again with a loud voice, yielded up the ghost. [43] And many women were there beholding afar off, which followed Jesus from Galilee, ministering unto him: [44] Among which was Mary Magdalene, and Mary the mother of James and Joses, and the mother of Zebedee's children.

LXIX. His Burial.

The Jews therefore, because it was the preparation, that the bodies should not remain upon the cross on the sabbath day, (for that sabbath day was an high day,) besought Pilate that their legs might be broken, and that they might be taken away. ² Then came the soldiers, and brake the legs of the first, and of the other which was crucified with him. ³ But when they came to Jesus, and was that he was dead already, they brake not his legs: ⁴ But one of the soldiers with a spear pierced his side, and forthwith came there out blood and water. ⁵ And after this Joseph of Arimathaea, being a disciple of Jesus, but secretly for fear of the Jews, besought Pilate that he might take away the body of Jesus: and Pilate gave him leave. He came therefore, and took the body of Jesus. ⁶ And there came also Nicodemus, which at the first came to Jesus by night, and brought a mixture of myrrh and aloes, about an hundred pound weight. ⁷ Then took they the body of Jesus, and wound it in linen clothes with the spices, as the manner of the Jews is to bury. ⁸ Now in the place where he was crucified there was a garden; and in the garden a new sepulchre, wherein never man yet laid. ⁹ There laid they Jesus: and rolled a great stone to the door of the sepulchre, and departed.

THE OPINIONS OF
THOMAS JEFFERSON

THE OPINIONS OF THOMAS JEFFERSON

ADAMS, JOHN. His vanity is a lineament in his character which has entirely escaped me. His want of taste I had observed. Notwithstanding all this, he has a sound head on substantial points, and I think he has integrity. I am glad, therefore, he is of the commission for negotiating peace and expect he will be useful in it. His dislike of all parties, and all men, by balancing his prejudices, may give them some fair play to his reason as would a general benevolence of temper. At any rate honesty may be extracted from poisonous weeds.

ADAMS, SAMUEL. A letter from you, my respectable friend, after three and twenty years of separation, has given me a pleasure I cannot express. It recalls to my mind the anxious days we then passed in struggling for mankind. Your principles have been tested in the crucible of time and have come out pure. You have proved that it was monarchy, and not merely British monarchy, you opposed. A government by representation, elected by the people at short periods, was our object; and our maxim at that day was "where annual election ends, tyranny begins;" nor have our departures from it been sanctioned by the happiness of their effect.

ADVICE. (1) This letter will, to you, be as one from the dead. The writer will be in the grave before you can weight its counsels. Your affectionate and excellent father has requested that I would address to you something which might possibly have a favorable influence on the course of life you have to run, and I, too, as a namesake, feel an interest in that course. Few words will be necessary, with good dispositions on your part. Adore God. Reverence and cherish your parents. Love your neighbor as yourself. Be just. Be true. Murmur not at the ways of Providence. So shall the life into which you have entered, be the portal to one of eternal and ineffable bliss.

ADVICE. (2) Never put off for tomorrow what you can do today. Never trouble another for what you can do yourself. Never spend your money before you have it. Never buy what you do not want, because it is cheap, it will be dear to you. Pride costs us more than hunger, thirst and cold. We never repent of having eaten too little. Nothing is troublesome that we do willingly. How much pain have cost us the evils which have never happened. Take things always by their smooth handle. When angry, count ten, before you speak; if very angry, a hundred.

AFFLICTION. Deeply practiced in the school of affliction, the human heart knows no joy which I have not lost, no sorrow of which I have not drunk! Fortune can present no grief of unknown form to me. Who then can so softly bind up the wound of another as he who has felt the same wound himself.

AGRICULTURE. To remove as much as possible the occasions of making war, it might be better for us to abandon the ocean altogether, that being the element whereon we shall be principally exposed to jostle with other nations; to leave to others to bring what we shall want, and to carry what we can spare. This would make us invulnerable to Europe, by offering none of our property to their prize, and would turn all our citizens to the cultivation of the earth; and I repeat it again, cultivators of the earth are the most virtuous and independent citizens.

ALIEN AND SEDITION LAWS. I consider the Alien and Sedition laws as merely an experiment of the American mind to see how far it will bear an avowed violation of the Constitution. If this goes down we shall immediately see attempted another act of Congress declaring that the President shall continue in office during life, reserving to another occasion the transfer of the succession to his heirs, and the establishment of the Senate for life. . . . That these things are in contemplation, I have no doubt; nor can I be confident of their failure, after the dupery of which our countrymen have shewn themselves susceptible.

ALLIANCES. I sincerely join you in abjuring all political connection with every foreign power; and though I cordially wish well to the progress of liberty in all nations, and would forever give it the weight of our countenance, yet they are not to be touched without contamination from their other bad principles. Commerce with all nations, alliance with none, should be our motto.

AMENDMENTS. None of the fundamental laws and principles of government shall be repealed or altered but by the personal consent of the people on summons to meet in their respective counties on one and the same day by an act of the legislature to be passed for every special occasion; and if in such county meetings the people of two-thirds of the counties shall give their suffrage for any particular alteration or repeal referred to them by the said act, the same shall be accordingly repealed or altered, and such repeal or alteration shall take its place among the fundamentals and stand on the same footing with them, in lieu of the article repealed or altered.

ANARCHY. The British ministry have so long hired their gazetteers to repeat and model into every form lies about our being in anarchy, that the world has at length believed them, the ministers themselves have come to believe them, and what is more wonderful we have believed them ourselves. Yet where does the anarchy exist? When did it ever exist except in the single instance of Massachusetts?

ANIMALS. The truth is, that a Pigmy and a Patagonian, a Mouse and a Mammoth, derive their dimensions from the same nutritive juices. The difference of increment depends upon circumstances unsearchable to beings with our capacities. Every race of animals seem to have received from their Maker certain laws of extension at the time of their formation. . . . Below these limits they cannot fall, nor rise above them. What intermediate station they shall take may depend on soil, on climate, on a careful choice of breeders. But all the manna of Heaven would never raise the Mouse to the bulk of the Mammoth.

THE APOCALYPSE. No man on earth has less taste or talent for criticism than myself, and least and last of all should I undertake to criticise works on the Apocalypse. It is between fifty and sixty years since I read it and then I considered it as merely the ravings of a maniac, no more worthy, nor capable of explanation than the incoherence of our own nightly dreams. I was, therefore, well pleased to see, in your first proof sheet, that it was said to be not the production of St. John, but of Cerinthus a century after the death of that apostle. Yet the change of the author's name does not lessen the extravagancies of the composition; come they from whomsoever they may, I cannot so far respect them as to consider them as an allegorical narration of events, past or subsequent. There is not coherence enough in them to countenance any suite of national ideas. You will judge, therefore, from this how impossible I think it that either your explanation or that of any man in "the Heavens above or on the earth beneath" can be a correct one. What has no meaning admits no explanation!

ARISTOCRACY. If anybody thinks that kings, nobles, or priests are good conservators of the public happiness send them here. It is the best school in the universe to cure them of their folly. They will see here with their own eyes that their descriptions of men are an abandoned confederacy against the happiness of the mass of people. The omnipotence of their effect cannot be better proved than in this country particularly, where notwithstanding the finest soil upon earth, the finest climate under heaven, and a people of the most benevolent, the most gay and amiable character of which the human form is susceptible, where such a people I say, surrounded by so many blessings from nature, are yet loaded with misery by kings, nobles and priests, and by them alone.

ATHEISM. As to the calumny of Atheism, I am so broken to calumnies of every kind, from every department of government, Executive, Legislative, and Judiciary, and from every mission of theirs holding office or seeking it, that I entirely disregard it. . . . It has been so impossible to contradict all their lies, that I am determined to contradict none; for while I should be engaged with one, they would publish twenty new ones.

BANKS. Like a dropsical man calling for water, water, our deluded citizens are clamoring for more banks, more banks. The American mind is now in that state of fever which the world has so often seen in the history of other nations. We are under the bank bubble, as England was under the South Sea bubble, France under the Mississippi bubble, and as every nation is liable to be, under whatever bubble, design, or delusion may puff up in moments when off their guard. We are now taught to believe that legerdemain tricks upon paper can produce as solid wealth as hard labor in the earth. It is vain for common sense to urge that nothing can produce but nothing, that it is an idle dream to believe in a philosopher's stone which is to turn everything into gold, and to redeem man from the original sentence of his Maker, "in the sweat of his brow shall he eat his bread."

BLOCKADE. Nor does this doctrine contravene the right of preventing vessels from entering a blockaded port. This right stands on other ground. When the fleet of a nation actually beleaguers the port of its enemy, no other has a right to enter their line, any more than their line of battle in the open sea, or their line, of circumvallation, or of encampment, or of battle array on land. The space included within their lines in any of those cases is either the property of their enemy, or it is common property assumed and possessed for the moment, which cannot be intruded on, even by a neutral, without committing the very trespass we are now considering, that of intruding into the lawful possession of a friend.

BONAPARTE, NAPOLEON. The penance he is now doing for all his atrocities must be soothing to every virtuous heart. It proves that we have a God in heaven. That He is just and not careless of what passes in the world. And we cannot but wish to this inhuman wretch a long, long life that time as well as intensity may fill up his sufferings to the measure of his enormities. But indeed what suffering can atone for his crimes against the liberties and happiness of the human race, for the miseries he has already inflicted on his own generation and on those yet to come on whom he has riveted the chains of despotism.

BRITAIN. Great Britain is the nation which can do us the most harm of any one, or all on earth; and with her on our side we need not fear the whole world. With her, then, we should most sedulously cherish a cordial friendship; and nothing would tend more to knit our affections than to be fighting once more, side by side, in the same cause. Not that I would purchase her amity at the price of taking part in her wars. But the war in which the present proposition might engage us, should that be its consequence, is not her war, but ours. Its object is to introduce and establish the American system, of keeping out of our land all foreign powers, of never permitting those of Europe to intermeddle with the affairs of our nation. It is to maintain our own principle, not to depart from it. And if, to facilitate this, we can effect a division in the body of the European powers, and draw over to our side its most powerful member, surely we should do it.

CALUMNY. If we suffer ourselves to be frightened from our post by mere lying, surely the enemy will use that weapon; for what one so cheap to those of whose system of politics morality makes no part? The patriot, like the Christian, must learn to bear revilings and persecutions as a part of his duty; and in proportion as the trial is severe, firmness under it becomes more requisite and praiseworthy. It requires, indeed, self-command. But that will be fortified in proportion as the calls for its exercise are repeated.

CANADA. I know your feelings on the present state of the world, and hope they will be cheered by the successful course of our war and the addition of Canada to our

Confederacy. The infamous intrigues of Great Britain to destroy our government . . . and with the Indians to tomahawk our women and children, prove that the cession of Canada must be a *sine qua non* at a treaty of peace.

CAPTIVES. But is an enemy so execrable, that though in captivity, his wishes and comforts are to be disregarded and even crossed? I think not. It is for the benefit of mankind to mitigate the horrors of war as much as possible. The practice, therefore, of modern nations, of treating captive enemies with politeness and generosity, is not only delightful in contemplation, but really interesting to all the world, friends, foes and neutrals.

CHARITY. We are all doubtless bound to contribute a certain portion of our income to the support of charitable and other useful public institutions. But it is a part of our duty also to apply our contributions in the most effectual way we can to secure this object. The question then is whether this will not be better done by each of us appropriating our whole contribution to the institutions within our reach, under our own eye, and over which we can exercise some useful control? Or would it be better that each should divide the sum he can spare among all the institutions of his State or the United States? Reason and the interest of these institutions themselves, certainly decide in favor of the former practice.

CHRISTIANITY. To the corruptions of Christianity I am indeed opposed; but not to the genuine precepts of Jesus himself. I am a Christian in the only sense he wished any one to be; sincerely attached to His doctrines in preference to all others; ascribing to Himself every human excellence; and believing he never claimed any other.

CHURCH AND STATE. Our sister States of Pennsylvania and New York have long subsisted without any establishment at all. The experiment was new and doubtful when they made it. It has answered beyond conception. They flourish infinitely. Religion is well supported; of various kinds indeed, but all good enough; all sufficient to preserve peace and order; or if a sect arises whose tenets would subvert morals, good sense has fair play, and reason laughs it out of doors, without suffering the State to be troubled with it. Their harmony unparalleled, and can be ascribed to nothing but their unbounded tolerance, because there is no other circumstance in which they differ from every nation on earth. They have made the happy discovery, that the way to silence religious disputes is to take no notice of them.

CITIES. When great evils happen, I am in the habit of looking out for what good may arise from them as consolations to us, and Providence has in fact so established the order of things as that most evils are the means of producing some good. The yellow fever will discourage the growth of great cities in our nation, and I view great cities as pestilential to the morals, the health, and the liberties of man. True they nourish some of the elegant arts, but the useful ones can thrive elsewhere and less perfection in the others with more health, virtue and freedom would be my choice.

CITIZENSHIP. The man who loves his country on its own account and not merely for its trappings of interest or power can never be divorced from it, can never refuse to come forward when he finds that she is engaged in dangers which he has the means of warding off. Make, then, an effort, my friend, to renounce your domestic comforts for a few months and reflect that to be a good husband and a good father at this moment you must also be a good citizen.

CIVIL POWER. To render these proceedings still more criminal against our laws, instead of subjecting the military to the civil powers, his majesty has expressly made the civil subordinate to the military. But can his majesty put down all law under his feet? Can he erect a power superior to that which erected himself? He has done it indeed by force, but let him remember that force cannot give right.

CIVIL RIGHTS. Our civil rights have no dependence on our religious opinions, any more than on our opinions in physics or geometry; and, therefore, the proscribing any citizen as unworthy the public confidence by laying upon him an incapacity of being called to offices of trust or emolument, unless he profess or renounce this or that religious opinion, is depriving him judicially of those privileges and advantages to which, in common with his fellow-citizens he has a natural right.

CLERGY. [F]rom the clergy I expect no mercy. They crucified their Saviour, who preached that their kingdom was not of this world; and all who practice on that precept must expect the extreme of their wrath. The laws of the present day withhold their hands from blood; but lies and slander still remain to them.

COLONIES. Ancient nations considered Colonies principally as receptacles for a too numerous population, and as natural and useful allies in times of war; but modern nations, viewing commerce as an object of first importance, value Colonies chiefly as instruments for the increase of that.

COMMERCE. All the world is becoming commercial. Were it practicable to keep our new empire separated from them we might indulge ourselves in speculating whether commerce contributes to the happiness of mankind. But we cannot separate ourselves from them. Our citizens have had too full a taste of the comforts furnished by the arts and manufactures to be debarred the use of them. We must then in our defense endeavor to share a large a portion as we can of this modern source of wealth and power.

COMPROMISE. A government held together by the bands of reason only, requires much compromise of opinion; that things even salutary should not be crammed down the throats of dissenting brethren, especially when they may be put into a form to be willingly swallowed, and that a great deal of indulgence is necessary to strengthen habits of harmony and fraternity.

CONFEDERACIES. Whether we remain in one Confederacy, or form into Atlantic and Mississippi Confederacies, I believe not very important to the happiness of either part. Those of the Western Confederacy will be as much children and descendants as those of the Eastern, and I feel myself as much identified with that country, in future time, as with this; and did I now foresee a separation at some future day, yet I should feel the duty and the desire to promote the Western interests as zealously as the Eastern, doing all the good for both portions of our future family which should fall within my power.

CONFIDENCE. It would be a dangerous delusion were a confidence in the men of our choice to silence our fears for the safety of our rights; confidence is everywhere the parent of despotism - free Government is founded on jealousy, and not in confidence; it is jealousy and not confidence which prescribes limited Constitutions to bind down those whom we are obliged to trust with power; our Constitution has accordingly fixed the limits to which, and no further, our confidence may go; and let the honest advocate of confidence read the Alien and Sedition acts and say if the Constitution has not been wise in fixing limits to the government it created, and whether we should be wise in destroying those limits. In questions of power, then, let no more be heard of confidence in man, but bind him down from mischief by the chains of the Constitution.

CONGRESS. Resolved unanimously that this Assembly of Virginia will not listen to any proposition or suffer any negotiation inconsistent with their national faith and Federal union, and that a proposition from the enemy for treating with any Assembly or body of men in America other than the Congress of these United States is insidious and inadmissible.

CONQUEST. It is an established principle that conquest gives inchoate right, which does not become perfect till confirmed by the treaty of peace, and by a renunciation or abandonment by the former proprietor.

THE CONSTITUTION. (1) I am glad to learn that the new Constitution will undoubtedly be received by a sufficiency of the States to set it a going. Were I in America, I would advocate it warmly till nine should have adopted it, and then as warmly take the other side to convince the remaining four that they ought not to come into it until the declaration of rights is annexed to it. By this means we should secure all the good of it and procure so respectable an opposition as would induce the accepting States to offer a bill of rights.

THE CONSTITUTION. (2) No society can make a perpetual Constitution or even a perpetual law. The earth belongs always to the living generation. They may manage it then, and what proceeds from it, as they please during their usufruct. They are masters, too, of their own persons, and consequently may govern them as they please. But persons and property make the sum of the objects of government. The Constitution and laws of their predecessors extinguished them, in their natural course, with those whose will gave them being. This could preserve that being till it ceased to be itself, and no longer. Every Constitution, then, and every law, naturally expires at the end of nineteen years. If it be enforced longer, it is an act of force and not of right.

CORPORATIONS. I hope we shall take warning from the example of England and crush in its birth the aristocracy of our moneyed corporations which dare already to challenge our Government to trial, and bid defiance to the laws of our country.

CREATION. I give one answer to all theorists - that is as follows: They all suppose the earth a created existence; they must suppose a Creator, then, and that he possessed power and wisdom to a great degree. As he intended the earth for the habitation of animals and vegetables, is it reasonable to suppose he made two jobs of the creation? That he first made a chaotic lump and set it in motion, and then, waiting ages necessary to form itself - that when it had done this he stepped in a second time to create the animals and plants which were to inhabit it? As a hand of a Creator is to be called in it may as well be called in at one stage of the process as another. We may as well suppose he created the earth at once nearly in the state in which we see it.

CRIMES AND PUNISHMENTS. In forming a scale of crimes and punishments, two considerations have considerable weight. 1. The atrocity of the crime. 2. The peculiar circumstances of a country which furnish greater temptations to commit it, or greater facilities for escaping detection. The punishment must be heavier to counterbalance this. Was the first the only consideration, all nations would form the same scale. But as the circumstances of a country have influence on the punishment, and no two countries exist precisely under the same circumstances, no two countries will form the same scale of crimes and punishments. For example, in America the inhabitants let their horses go at large in the uninclosed lands which are so extensive as to maintain them altogether. It is easy, therefore, to steal them and easy to escape. Therefore, the laws are obliged to oppose these temptations with a heavier degree of punishment. For this reason the stealing of a horse in America is punished more severely than stealing the same value in any other form. In Europe, where horses are confined so securely that it is impossible to steal them, that species of theft need not be punished more severely than any other. In some countries of Europe, stealing fruit from trees is punished capitally. This to an unreflecting American appears the most enormous of all the abuses of power; because he has been used to see fruit hanging in such quantities, that if not taken by men they would rot.

CRIMINALS. The reformation of offenders, though an object worthy of the attention of the laws, is not effected at all by capital punishments which exterminate instead of reforming, and should be the last melancholy resource against those whose existence is become inconsistent with the safety of their fellow-citizens; which also weaken the State by cutting off so many, who, if reformed, might be restored sound members of society, who even under a course of correction, might be rendered useful in various labors for the public, and would be living and long-continued spectacles to deter others from committing like offenses.

CUBA. Do we wish to acquire to our own Confederacy any one or more of the Spanish provinces? I candidly confess, that I have ever looked on Cuba as the most interesting addition which could ever be made to our system of States. The control which, with Florida Point, this island would give us over the Gulf of Mexico, and the countries and isthmus bordering on it, as well as all those whose waters flow into it, would fill up the measure of our political well-being. Yet, as I am sensible that this can never be obtained, even with her own consent, but by war; and its independence, which is our second interest (and especially its independence of England), can be secured without it, I have no hesitation in abandoning my first wish to future chances, and accepting its independence, with peace and the friendship of England, rather than its association, at the expense of war and her enmity.

DEBT. Whether one generation of men has a right to bind another is a question of such consequence as not only to merit decision, but place also, among the fundamental principles of every government. That no such obligation can be transmitted I think very capable of proof. I set out on this ground which I suppose to be self evident: that the earth belongs in usufruct to the living, that the dead have neither right nor power over it. The portion occupied by any individual ceases to be his when himself ceases to be, and reverts to the society. If the society has formed no rules for the appropriation of its lands in severalty, it will be taken by the first occupants. These will generally be the wife and children of the decedent. If they have formed rules of appropriation, those rules may give it to the wife and children, or to some of them, or to the legatee of the deceased. So they may give it to his creditors. But the child, the legatee or creditor take it, not by any natural right, but by a law of the society of which they are members, and to which they are subject. Then no man can by natural right oblige the lands he occupied, or the persons who succeed him in that occupation, to the payment of debts contracted by him. For if he could, he might during his own life eat up the usufruct of the land for several generations to come, and then the lands would belong to the dead and not to the living which is the reverse of the principle. What is true of every member of the society individually, is true of them all collectively, since the rights of the whole can be no more than the sum of the rights of individuals. Then no generation can contract debts greater than may be paid during the course of its own existence.

DEBT, NATIONAL. We are ruined, Sir, if we do not overrule the principles that "the more we owe, the more prosperous we shall be," that a public debt furnishes the means of enterprise, that if ours should be once paid off, we should incur another by any means however extravagant, etc.

DEMOCRACY. The introduction of this new principle of representative Democracy has rendered useless almost everything written before on the structure of government; and, in a great measure, relieves our regret, if the political writings of Aristotle, or of any other ancient, have been lost, or are unfaithfully rendered or explained to us. My most earnest wish is to see the Republican element of popular control pushed to the maximum of its practicable exercise. I shall then believe that our Government may be pure and perpetual.

DEVICE. A proper device (instead of arms) for the American States would be the father presenting the bundle of rods to his son, with the motto, "Insuperabiles si inseparabiles."

DISSENSION. Political dissension is doubtless a less evil than the lethargy of despotism, but still it is a great evil, and it would be as worthy the efforts of the patriot as of the philosopher to exclude its influence if possible from social life. The good are rare enough at best. There is no reason to sub-divide them by artificial lines. But whether we shall ever be able to perfect the principles of society as that political opinions shall be as inoffensive as those of philosophy, mechanics, or any other may well be doubted.

EDUCATION. If all the sovereigns of Europe were to set themselves to work to emancipate the minds of their subjects from their present ignorance and prejudices, and that as zealously as they now endeavor to the contrary, a thousand years would not place them on that high ground on which our common people are now setting out. Ours could not have been so fairly put into the hands of their own common sense had they not been separated from their parent stock and kept from contamination, either from them, or the other people of the old world, by the intervention of so wide an ocean. I think by far the most important bill in our whole code is that for the diffusion of knowledge among the people. No other sure foundation can be devised for the preservation of freedom and happiness.... Preach, my dear sir, a crusade against ignorance; establish and improve the law for educating the common people. Let our countrymen know that the people alone can protect us against those evils, and that the tax which will be paid for this purpose is not more than the thousandth part of what will be paid to kings, priests, and nobles who will rise up among us if we leave the people in ignorance.

ELECTIONS. From a very early period of my life I determined never to intermeddle with elections of the people, and have invariably adhered to this determination. In my own country, where there have been so many elections in which my inclinations were enlisted, I yet never interfered.

EMANCIPATION. I concur entirely in your leading principles of gradual emancipation, of establishment on the coast of Africa, and the patronage of our Nation until the emigrants shall be able to protect themselves. The subordinate detail might be easily arranged. But the bare proposition of purchase by the United States generally, would excite infinite indignation in all the States north of Maryland. The sacrifice must fall on the States alone which hold them; and the difficult question will be how to lessen this so as to reconcile our fellow citizens to it. Personally I am ready and desirous to make any sacrifice which shall ensure their gradual but complete retirement from the State, and effectually at the same time, establish them elsewhere in freedom and safety. But I have not perceived the growth of this disposition in the rising generation, of which I once had sanguine hopes.

EMBARGO. It is true that the embargo laws have not had all the effect in bringing the powers of Europe to a sense of justice which a more faithful observance of them might have produced. Yet they have had the important effects of saving our seamen and property, of giving time to prepare for defense; and they will produce the further inestimable advantage of turning the attention and enterprise of our fellow citizens, and the patronage of our State Legislatures to the establishment of useful manufactures in our country. They will have hastened the day when an equilibrium between the occupations of agriculture, manufacture and commerce shall simplify our foreign concerns to the exchange only of that surplus which we cannot consume for those articles of reasonable comfort or convenience which we cannot produce.

ENGLAND. (1) In spite of treaties, England is still our enemy. Her hatred is deep rooted and cordial, and nothing is wanted with her but the power to wipe us and the land we live on out of existence. Her interest, however, is her ruling passion; and the late American measures have struck at that so vitally, and with an energy, too, of which she thought us quite incapable, that a possibility seems to open of forming some arrangement with her when they shall see decidedly, that, without it we shall suppress their commerce with us, they will be agitated by their avarice, on the one hand, and their hatred and their fear of us on the other. The result of this conflict of dirty passion is yet to be awaited. The body of people of this country love us cordially, but ministers and merchants love nobody. The merchants here are endeavoring to exclude us from their islands. The ministers will be governed in it by political motives, and will do it or not do it, as these shall appear to dictate, without love or hatred to anybody.

ENGLAND. (2) I consider the English as our natural enemies and the only nation on earth who wish us ill from the bottom of their souls. And I am satisfied that were our continent to be swallowed up by the ocean, Great Britain would be a bonfire from one end to the other.

EXPANSION. I am aware of the force of the observations you make on the power given by the Constitution to Congress to admit new States into the Union without restraining the subject to the territory then constituting the United States. But when I consider that the limits of the United States are precisely fixed by the treaty of 1783, that the Constitution expressly declares itself to be made for the United States, I cannot help believing the intention was not to permit Congress to admit into the Union new States which should be formed out of the territory for which and under whose authority alone they were then acting. I do not believe it was meant that they might receive England, Ireland, Holland, etc., into it, which would be the case under your construction.

EXERCISE. Give about two hours every day to exercise; for health must not be sacrificed to learning. A strong body makes the mind strong. As to the species of exercise, I advise the gun. While this gives a moderate exercise to the body, it gives boldness, enterprise, and independence to the mind. Games played with the ball, and others of that nature, are too violent for the body, and stamp no character on the mind. Let your gun, therefore, be the constant companion of your walks. Never think of taking a book with you. The object of walking is to relax the mind. You should, therefore, not permit yourself even to think while you walk; but direct yourself by the objects surrounding you. Walking is the best possible exercise. Habituate yourself to walk very far. The

Europeans value themselves on having subdued the horse to the uses of man; but I doubt whether we have not lost more than we have gained by the use of this animal. No one has occasioned so much the degeneracy of the human body. An Indian goes on foot nearly as far in a day for a long journey as an enfeebled white does on his horse; and he will tire the best horses. There is no habit you will value so much as that of walking far without fatigue. I would advise you to take your exercise in the afternoon; not because it is the best time for exercise, for certainly it is not; but because it is the best time to spare from your studies; and habit will soon reconcile it to health, and render it nearly as useful as if you gave to that the more precious hours of the day. A little walk of half an hour in the morning when you first rise is advisable also. It shakes off sleep and produces other good effects in the animal economy.

FARMERS. (1) An industrious farmer occupies a more dignified place in the scale of beings, whether moral or political, than a lazy lounger, valuing himself on his family, too proud to work, and drawing out a miserable existence by eating on that surplus of other men's labour which is the sacred fund of the helpless poor.

FARMERS. (2) Farmers are the true representatives of the great American interest and are alone to be relied on for expressing the proper American sentiments.

THE FEDERALIST. With respect to the Federalist, the three authors had been named to me. I read it with care, pleasure and improvement, and was satisfied there was nothing in it by one of these hands and not a great deal by a second. It does the highest honor to the third, as being in my opinion, the best commentary on the principles of government which ever was written. In some parts it is discoverable that the author means only to say what may be best said in defense of opinions in which he did not concur. But in general it establishes firmly the plan of government. I confess it has rectified me in several points.

FICTION. A little attention to the nature of the human mind evinces that the entertainments of fiction are useful as well as pleasant. A lively and lasting sense of filial duty is more effectually impressed on the mind of a son or daughter by reading King Lear, than by all the dry volumes of ethics and divinity that ever were written.

FOREIGN ENTANGLEMENTS. Determined as we are to avoid if possible wasting the energies of our people in war and destruction,we shall avoid implicating ourselves with the powers of Europe even in the support of principles which we mean to pursue. They have so many other interests different from ours that we must avoid being entangled in them.

FRANCE. Be assured, Sir, that the government and citizens of the United States view with the most sincere pleasure every advance of your nation towards its happiness, an object essentially connected with its liberty, and they consider the union of principles and pursuits between our two countries as a link which binds still closer than interests and affections. The genuine and general effusion of joy which you saw overspread our country on their seeing the liberties of yours rise superior to foreign invasion and domestic trouble has proved to you that our sympathies are great and sincere, and we earnestly wish on our part that there our mutual dispositions may be improved to mutual good by establishing our commercial intercourse on principles as friendly to natural right and freedom as are those of our government.

FRANCE AND ENGLAND. When of two nations the one has engaged herself in a ruinous war for us, has spent her blood and money to save us, has opened her bosom to us in peace, and received us almost on the footings of her own citizens, while the other has moved heaven, earth and hell to exterminate us in war, has insulted us in all her councils in peace, shut her doors to us in every port where her interests would admit it, libeled us in foreign nations, endeavored to poison them against the reception of our most precious commodities; to place these two nations on a footing, is to give a great deal more to one than to the other if the maxim be true that to make unequal quantities equal you must add more to the one than to the other. To say in excuse that gratitude is never to enter into the motives of national conduct is to revive a principle which has been buried for centuries with its kindred principles of the lawfulness of assassination, poison, prying, etc.

FRANKLIN, BENJAMIN. The succession to Dr. Franklin, at the court of France, was an excellent school of humility. On being represented to any one as the Minister of America, the commonplace question used in such cases was "C'est vous, Monsieur, qui remplace le Docteur Franklin;" "It is you, Sir, who replace Dr. Franklin." I generally answered, "No one can replace him, Sir; I am only his successor."

FREEDOM. The station which we occupy among the nations of the earth is honorable, but awful. Trusted with the destinies of this solitary republic of the world, the only monument of human rights and the sole depository of the sacred fire of freedom and self-government, from hence it is to be lighted up in other regions of the earth, if other regions of the earth ever become susceptible of its benign influence. All mankind ought then, with us, to rejoice in its prosperous, and sympathize in its adverse fortunes, as involving everything that is dear to man. And to what sacrifices of interest, or commerce ought not these considerations to animate us? To what compromises of opinion and inclination, to maintain harmony and union among ourselves, and to preserve from all danger this hallowed ark of human hope and human happiness. That differences of opinion should arise among men, on politics, on religion, and on every other topic of human inquiry, and that these should be freely expressed in a country where all our faculties are free, is to be expected.

FREEDOM OF THE PRESS. As to myself, conscious that there was not a truth on earth which I feared should be known, I have lent myself willingly as the subject of a great experiment, which was to prove that an administration, conducting itself with integrity and common understanding, cannot be battered down, even by the falsehoods of a licentious press, and consequently still less by the press, as restrained within the legal and wholesome limits of truth. This experiment was wanting for the world to demonstrate the falsehood of the pretext that freedom of the press is incompatible with orderly government. I have never therefore even contradicted the thousands of calumnies so industriously propagated against myself. But the fact being once established, that the press is impotent when it abandons itself to falsehood, I leave to others to restore it to its strength, by recalling it within the pale of truth. Within that, it is a noble institution, equally the friend of science and of civil liberty. If this can once be effected in your State, I trust we shall soon see its citizens rally to the republican principles of our Constitution, which unite their sister states into one family.

FRENCH REVOLUTION. (1) I still hope the French revolution will issue happily. I feel that the permanence of our own leans in some degree on that, and that failure there would be a powerful argument to prove a failure here.

FRENCH REVOLUTION. (2) We surely cannot deny to any nation the right whereon our own government is founded, that every one may govern itself under whatever form it pleases, and change these forms at its own will, and that it may transact its business with foreign nations through whatever organ it thinks proper, whether King, convention, assembly, committee, President, or whatever else it may choose. The will of the nation is the only thing essential to be regarded.

FRIENDSHIP. When languishing under disease, how grateful is the solace of our friends! How we are penetrated with their assiduities and attentions! How much are we supported by their encouragement and kind offices! When heaven has taken from us some object of our love, how sweet it is to have a bosom whereon to recline our heads and into which we may pour the torrent of our tears! Grief, with such a comfort, is almost a luxury! Friendship is precious, not only in the shade but in the sunshine of life; and thanks to a benevolent arrangement of things, the greater part of life is sunshine. I will recur for proof to the days we have lately passed. On these indeed the sun shone brightly. How gay did the face of nature appear! Hills, valleys, chateaux, gardens, rivers, every object wore its loveliest hue! Whence did they borrow it? From the presence of our charming companion. They were pleasing because she seemed pleased. Alone the scene would have been dull and insipid; the participation of it with her gave relish. Let the gloomy monk, sequestered from the world, seek unsocial pleasures in the bottom of his cell; let the sublimated philosopher grasp visionary happiness while pursuing phantoms dressed in the garb of truth. Their supreme wisdom is supreme folly. Had they ever felt the solid pleasure of one generous spasm of the heart, they would exchange it for all the frigid speculations of their lives. Believe me, then, my friend, that that is a miserable arithmetic which could estimate friendship at nothing.

GENIUS. I hold it to be one of the distinguishing excellencies of election over hereditary successions that the talents which nature has provided in sufficient proportion should be selected by the society for the government of their affairs, rather than this should be transmitted through the lions of knaves and fools, passing from debauches of the table to those of the bed.

GOVERNMENT. (1) In every government on earth is some trace of human weakness, some germ of corruption and degeneracy, which cunning will discover, and wickedness insensibly open, cultivate and improve. Every government degenerates when trusted to the rulers of the people alone. The people, themselves, therefore, are its only safe depositaries. And to render even them safe, their minds must be improved to a certain degree.

GOVERNMENT. (2) But when we come to the moral principles on which the government is to be administered, we come to what is proper for all conditions of society.

I meet you there in all the benevolence and rectitude of your native character; and I love myself always most where I concur most with you.   Liberty, truth, probity, honor, are declared to be the four cardinal principles of your society.   I believe with you that morality, compassion, generosity, are innate elements of the human constitution; that there exists a right independent of force; that a right to property is founded in our natural wants, in the means with which we are endowed to satisfy these wants, and the right to what we acquire by those means without violating the similar rights of other sensible beings; that no one has a right to obstruct another, exercising his faculties innocently for the relief of sensibilities made a part of his nature; that justice is the fundamental law of society; that the majority, oppressing an individual, is guilty of a crime, abuses its strength, and by acting on the law of the strongest breaks up the foundations of society; that action by the citizens in person, in affairs within their reach and competence, and in all others by representatives, chosen immediately, and removable by themselves, constitutes the essence of a republic; that all governments are more or less Republican in proportion as their principle enters more or less into their composition; and that a government by representation is capable of extension over a greater surface of country than one of any other form. These, my friend, are the essentials in which you and I agree; however, in our zeal for their maintenance, we may be perplexed and divaricate, as to the structure of society most likely to secure them.

GRIEF. I have often wondered for what good end the sensation of grief could be intended.   All other passions, within proper bounds, have a useful object.   And the perfection of the moral character is, not in a stoical apathy, so hypocritically vaunted, and so truly too, because impossible, but in a just equilibrium of all the passions. I wish the pathologist then would tell us what is the use of grief in the economy, and of what good it is the cause, proximate or remote.

HABEAS CORPUS. Why suspend the Habeas Corpus in insurrections and rebellions? If public safety requires that the Government should have a man imprisoned on less probable testimony in those than in other emergencies, let him be taken and tried, retaken and retried, while the necessity continues, only giving him redress against the Government for damages. Examine the history of England. See how few of the cases of the suspension of the Habeas Corpus law have been worthy of that suspension. They have been either real treason wherein the parties might as well have been charged at once, or sham plots where it was shameful they should ever have been suspected. Yet for the few cases wherein the suspension of the Habeas Corpus has done real good, that operation is now become habitual, and the minds of the nation almost prepared to live under its constant suspension.

HAMILTON, ALEXANDER. (1) That I have utterly in my private conversations disapproved of the system of the Secretary of the Treasury, Alexander Hamilton, I acknowledge and avow; and this was not a merely speculative difference. His system flowed from principles adverse to liberty and was calculated to undermine and demolish the republic, by creating an influence of his department over the members of the Legislature. I saw this influence actually produced, and its first fruits to be the establishment of the great outlines of his project by the votes of the very persons who, having swallowed his bait, were laying themselves out to profit by his plans; and that had these persons withdrawn as those interested in a question ever should, the vote of the disinterested majority was clearly the reverse of what they made it. These were no longer then the votes of the representatives of the people, but of deserters from the rights and interests of the people.

HAMILTON, ALEXANDER. (2)   My objection to the Constitution was that it wanted a bill of rights securing freedom of religion, freedom of the press, freedom from standing armies, trial by jury, and a constant Habeas Corpus act.   Colonel Hamilton's was that it wanted a king and house of lords.   The sense of America has approved my objection and added the bill of rights, not the king and lords.   I   also   thought   a   longer   term   of   service, insusceptible of renewal would have made a President more independent.   My country has thought otherwise, and I have acquiesced implicitly.   He wishes the general government should have power to make laws binding the States in all cases whatever.   Our country has thought otherwise. Has he acquiesced?

HEALTH. (1) Knowledge indeed is a desirable, a lovely possession, but I do not scruple to say that health is more so.   It is of little consequence to store the mind with science if the body be permitted to become debilitated. If the body be feeble, the mind will not be strong.   The sovereign invigorator of the body is exercise and of all exercises, walking is the best.

HEALTH. (2) An attention to health should take place of every other object. The time necessary to secure this by active exercises, should be devoted to it in preference to every other pursuit. I know the difficulty with which a studious man tears himself from his studies at any given moment of the day. But his happiness and that of his family depend on it. The most uninformed mind with a healthy body, is happier than the wisest valetudinarian.

HISTORY. (1) The most effectual means of preventing tyranny is to illuminate, as far as practicable, the minds of the people at large, and more especially to give them knowledge of those facts, which history exhibiteth, that possessed thereby of the experience of other ages and countries, they may be able to know ambition under all its shapes, and prompt to exert their natural powers to defeat its purposes.

HISTORY. (2) But of all the views of this law relating to popular education none is more important, none more legitimate, than that of rendering the people the safe, as they are the ultimate, guardians of their own liberties. For this purpose the reading in the first stage, where they will receive their whole education, is proposed to be chiefly historical. History, by apprising them of the past, will enable them to judge of the future; it will avail them of the experience of other times and other nations; it will qualify them as judges of the actions and designs of men; it will enable them to know ambition under every disguise it may assume; and knowing it to defeat its views.

IMMIGRATION. The present desire of America is to produce rapid population by as great importation of foreigners as possible. But is this founded in good policy? The advantage proposed is the multiplication of numbers. But are there no inconveniences to be thrown into the scale against this advantage? It is for the happiness of those united in society to harmonize as much as possible in matters which they must of necessity transact together.

Civil government being the sole object of forming societies, its administration must be conducted by common consent. Every species of government has its specific principles. Ours perhaps are more peculiar than those of any other in the universe. It is a composition of the finest principles of the English Constitution, with others derived from natural right and natural reason. To these nothing can be more opposed than the maxims of absolute monarchies. Yet from such are we to expect the greatest number of emigrants. They will bring with them the principles of governments they leave, imbibed in their early youth; or, if able to throw them off, it will be in exchange for an unbounded licentiousness, passing as is usual from one extreme to another. These principles, with their language, they will transmit to their children. In proportion to their numbers, they will share with us in the legislation. They will infuse into it their spirit, warp and bias its directions, and render it a heterogeneous, incoherent, distracted mass.

IMMORTALITY. I will not, therefore, by useless condolences, open fresh the sluices of your grief, nor, although mingling sincerely my tears with yours, will I say a word more where words are vain, but that it is of some comfort to us both, that the time is not very distant, at which we are to deposit in the same cerement, our sorrows and suffering bodies, and to ascend in essence to an ecstatic meeting with the friends we have loved and lost, and whom we shall still love and never lose again.

INDEPENDENCE. Not only the principles of common sense, but the feelings of human nature, must be surrendered up before his Majesty's subjects here can be persuaded to believe that they hold their political existence at the will of a British Parliament. Shall these governments be dissolved, their property annihilated, and their people reduced to a state of nature at the imperious breath of a body of men whom they never saw, in whom they never confided, and over whom they have no power of punishment or removal, let their crimes against American public be ever so great? Can any one reason be assigned why 160,000 electors in the Island of Great Britain should give law to four millions in the States of America, every individual of whom is equal to every individual of them, in virtue, in understanding, and in bodily strength?

INDIANS. (1) In truth, the ultimate point of rest and happiness for them is to let our settlements and theirs meet and blend together, to intermix, and become one people. Incorporating themselves with us as citizens of the United States, this is what the natural progress of things will of course bring on, and it will be better to promote than retard it. Surely it will be better for them to be identified with us, and preserved in the occupation of their lands, than be exposed to the many casualties which may endanger them while a separate people.

INDIANS. (2) My friends and children, I have now an important advice to give you. I have already told you that you and all the red men are my children, and I wish you to live in peace and friendship with one another as brethren of the same family ought to do. How much better is it for neighbors to help than to hurt one another; how much happier must it make them. If you will cease to make war on one another, if you will live in friendship with all mankind, you can employ all your time in providing food and clothing for yourselves and your families. Your men will not be destroyed in war, and your women and children will lie down to sleep in their cabins without fear of being surprised by their enemies and killed or carried away. Your numbers will increase instead of diminishing, and you will live in plenty and in quiet. My children, I have given this advice to all your red brethren on this side of the Mississippi; they are following it, they are increasing in their numbers, are learning to clothe and provide for their families as we do. Remember then my advice, my children; carry it home to your people, and tell them that from the day that they have become all of the same family, from the day that we become father to them all, we wish, as a true father should do, that we may all live together as one household, and that before they strike one another, they should go to their father and let him endeavor to make up the quarrel.

INDUSTRY. A mind always employed is always happy. This is the true secret, the grand recipe for felicity. The idle are only the wretched. In a world which furnishes so many employments which are useful, so many which are amusing, it our own fault if we ever know what ennui is, or if we are ever driven to the miserable resources of gaming, which corrupts our dispositions, and teaches us a habit of hostility against all mankind.

JESUS CHRIST. In this state of things among Jews, Jesus appeared. His parentage was obscure; his condition poor; his education null; his natural endowments great; his life correct and innocent; he was meek, benevolent, patient, firm, disinterested and of the sublimest eloquence.

The disadvantages under which his doctrine appeared are remarkable.

1. Like Socrates and Epictetus, he wrote nothing himself.

2. But he had not, like them, a Xenophon or an Arrian to write for him. On the contrary, all the learned of his country, entrenched in its power and riches, were opposed to him, lest his labors should undermine their advantages; and the committing to writing his life and doctrines fell on the most unlettered and ignorant men, who wrote, too, from memory, and not till long after the transaction had passed.

3. According to the ordinary fate of those who attempt to enlighten and reform mankind, he fell an early victim to the jealousy and combination of the altar and the throne, at about 33 years of age, his reason having not yet attained the maximum of its energy, nor the course of his preaching, which was but of three years at most, presented occasions for developing a complete set of morals.

4. Hence the doctrines which he really delivered were defective as a whole, and fragments only of what he did deliver have come to us mutilated, misstated and often unintelligible.

5. They have been still more disfigured by the corruptions of schismatising followers, who have found an interest in sophisticating and perverting the simple doctrines he taught by engrafting on them the mysticisms of a Grecian sophist, frittering them into subtilities and obscuring them with jargon, until they have caused good men to reject the whole in disgust and view Jesus himself as an impostor.

Notwithstanding these disadvantages, a system of morals is presented to us, which, if filled up in the true style and spirit of the rich fragments he left us, would be the most perfect and sublime that has ever been taught by man.

The question of his being a member of the Godhead, or in direct communication with it, claimed for him by some of his followers and denied by others, is foreign to the present view, which is merely an estimate of the intrinsic merit of his doctrines.

1. He corrected the deism of the Jews, confirming them in their belief of one only God, and giving them juster notions of his attributes and government.

2. His moral doctrines, relating to kindred and friends, were more pure and perfect than those of the most correct philosophers, and greatly more so than those of the Jews; and they went far beyond both in inculcating universal philanthropy, not only to kindred and friends, to neighbors and countrymen, but to all mankind, gathering all into one family, under the bonds of love, charity, peace, common wants and common aids. A development of this head will evince the peculiar superiority of the system of Jesus over all others.

3. The precepts of philosophy and of the Hebrew code, laid hold of actions only. He pushed his scrutinies into the heart of man; erected his tribunal in the region of his thoughts, and purified the waters at the fountain head.

4. He taught emphatically the doctrines of a future state, which was either doubted or disbelieved by the Jews; and wielded it with efficacy as an important incentive, supplementary to the other motives to moral conduct.

JUDICIARY. The dignity and stability of government in all its branches, the morals of the people, and every blessing of society, depend so much upon an upright and skilful administration of justice that the judicial power ought to be distinct from both the legislature and executive, and independent upon both, that so it may be a check upon both, as both should be a check upon that. The judges, therefore, should be men of learning and experience in the laws, of exemplary morals, great patience, calmness and attention; their minds should not be distracted with jarring interests; they should not be dependent upon any man or body of men. To these ends they should hold estates for life in their offices, or, in other words, their commissions should be during good behavior, and their salaries ascertained and established by law.

KINGS. So much for the blessings of having kings and magistrates who would be kings. From these events our growing Republic may learn useful lessons, never to call on foreign powers to settle their differences, to guard against hereditary magistrates, to prevent their citizens from becoming so established in wrath and power as to be thought worthy of alliance by marriage with the nieces, sisters, etc., of kings, and, in short, to besiege the throne of heaven with eternal prayers, to extirpate from creation this class of human lions, tigers and mammoth called kings; from whom let him perish who does not say, "Good Lord, deliver us."

LAND. The earth is given a common stock for man to labor and live on. If for the encouragement of industry we allow it to be appropriated, we must take care that other employment be provided to those excluded from the appropriation. If we do not, the fundamental right to labor the earth returns to the unemployed. It is too soon yet in our country to say that every man who can not find employment but who can find uncultivated land shall be at liberty to cultivate it, paying a wholesale rent. But it is not too soon to provide by every possible means that as few as possible shall be without a little portion of land. The small land holders are the most precious part of a State.

LAWYERS. But was there ever a profound common lawyer known in any of the Eastern States? There never was, nor can be one from those States. The basis of their law is neither common nor civil; it is an original, if any compound can so be called. Its foundation seems to have been laid in the spirit and principles of Jewish law, incorporated with some words and phrases of common law, and an abundance of notions of their own. This makes an amalgam *sui generis*, and it is well known that a man, first and thoroughly initiated into the principles of one system of law, can never become pure and sound in any other.

LEGISLATURES. Our legislatures are composed of two houses, the Senate and Representatives, elected in different modes, and for different periods, and in some States, with a qualified veto in the executive chief. But to avoid all temptation to superior pretensions of the one over the other house, and the possibility of either erecting itself into a privileged order, might it not be better to choose at the same time and in the same mode, a body sufficiently numerous to be divided by lot into two separate houses, acting as independently as the two houses in England, or in our governments, and to shuffle their names together and redistribute them by lot, once a week, or a fortnight? This would equally give the benefit of time and separate deliberation, guard against an absolute passage by acclamation, derange cabals, intrigues, and the count of noses, disarm the ascendency which a popular demagogue might at any time obtain over either house, and render impressible all disputes between the two houses, which often form such obstacles to business.

LIBELS. I had no conception there were persons enough to support a paper whose stomachs could bear such aliment as the enclosed papers contain. They are far beyond even the Washington Federalists. To punish, however, is impracticable until the body of the people from whom injuries are to be taken get their minds to rights; and even then I doubt its expediency. While a full range is proper for actions by individuals, either private or public, for slanders affecting them, I would wish much to see the experiment tried of getting along without public prosecutions for libels. I believe we can do it. Patience and well doing, instead of punishment, if it can be found sufficiently efficacious, would be a happy change in the instruments of government.

LIBERTY. This ball of liberty is now so well in motion that it will roll round the globe. At least the enlightened part of it, for light and liberty go together. It is our glory that we first put it into motion, and our happiness that, being foremost, we had no bad examples to follow.

LIBRARIES. I have often thought that nothing would do more extensive good at small expense than the establishment of a small circulating library in every county, to consist of a few well-chosen books to be lent to the people of the county, under such regulations as would secure their safe return in due time. These should be such as would give them a general view of other history, and a particular view of that of their own country, a tolerable knowledge of geography, the elements of natural philosophy, of agriculture and mechanics.

MANUFACTURER. We must now place the manufacturer by the side of the agriculturist. The former question is suppressed or assumes a new form. Shall we make our own comforts, or go without them, at the will of a foreign nation? He, therefore, who is against domestic manufacture, must be for reducing us either to dependence on that foreign nation, or to be clothed in skins, and to live like wild beasts in dens and caverns. I am not one of these; experience has taught me that manufactures are now as necessary to our independence as to our comfort; and if those who quote me as of a different opinion, will keep pace with me in purchasing nothing foreign where an equivalent of domestic fabric can be obtained, without regard to difference of price, it will not be our fault if we do not soon have a supply at home equal to our demand, and wrest that weapon of distress from the hand which has wielded it.

METEMPSYCHOSIS. It is not for me to pronounce on the hypothesis you present of a transmigration of souls from one body to another in certain cases. The laws of nature have withheld from us the means of physical knowledge of the country of spirits, and revelation has, for reasons unknown to us, chosen to leave us in the dark as we were. When I was young I was fond of the speculations which seemed to promise some insight into that hidden country, but observing at length that they left me in the same ignorance which they found me, I have for many years ceased to read or think concerning them, and have reposed my head on that pillow of ignorance which a benevolent Creator has made so soft for us, knowing how much we should be forced to use it. I have thought it better by nourishing the good passion and destroying the bad, to merit an inheritance in a state of being of which I can know so little, and to trust for the future to him who has been so good for the past.

MISSISSIPPI RIVER. I never had any interest westward of the Allegheny and I never will have any. But I have had great opportunities of knowing the character of the people who inhabit that country, and I will venture to say that the act which abandons the navigation of the Mississippi is an act of separation between the Eastern and Western country. It is a relinquishment of five parts out of eight of the territory of the United States, and abandonment of the fairest subjects for the payment of our public debts, and the chaining those debts on our own necks *in perpetuam.* If they declare themselves a separate people, we are incapable of a single effort to retain them.

MISSOURI QUESTION. The Missouri is not a moral question, but one merely of power. Its object is to raise a geographical principle for the choice of a President, and the noise will be kept up until that is effected. All know that permitting the slaves of the South to spread into the West will not add one being to that unfortunate condition, that it will increase the happiness of those existing, and by spreading them over a larger surface, will dilute the evil everywhere, and facilitate the means of getting finally rid of it, an event more anxiously wished by those on whom it presses than by the noisy pretenders to exclusive humanity. In the meantime, it is a ladder for rivals climbing to power.

MONARCHY. The perpetual reeligibility of the President I fear will make an office for life and then hereditary. I was much an enemy to monarchy before I came to Europe. I am ten thousand times more so since I have seen what they are. There is scarcely an evil known in these countries which may not be traced to their King as its source, nor a good which is not derived from the small fibers of Republicanism existing among them. I can further say with safety there is not a crowned head in Europe whose talents or merits would entitle him to be elected a vestryman by the people of any parish in America.

MONEY. I should say, put down all banks, admit none but a metallic circulation, that will take its proper level with the like circulation in other countries, and then our manufacturers may work in fair competition with those of other countries, and the import duties which the government may lay for the purposes of revenue will so far place them above equal competition.

MONROE DOCTRINE. I could honestly, therefore, join in the declaration proposed, that we aim not at the acquisition of any of those possessions, that we will not stand in the way of any amicable arrangement between them and the mother country; but that we will oppose, with all our means, the forcible interposition of any other power, as auxiliary, stipendiary, or under any other form or pretext, and most especially, their transfer to any power by conquest, cession or acquisition in any other way.

MONTICELLO. And our own dear Monticello, where has nature spread so rich a mantle under the eye? Mountains, forests, rocks, rivers. With what majesty do we there ride above the storms! How sublime to look down into the workhouse of nature, to see her clouds, hail, snow, rain, thunder, all fabricated at our feet! And the glorious sun when rising as if out of a distant water, just gilding the tops of the mountains, and giving life to all nature.

MORALITY. The moral sense or conscience is as much a part of man as his leg or arm. It is given to all human beings in a stronger or weaker degree, as force of members is given them in a greater or less degree. It may be strengthened by exercise, as may any particular limb of the body. This sense is submitted indeed in some degree to the guidance of reason; but it is a small stock which is required for this; even a less one than what we call common sense. State a moral case to a ploughman and a professor. The former will decide it as well, and often better, than the latter, because he has not been led astray by artificial rules.

MUSIC. If there is a gratification which I envy any people in this world it is to your country its music. This is the favorite passion of my soul and fortune has cast my lot in a country where it is in a state of deplorable barbarism.

NATIONAL GOVERNMENT. It is a singular phenomenon that while our State governments are the very best in the world, without exception or comparison, our general government has in the rapid course of nine or ten years become more arbitrary and has swallowed up more of the public liberty than even that of England.

NAVY. We have two plans to pursue. The one to carry nothing for ourselves and thereby render ourselves invulnerable to the European states, the other (which our country will be for) is to carry as much as possible. But this will require a protecting force on the sea. Otherwise the smallest power in Europe, every one which possesses a single ship of the line, may dictate to us and enforce their demands by captures on our commerce. Some naval force, then, is necessary if we mean to be commercial.

NEGROES. It will probably be asked, "Why not retain and incorporate the blacks (after the proposed emancipation) into the State and thus save the expense of supplying by importation of white settlers, the vacancies they will leave?" Deep rooted prejudices entertained by the whites; ten thousand recollections by the blacks, of the injuries they have sustained; new provocations; the real distinctions which nature has made; and many other circumstances will divide us into parties, and produce convulsions, which will probably never end but in the extermination of the one or the other race.

NEIGHBORS. The testimony of my native country, of the individuals who have known me in private life, to my conduct in its various duties and relations, is the more grateful, as proceeding from eye witnesses and observers, from triers of the vicinage. Of you, then, my neighbors, I may ask, in the face of the world, "Whose ox have I taken, or whom have I defrauded? Whom have I oppressed, or of whose hand have I received a bribe to blind my eyes therewith?" On your verdict I rest with conscious security.

NEPOTISM. In the course of the trusts I have exercised through life with powers of appointment, I can say with truth, and with unspeakable comfort, that I never did appoint a relation to office, and that merely because I never saw the case in which some one did not offer, or occur, better qualified.

NEWSPAPERS. At a very early period of my life I determined never to put a sentence into any newspaper. I have religiously adhered to the resolution through my life and have great reason to be contented with it. Were I to undertake to answer the calumnies of the newspapers it would be more than all my time and twenty aids could effect. For, while I should be answering one, twenty new ones would be invented. I have thought it better to trust to the justice of my countrymen that they would judge me by what they see of my conduct on the stage where they have placed me.

NOVELS. A great obstacle to good education is the inordinate passion prevalent for novels, and the time lost in that reading which should be instructively employed. When this passion infects the mind, it destroys its tone and revolts it against wholesome reading. Reason and fact, plain and unadorned, are rejected. Nothing can gain attention unless dressed in all the figments of fancy, and nothing so bedecked comes amiss. The result is a bloated imagination, sickly judgment, and disgust towards all the real business of life. This mass of trash, however, is not without some distinction; some few modelling their narratives, although fictitious, on the incidents of real life, have been able to make them interesting and useful vehicles of a sound morality. Such, I think, are Marmontel's new moral-tales, but not his old ones; which are really immoral. Such are the writings of Miss Edgeworth, and some of those of Madame Genlis. For a like reason, too, much poetry should not be indulged. Some is useful for forming style and taste. Pope, Dryden, Thompson, Shakespeare, and of the French, Moliere, Racine, the Corneilles, may be read with pleasure and improvement.

OPINION. For even if we differ in the principle more than I believe we do, you and I know too well the texture of the human mind and the slipperiness of human reason to consider differences of opinion otherwise than differences of form or feature. Integrity of views more than their soundness is the basis of esteem.

PAINE, THOMAS. A writer under the name of Publicola (J.Q. Adams) in attacking all Paine's principles, is very desirous of involving me in the same censure with the author. I certainly merit the same, for I profess the same principles, but it is equally certain I never meant to have entered as a volunteer into the cause.

PAPER MONEY. I wish it were possible to obtain a single amendment to our Constitution. I would be willing to depend on that alone for the reduction of the administration of our government to the genuine principles of its Constitution; I mean an additional article taking from the Federal Government the power of borrowing. I now deny their power of making paper money or anything else a legal tender. I know that to pay all proper expenses within the year would in case of war be hard upon us. But not so hard as ten wars instead of one.

PARDONS. I have made it a rule to grant no pardon in any criminal case, but on the recommendation of the judges who sat on trial, and the district attorney, or two of them. I believe it a sound rule, and not to be departed from but in extraordinary cases.

PARLIAMENT. We conceive that the British Parliament has no right to intermeddle with our provisions for the support of civil government or administration of justice. The provisions we have made are such as please ourselves; they answer the substantial purposes of government and justice, and other purposes than these should not be answered. While Parliament pursue their plan of civil government within their own jurisdiction, we hope also to pursue ours without molestation.

PARTIES. (1) Were parties here divided merely by a greediness for office, as in England, to take a part with either would be unworthy of a reasonable or moral man, but where the principle of difference is as substantial and as strongly pronounced as between the Republicans and the Monocrats of our country, I hold it as honorable to take a firm and decided part, and as immoral to pursue a middle line as between the parties of honest men and rogues into which every country is divided.

PARTIES. (2) When a Constitution like ours wears a mixed aspect of monarchy and Republicanism its citizens will naturally divide into two classes of sentiment, according as their tone of body or mind, their habits, connections and callings induce them to wish to strengthen either the monarchial or Republican features of the Constitution. Some will consider it as an elective monarchy, which had better be made hereditary, and therefore endeavor to lead towards that all the forms and principles of its administration. Others will view it as an energetic republic, turning in all its points on the pivot of free and frequent elections. The great body of our native citizens are unquestionably of the Republican sentiment.

PATENTS. Certainly an inventor ought to be allowed a right to the benefit of his invention for some certain time. It is equally certain it ought not to be perpetual; for to embarrass society with monopolies for every utensil existing, and in all the details of life, would be more injurious to them than had the supposed inventors never existed; because the natural understanding of its members would have suggested the same things or others as good.

How long the term should be is the difficult question. Our legislators have copied the English estimate of the term, perhaps without sufficiently considering how much longer, in a country so much more sparsely settled, it takes for an invention to become known, and used to an extent profitable to the inventor. Nobody wishes more than I do that ingenuity should receive a liberal encouragement.

PEACE. Never was so much false arithmetic employed on any subject, as that which has been employed to persuade nations that it is their interest to go to war. Were the money which it has cost to gain, at the close of a long war, a little town, or a little territory, the right to cut wood here, or to catch fish there, expended in improving what they already possess, in making roads, opening rivers, building ports, improving the arts and finding employment for their idle poor, it would render them much stronger, much wealthier and happier. This I hope will be our wisdom.

THE PEOPLE. I am myself persuaded that the good sense of the people will always be found to be the best army. They may be led astray for a moment, but will soon correct themselves. The people are the only censors of their governors; and even their errors will tend to keep these to the true principles of their institution. To punish their errors too severely would be to suppress the only safeguard to public liberty.

PLEASURE. Do not bite at the bait of pleasure until you know there is no hook beneath it. The art of life is the art of avoiding pain; and he is the best pilot who steers clearest of the rocks and shoals with which he is beset. Pleasure is always before us; but misfortune is at our side; while running after that, this arrests us. The most effectual means of being secure against pain is to retire within ourselves, and to suffice with our own happiness. These, which depend on ourselves, are the only pleasures a wise man will count on; for nothing is ours which another may deprive us of.

POETRY. To my own mortification of all living men, I am the last who should undertake to decide as to the merits of poetry. In early life I was fond of it and easily pleased. But as age and cares advanced the powers of fancy have declined. Every year seems to have plucked a feather from her wings till she can no longer waft one to those sublime heights to which it is necessary to accompany the poet.

POLITENESS. In truth, politeness is artificial good humor, it covers the natural want of it, and ends by rendering habitual a substitute nearly equivalent to the real virtue. It is the practice of sacrificing to those whom we meet in society, all the little conveniences and preferences which will gratify them, and deprive us of nothing worth a moment's consideration; it is the giving a pleasure and flattering turn to our expressions, which will conciliate others, and make them pleased with us as well as themselves. How cheap a price for the good will of another! When this is in return for a rude thing said by another, it brings him to his senses, it mortifies and corrects him in the most salutary way, and places him at the feet of your good nature, in the eyes of the company.

POWER. An honest man can feel no pleasure in the exercise of power over his fellow citizens. And considering as the only offices of power those conferred by the people directly, that is to say, the executive and legislative functions of the general and the State governments, the common refusal of these, and multiplied resignations, are proofs sufficient that power is not alluring to pure minds, and is not, with them, the primary principle of contest. This is my belief of it; it is that on which I have acted; and had it been a mere contest who should be permitted to administer the government according to its genuine Republican principles, there has never been a moment of my life in which I should have relinquished for it the enjoyment of my family, my poems, my friends and books.

PRESIDENCY. General Washington set the example of voluntary retirement after eight years. I shall follow it, and a few more precedents will oppose the obstacle of habit to anyone after a while who shall endeavor to extend his term. Perhaps it may beget a disposition to establish it by an amendment of the Constitution.

THE PRESS. No Government ought to be without censors; and when the press is free, no one ever will. Nature has given to man no other means of sifting out the truth either in religion, law or politics. I think it as honorable to the government neither to know nor notice its sycophants or censors as it would be undignified and criminal to pamper the former and persecute the latter.

PROGRESS. The Gothic idea that we are to look backwards instead of forwards for the improvement of the human mind, and to recur to the annals of our ancestors for what is not perfect in government, in religion and in learning is worthy of those bigots in religion and government by whom it has been recommended and whose purposes it would answer. But it is not an idea which this country will endure.

PUBLIC OPINION. It will always be interesting to me to know the impression made by any particular thing on the public mind. My idea is that when two measures are equally right, it is a duty of the people to adopt that one which is most agreeable to them; and where a measure not agreeable to them has been adopted, it is desirable to know it, because it is an admonition to a review of that measure to see if it has been really right, and to correct it if mistaken. It is rare that the public sentiment decides universally or unwisely, and the individual who differs from it ought to distrust and examine well his own opinion.

PUBLIC SERVICE. The happiest moments of my life have been the few which I have passed at home in the bosom of my family. Employment anywhere else is a mere [waste] of time; it is burning the candle of life in perfect waste for the individual himself. I have no complaint against anybody. I have had more of the confidence of my country than my share. I only say that public employment contributes neither to advantage or happiness. It is but honorable exile from one's family and affairs.

PUNISHMENTS. It frequently happens that wicked and dissolute men, resigning themselves to the dominion of inordinate passions, commit violations on the lives, liberties, and property of others, and the secure enjoyments of these having principally induced men to enter into society, government would be defective in its principal purpose were it not to restrain such criminal acts by inflicting due punishments on those who perpetrate them.

REBELLION. We have had thirteen independent States eleven years. There has been one rebellion. That comes to one rebellion in a century and a half for each State. What country before ever existed a century and a half without a rebellion? And what country can preserve its liberties if their rulers are not warned from time to time that their people preserve the spirit of resistance? Let these take arms. The remedy is to set them right as to facts, pardon and pacify them. What signify a few lives lost in a century or two? The tree of liberty must be refreshed from time to time with the blood of patriots and tyrants. It is its natural manure.

RELIGION. (1) If I be marching on with my utmost vigor in that way which according to sacred geography leads to Jerusalem straight, why am I beaten and ill used by others because my hair is not of the right cut; because I have not been dressed right; because I eat flesh on the road; because I avoid certain by-ways which seem to lead into briars; because I avoid travelers less grave and keep company with others who are more sour and austere? Yet these are the frivolous things which keep Christians at war.

RELIGION. (2) To compel a man to furnish contributions of money for the propagations of opinions which he disbelieves and abhors, is sinful and tyrannical; the forcing him to support this or that teacher of his own religious persuasion, is depriving him of the comfortable liberty of giving his contributions to the particular pastor whose morals he would make his pattern, and whose power he feels most persuasive to righteousness; and is withdrawing from the ministry those temporary rewards, which proceeding from an approbation of their personal conduct, are an additional incentive to earnest and unremitting labours for the instruction of mankind.

RELIGION, FREEDOM OF. I am really mortified to be told that, in the United States of America, a fact like this can become a subject of inquiry, and a criminal inquiry too, as an offense against religion; that a question about the sale of a book can be carried before the civil magistrate. Is this then our freedom of religion? And are we to have a censor whose imprimatur shall say what books may be sold, and what we may buy? And who is thus to dogmatize religious opinions for our citizens? Whose foot is to be the measure to which ours are all to be cut or stretched? Is a priest to be our inquisitor, or shall a layman simple as ourselves, set up his reason as the rule for what we are to read, and what we must believe? It is an insult to our citizens to question whether they are rational beings or not, and blasphemy against religion to suppose it cannot stand the test of truth and reason. If M. de Becourt's book be false in its facts, disprove them; if false in its reasoning, refute it. But, for God's sake, let us freely hear both sides, if we choose.

REPRESENTATION. When the representative body have lost the confidence of their constituents, when they have notoriously made sale of their most valuable rights, when they have assumed to themselves powers which the people never put into their hands, then indeed their continuing in office becomes dangerous to the State, and calls for an exercise of the power of dissolution.

REPUBLICS. Perhaps it will be found that to obtain a just republic (and it is to secure our just rights that we resort to government at all) it must be so extensive as that local egoisms may never reach its greater part; that on every particular question a majority may be found in its councils free from particular interests and giving therefore an uniform prevalence to the principles of justice. The smaller the societies, the more violent and convulsive their schisms. We have chanced to live in an age which will probably be distinguished in history for its experiments in government on a larger scale than has as yet taken place. But we shall not live to see the result. The grosser absurdities such as hereditary magistracies, we shall see exploded in our day. But what is to be the substitute? This our children or grandchildren will answer. It is unfortunate that the efforts of mankind to recover the freedom of which they have been so long deprived will be accompanied with violence, with errors and even with crimes. But while we weep over the means, we may pray for the end.

RETIREMENT. Within a few days I retire to my family, my books and farms; and having gained the harbor myself, I shall look on my friends still buffeting the storm with anxiety indeed, but not with envy. Never did a prisoner, released from his chains, feel such relief as I shall on shaking off the shackles of power. Nature intended me for the tranquil pursuits of science, by rendering them my supreme delight. But the enormities of the times in which I have lived, have forced me to take a part in resisting them, and to commit myself on the boisterous ocean of political passions. I thank God for the opportunity of retiring from them without censure, and carrying with me the most consoling proofs of public approbation.

REVENUE. Is it consistent with good policy or free government to establish a perpetual revenue? Is it not against the practice of our wise British ancestors? Have not the instances in which we have departed from this in Virginia been constantly condemned by the universal voice of our country? Is it safe to make the governing power when once seated in office, independent of its revenue?

RIGHTS. Our legislators are not sufficiently apprised of the rightful limits of their power; that their true office is to declare and enforce only our natural rights and duties, and to take none of them from us. No man has a natural right to commit aggression on the equal rights of another; and this is all from which the laws ought to restrain him; every man is under the natural duty of contributing to the necessities of the society; and this is all the laws should enforce on him; and, no man having a natural right to be the judge between himself and another, it is his natural duty to submit to the umpirage of an impartial third. When the laws have declared and enforced all this, they have fulfilled their functions; and the idea is quite unfounded, that on entering into society we give up any natural right.

SALVATION. The care of every man's soul belongs to himself. But what if he neglect the care of it? Well, what if he neglect the care of his health or estate, which more nearly relate to the state? Will the magistrate make a law that he shall not be poor or sick? Laws provide against injury from others; but not from ourselves. God himself will not save men against their wills.

SECESSION. Should the schism be pushed to separation, it will be for a short term only; two or three years' trial will bring them back, like quarrelling lovers, to renewed embraces, and increased affections. The experiment of separation would soon prove to both that they had mutually miscalculated their best interests. And even were the parties in Congress to secede in a passion, the soberer people would call a convention and cement against the severance attempted by the insanity of their functionaries. With this consoling view, my greatest grief would be for the fatal effect of such an event on the hopes and happiness of the world. We exist, and are quoted, as standing proofs that a government, so modelled as to rest continually on the will of the whole society, is a practicable government. Were we to break to pieces, it would damp the hopes and the efforts of the good, and give triumph to those of the bad, through the whole enslaved world.

SECRECY. No ground of support of the Executive will ever be so sure as a complete knowledge of their proceedings by the people; and it is only in cases where the public good would be injured, and because it would be injured that proceedings should be secret.

SEDITION LAW. I considered, and now consider, that law to be a nullity, as absolute and as palpable as if Congress had ordered us to fall down and worship a golden image; and that it was as much my duty to arrest its execution in every stage, as it would have been to have rescued from the fiery furnace those who should have been cast into it for refusing to worship their image. It was accordingly done, in every instance, without asking what the offenders had done, or against whom they had offended, but whether the pains they were suffering were inflicted under the pretended sedition law.

SELF-GOVERNMENT. Every man and every body of men on earth possess the right of self-government. They receive it with their being from the hand of nature.

Individuals exercise it by their single will; collections of men that of their majority; for the law of the majority is the natural law of every society of men. When a certain description of men are to transact together a particular business, the times and places of their meeting and separating depend on their own will; they make a part of the natural right of self-government. This, like all other natural rights, may be abridged or modified in its exercise by their own consent, or by the law of those who depute them, and if they meet in the rights of others; but as far as it is not abridged or modified, they retain it as a natural right, and may exercise it in what form they please, either exclusively by themselves or in association with others, or by others altogether, as they shall agree.

SERVICE. Nothing could so completely divest us of liberty as the establishment of opinion that the State has a perpetual right to the services of all its members. This to men of certain ways of thinking would be to annihilate the blessings of existence; to contradict the giver of life who gave it for happiness, not for wretchedness; and certainly to such it were better that they had never been born.

SLAVERY. (1) It is impossible to be temperate and pursue this subject through the various considerations of policy, of morals, or history, natural and civil. We must be contented to hope they will force their way into everyone's mind. I think a change already perceptible, since the origin of the present revolution. The spirit of the master is abating, that of the slave rising from the dust, his condition mollifying, the way I hope preparing under the auspices of heaven, for a total emancipation, and that this is disposed, in the order of events, to be with the consents of the masters, rather than by their extirpation.

SLAVERY. (2) I tremble for my country when I reflect that God is just: that his justice cannot sleep forever: that considering members, nature, and natural means only, a revolution of the wheel of fortune, an exchange of situation, is among possible events; that it may become probable by supernatural interference. The Almighty has no attribute which can take side with us in such a contest (with slaves).

SOVEREIGNTY. It is the right of every nation to prohibit acts of sovereignty from being exercised by any other within its limits; and the duty of a neutral nation to prohibit such as would injure one of the warring powers; the granting military commissions within the United States by any other authority than their own is an infringement on their sovereignty, and particularly so when granted to their own citizens to lead them to commit an act contrary to the duties they owe their own country.

SPIRIT OF THE LAW. Substance not circumstance is to be regarded while we have so many foes in our bowels and environing us on every side. He is a bad citizen who can entertain a doubt whether the law will justify him in saving his country or who will scruple to risk himself in support of the spirit of the law where avoidable accidents have prevented a literal compliance with it.

STATE'S RIGHTS. I wish to preserve the line drawn by the Federal Constitution between the general and particular governments as it stands at present, and to take every prudent means of preventing either from stepping over it. It is easy to foresee from the nature of things that the encroachments of the State government will tend to an excess of liberty which will correct itself, while those of the general government will tend to monarchy, which will fortify itself from day to day, instead of working its own cure, as all experience shows. I would rather be exposed to the inconveniences attending too much liberty than those attending too small a degree of it.

SUFFRAGE. However nature may by mental or physical disqualifications have marked infants and the weaker sex for the protection rather than the direction of government, yet among the men who either pay or fight for their country, no line of right can be drawn. The exclusion of a majority of our freemen from the right of representation is merely arbitrary, and an usurpation of the minority over the majority; for it is believed that the non-freeholders compose the majority of our free and adult male citizens.

TALENT. Men possessing minds of the first order, who have had opportunities of being known and acquiring the general confidence, do not abound in any country beyond the wants of the country.

TAXATION. But would it not be better to simplify the system of taxation rather than to spread it over such a variety of subjects, and pass the money through so many hands? Taxes should be proportioned to what may be annually spared by the individual. The simplest system of taxation yet adopted is that of levying on the land and the laborer. But it would be better to levy the same sums on the produce of that labor when collected in the barn of the farmer; because then if through the badness of the year he made little, he would pay little. It would be better yet to levy it not in his hands, but in those of the merchant purchaser; because though the farmer would in fact pay it, as the merchant purchaser would deduct it from the original price of his produce, yet the farmer would not be sensible that he paid it.

TITLES. In America no other distinction between man and man had ever been known, but that of persons in office exercising powers by authority of the laws, and private individuals. Among these last the poorest laborer stood on equal ground with the wealthiest millionaire, and generally on a more favored one whenever their rights seem to jar. Of distinction by birth or badge they had no more idea than they had of the mode of existence in the moon or planets. They had heard only that there were such, and they knew that they must be wrong. A due horror of the evils which flow from these distinctions could be excited in Europe only, where the human species is classed into several stages of degradation, where the many are crushed under the weight of the few, and where the order established can present to the contemplation of a thinking being no other picture than that of God Almighty and His angels trampling under foot the hosts of the damned.

TOBACCO. It is a culture of infinite wretchedness. Those employed in it are in a continual state of exertion beyond the power of nature to support. Little food of any kind is raised by them; so that the men and animals on these farms are illy fed, and the earth is rapidly impoverished. The cultivation of wheat is the reverse in every circumstance. Besides clothing the earth with herbage and preserving its fertility, it feeds the laborers plentifully, requires from them only a moderate foil, except in the season of the harvest, raises great numbers of animals for food and service, and diffuses plenty and happiness among the whole.

TOLERATION. How far does the duty of toleration extend? First, no church is bound by the duty of toleration to retain within her bosom obstinate offenders against her laws. Second, we have no right to prejudice another in his civil enjoyments because he is of another church. If any man err from the right way, it is his own misfortune, no injury to thee; nor therefore art thou to punish him in the things of this life because thou supposeth he will be miserable in that which is to come.

TRAVEL. Traveling makes men wiser, but less happy. When men of sober age travel, they gather knowledge which they may apply usefully for their country, but they are subject ever after to recollections mixed with regret, their affections are weakened by being extended over more objects, and they learn new habits which cannot be gratified when they return home.

TREASON. Most codes do not distinguish between acts against the government and acts against the oppression of the government. The latter are virtues; yet have furnished more victims to the executioner than the former. The unsuccessful struggles against tyranny have been the chief martyrs against treason laws in all countries. We should not wish them to give up to the executioner the patriot who fails and flees to us.

TRUTH. Truth will do well enough if left to shift for herself. She seldom has received much aid from the power of great men to whom she is rarely known and seldom welcome. She has no need of force to procure entrance into the minds of men. Error indeed has often prevailed by the assistance of power or force. Truth is the proper and sufficient antagonist to error.

TYRANNY. Human nature is the same on every side of the Atlantic, and will be alike influenced by the same causes. The time to guard against corruption and tyranny is before they have gotten hold of us. It is better to keep the wolf out of the fold than to trust to drawing his teeth and talons after he shall have entered.

UNIFORMITY. Truth can stand by itself. Subject opinion to coercion: whom will you make your inquisitors? Fallible men; men governed by bad passions, by private as well as public reasons. And why subject it to coercion? To produce uniformity. But is uniformity of opinion desirable? No more than of face and stature. Difference in opinion is advantageous in religion. The several sects perform the office of a censor over each other. Is uniformity attainable? Millions of innocent men, women and children, since the introduction of Christianity have been burnt, tortured, fined, imprisoned; yet we have not advanced one inch towards uniformity.

UNION. We are now represented in General Congress by members approved by this House where the former union, it is hoped, will be so strongly cemented that no partial applications can produce the slightest departure from the common cause. We consider ourselves as bound in honor, as well as interest, to share one general fate with our sister colonies; and should hold ourselves base deserters of that union to which we have acceded, were we to agree on any measure distinct and apart from them.

UNION. We shall never give up our Union, the last anchor of our hope, and that alone which is to prevent this heavenly country from becoming an arena of gladiators. Much as I abhor war, and view it as the greatest revenge of mankind, and anxiously as I wish to keep out of the broils of Europe, I would yet go with my brethren into these rather than separate from them.

UNIVERSITY OF VIRGINIA. We wish to establish in the upper and healthier country and more centrally for the State an university on a plan so broad and liberal and modern as to be worth patronizing with the public support, and be a temptation to the youth of other States to come and drink of the cup of knowledge and fraternize with us. The first step is to obtain a good plan; that is a judicious selection of the sciences and a practicable grouping of them together. I will venture to sketch the sciences which seem useful and practicable for us, as they occur to me while holding my pen. Botany, Chemistry, Zoology, Anatomy, Surgery, Medicine, Natural Philosophy, Agriculture, Mathematics, Astronomy, Geology, Geography, Politics, Commerce, History, Ethics, Law, Arts, Fine Arts. This list is imperfect because I make it hastily, and because I am unequal to the subject. It is evident that some of these articles are too much for one professor and must therefore be ramified; others may be ascribed in groups to a single professor.

VICE-PRESIDENCY. The idea that I would accept the office of President but not that of Vice-President of the United States had not its origin with me. I never thought of questioning the free exercise of the right of my fellow citizens to marshal those whom they call into their service according to their fitness, nor ever presumed that they were not the best judges of these. Had I indulged in a wish in what manner they should dispose of me, it would precisely have coincided with what they have done.

WAR. I do not recollect in all the animal kingdom a single species but man which is eternally and systematically engaged in the destruction of its own species. What is called civilization seems to have no other effect on him than to teach him to pursue the principle of *bellum omnium in omnia* on a larger scale, and, in place of the little contests of tribe against tribe, to engage all the quarters of the earth in the same work of destruction. When we add to this that as the other species of animals the lions and tigers are mere lambs compared with man as a destroyer, we must conclude that it is in man alone that nature has been able to find a sufficient barrier against the too great nullification of other animals and of man himself, an equilibrating power against the fecundity of generation.

WHISKY. Considering it only as a fiscal measure, this was right. But the prostration of body and mind which the cheapness of this liquor is spreading through the mass of our citizens, now calls the attention of the legislator on a very different principle. One of his important duties is as guardian of those who from causes susceptible of precise definition, cannot take care of themselves. Such are infants, maniacs, gamblers, drunkards. The last as much as the maniac, requires restrictive measures to save him from the fatal infatuation under which he is destroying his health, his morals, his family, and his usefulness to society. One powerful obstacle to his ruinous self-indulgence would be a price beyond his competence. As a sanatory measure, therefore, it becomes one of duty in the public guardians. Yet I do not think it follows that imported spirits should be subjected to similar enhancement until they become as cheap as they are made at home. A tax on whisky is to discourage its consumption; a tax on foreign spirits encourages whisky by removing its rival from competition. The price and present duty throw foreign spirits already out of competition with whisky, and accordingly they are used but to a salutary extent. You see no persons besotting themselves with imported spirits, wines and liquors, cordials, etc. Whisky claims to itself alone the exclusive office of sot-making. Foreign spirits, wines, teas, coffee, sugars, salt, are articles of as innocent consumption as broadcloths and silks; and ought like them, to pay but the average *ad valorem* duty of other important comforts.

WOMEN. But our good ladies, I trust have been too wise to wrinkle their foreheads with politics. They are contented to soothe and calm the minds of their husbands returning ruffled from political debate. They have the good sense to value domestic happiness above all others, and the art to cultivate it above all others. There is no part of the earth where as much of this is enjoyed as in America. Recollect the women of this capital [Paris], some on foot, some on horses, and some in carriages hunting pleasure in the streets, in routs and assemblies, and forgetting what they have left behind them in their nurseries; compare them with our own countrywomen occupied in the tender and tranquil amusements of domestic life, and confess that it is a comparison of Americans and Angels.

BIBLIOGRAPHY

Adams, Dickinson W., Editor. *Jefferson's Extracts from the Gospels: "The Philosophy of Jesus" and "The Life and Morals of Jesus."* Princeton, NJ: Princeton University Press, 1986.

Adams, William H. *Jefferson's Monticello.* New York, NY: Abbeville Press, 1988.

Arrowood, Charles F. *Thomas Jefferson and Education in a Republic.* New York, NY: McGraw-Hill Co., 1930.

Bear, James A., Jr., Editor. *Jefferson at Monticello.* Charlottesville, VA: University Press of Virginia, 1967.

Becker, Carl. *Declaration of Independence: A Study in the History of Political Ideas.* New York, NY: Random House, 1958.

Beilenson, Nick, Editor. *Thomas Jefferson: His Life and Words.* White Plains, NY: Peter Pauper, 1986.

Bestor, Arthur. "Thomas Jefferson and the Freedom of Books." *Three Presidents and Their Books.* Urbana, IL: University of Illinois Press, 1955.

Betts, Edwin M. & James A. Bear, Jr., Editors. *The Family Letters of Thomas Jefferson.* Charlottesville, VA: University Press of Virginia, 1986.

Bober, Natalie. *Thomas Jefferson: Man on a Mountain.* New York, NY: Macmillan, 1988.

Boorstin, Daniel J. *The Lost World of Thomas Jefferson.* Chicago, IL: University of Chicago Press, 1981.

Boyd, Julian P., Editor. *The Papers of Thomas Jefferson.* Princeton, NJ: Princeton University Press, 1950.

Boyd, Julian P. *The Declaration of Independence: The Evolution of the Text.* Princeton, NJ: Princeton University Press, 1945.

Brodie, Fawn M. *Thomas Jefferson: An Intimate History.* New York, NY: Bantam Books, 1975.

Bruns, Roger. *Thomas Jefferson.* New York, NY: Chelsea House, 1986.

Bush, Alfred L. *The Life Portraits of Thomas Jefferson.* Charlottesville, VA: University Press of Virginia, 1988.

Cappon, Lester J., Editor. *The Adams-Jefferson Letters: The Complete Correspondence between Thomas Jefferson and Abigail and John Adams.* Chapel Hill, NC: University of North Carolina, 1959.

Cary, Wilson Miles, Editor. "Some Family Letters of Thomas Jefferson." *Scribner's Magazine,* XXXVI (November 1904), pp. 573-586.

Catchings, Benjamin S. *Master Thoughts of Thomas Jefferson.* New York, NY: The Nation Press, 1907.

Chinard, Gilbert, Editor. *The Commonplace Book of Thomas Jefferson.* Baltimore, MD: Johns Hopkins Press, 1926.

Chinard, Gilbert, Editor. *The Literary Bible of Thomas Jefferson.* Baltimore, MD: Johns Hopkins Press, 1928.

Chinard, Gilbert, Editor. *The Letters of Lafayette and Jefferson.* Baltimore, MD: Johns Hopkins Press, 1929.

Chinard, Gilbert, Editor. The Correspondence of Jefferson and Du Pont de Nemours. Baltimore, MD: Johns Hopkins Press, 1931.

Chinard, Gilbert. *Thomas Jefferson, the Apostle of Americanism.* Boston, MA: Little, Brown & Co., 1929.

Commager, Henry Steele. *Jefferson, Nationalism, and the Enlightenment.* New York, NY: George Brazilier, 1975.

Conant, James B. *Thomas Jefferson and the Development of American Public Education.* Berkeley, CA: University of California Press, 1962.

Cunningham, Noble E., Jr. *In Pursuit of Reason: The Life of Thomas Jefferson.* Baton Rouge, LA: Louisiana State University Press, 1987.

Cunningham, Noble E., Jr. *The Process of Government under Jefferson.* Princeton, NJ: Princeton University Press, 1978.

Curtis, William E. *The True Thomas Jefferson.* Philadelphia, PA: J.B. Lippincott Co., 1901.

Dewey, Frank L. *Thomas Jefferson, Lawyer.*
Charlottesville, VA: University Press of Virginia, 1986.

Donovan, Frank. *Mr. Jefferson's Declaration: The Story Behind the Declaration of Independence.* New York, NY: Dodd, Mead & Co., 1968.

Dumbauld, Edward. *Thomas Jefferson & the Law.* Norman, OK: University of Oklahoma Press, 1978.

Dumbauld, Edward. *Thomas Jefferson: American Tourist.* Norman, OK: University of Oklahoma Press, 1946.

Falkner, Leonard. *For Jefferson and Liberty.* New York, NY: Knopf, 1972.

Fleming, Thomas. *The Man from Monticello: An Intimate Life of Thomas Jefferson.* New York, NY: Morrow, 1969.

Foley, John P., Editor. *The Jefferson Cyclopedia..* New York, NY: Funk & Wagnalls, 1900.

Foote, Henry Wilder, Editor. *The Life and Morals of Jesus of Nazareth.* Boston, MA: Beacon Press, 1951.

Ford, Paul L., Editor. *The Writings of Thomas Jefferson.* New York, NY: G.P. Putnam's Sons, 1892-1899.

Ford, Paul L., Editor. *The Works of Thomas Jefferson.* New York, NY: G.P. Putnam's Sons, 1904.

Ford, Paul L., Editor. *The Autobiography of Thomas Jefferson.* New York, NY: G.P. Putnam's Sons, 1914.

Ford, W.C. *Thomas Jefferson's Correspondence.* Boston, MA, 1916.

Forman, Samuel E. *The Life and Writings of Thomas Jefferson.* Indianapolis, IN: The Bowen-Merrill Co., 1900.

Henderson, John C. *Thomas Jefferson's Views on Public Education.* New York, NY: G.P. Putnam's Sons, 1890.

Hirst, Francis W. *Life and Letters of Thomas Jefferson.* New York, NY: Macmillan, 1926.

Honeywell, Roy J. *The Educational Work of Thomas Jefferson.* Boston, MA: Harvard University Press, 1931.

Howell, Wilbur S., Editor. *Jefferson's Parliamentary Writings.* Princeton, NJ: Princeton University Press, 1988.

Huddleston, Eugene L.. *Thomas Jefferson: A Reference Guide.* Boston, MA: G.K. Hall, 1982.

Jackson, Donald. *A Year at Monticello: 1795.* Golden, CO: Fulcrum Pub., 1989.

Jefferson, Thomas. *Life & Selected Writings.* New York, NY: Random House, 1978.

Johnson, Allen. *Jefferson & His Colleagues.* Northford, CT: Elliots Books, 1921.

Kaplan, Lawrence S. *Jefferson & France: An Essay on Politics & Political Ideas.* New York, NY: Greenwood Press, 1980.

Kean, R.G. "Thomas Jefferson as a Legislator." *Virginia Law Journal.* December 1887.

Kimball, Marie. *Jefferson, the Road to Glory.* New York, NY: Greenwood Press, 1977.

Koch, Adrienne, and William Peden, Editors. *The Life and Selected Writings of Jefferson.* New York, NY: The Modern Library, 1982.

Koch, Adrienne. *The Philosophy of Thomas Jefferson.* New York, NY: Columbia University Press, 1943.

Lehmann, Karl. *Thomas Jefferson, American Humanist.* Charlottesville, VA: University Press of Virginia, 1985.

Levy, Leonard W. *Jefferson & Civil Liberties: The Darker Side.* Chicago, IL: Ivan R. Dee, 1989.

Lewis, Jan. *The Pursuit of Happiness: Family & Values in Jefferson's Virginia.* Cambridge, MA: Cambridge University Press, 1985.

Linn, William. *The Life of Thomas Jefferson.* Ithaca, NY: Mack & Andrus, 1834.

Lipscomb, Andrew A., and Albert E. Bergh, Editors. *The Writings of Thomas Jefferson* (20 volumes). Washington, DC, 1903.

McDonald, Forrest. *The Presidency of Thomas Jefferson.* Lawrence, KS: University Press of Kansas, 1976.

McLaughlin, Jack. *Jefferson & Monticello: The Biography of a Builder.* New York, NY: H. Holt & Co., 1990.

McLaughlin, Jack. *To His Excellency Thomas Jefferson: Letters to a President.* New York, NY: W.W. Norton & Co., 1991.

Malone, Dumas. *Jefferson & His Time:* The Sage of His Monticello. New York, NY: Little, Brown & Co., 1982.

Malone, Dumas. *Jefferson & The Ordeal of Liberty.* New York, NY: Little, Brown & Co., 1969.

Malone, Dumas. *Jefferson & The Rights of Man.* New York, NY: Little, Brown & Co., 1968.

Malone, Dumas. *Jefferson the President: First Term, 1801-1805.* New York, NY: Little, Brown & Co., 1971.

Malone, Dumas. *Jefferson the President: Second Term, 1805-1809.* New York, NY: Little, Brown & Co., 1975.

Malone, Dumas. *Jefferson the Virginian.* New York, NY: Little, Brown & Co., 1967.

Malone, Dumas. *Thomas Jefferson as Political Leader,* New York, NY: Greenwood, 1979.

Mansfield, Harvey C., Jr., Editor. *Thomas Jefferson: Selected Writings.* Arlington Heights, IL: Harlan Davidson, 1979.

Mapp, Alf J., Jr. *Thomas Jefferson: Passionate Pilgrim, the Presidency, the Founding of the University, and the Private Battle.* Lanham, MD: Madison Books, 1991.

Martin, Edwin T. *Thomas Jefferson: Scientist.* New York, NY: Macmillan, 1961.

Matthews, Richard K. *The Radical Politics of Thomas Jefferson: A Revisionist View.* Lawrence, KS: University Press of Kansas, 1984.

Mayo, Bernard. *Jefferson Himself: The Personal Narrative of a Many-Sided American.* Charlottesville, VA: University Press of Virginia, 1970.

Mellon, George F. "Thomas Jefferson and Higher Education." *New England Magazine.* July 1902.

Meltzer, Milton. *Thomas Jefferson: The Revolutionary Aristocrat.* New York, NY: Watts, 1991.

Merwin, Henry C. *Thomas Jefferson.* Boston, MA: Houghton Mifflin Co., 1901.

Miller, John Chester. *The Wolf by the Ears: Thomas Jefferson and Slavery.* New York, NY: Free Press, 1977.

Minningerode, Meade. *Jefferson, Friend of France.* New York, NY: G.P. Putnam's Sons, 1928.

Morse, David S. *Thomas Jefferson.* Boston, MA: Houghton Mifflin Co., 1883.

Muzzey, David S. *Thomas Jefferson.* New York, NY: C. Scribner's Sons, 1918.

Nichols, Frederick D., and James A. Bear, Jr. *Monticello.* Charlottesville, VA: Thomas Jefferson Memorial Foundation, 1967.

Nock, Albert J. *Jefferson.* New York, NY: Harcourt, Brace & Co., 1926.

Padover, Saul K. *Jefferson.* New York, NY: Harcourt, Brace & Co., 1942.

Padover, Saul K., Editor. *The Complete Jefferson.* New York, NY: Duell, Sloan & Pearce, 1943.

Parton, James. *Life of Thomas Jefferson.* Boston, MA: J.R. Osgood & Co., 1874.

Peden, William, Editor. *Notes on the State of Virginia.* Chapel Hill, NC: University of North Carolina Press, 1955.

Peterson, Merrill D. *Thomas Jefferson & the New Nation: A Biography.* New York, NY: Oxford University Press, 1986.

Peterson, Merrill D., Editor. *The Portable Thomas Jefferson.* New York, NY: Viking Penguin, 1977.

Peterson, Merrill D., Editor. *Public & Private Papers.* New York, NY: Random House, 1990.

Peterson, Merrill D. *The Jefferson Image in the American Mind.* New York, NY: Oxford University Press, 1960.

Peterson, Merrill D. *Thomas Jefferson: A Profile.* New York, NY: Hill & Wang, 1967.

Powell, E.P. "Thomas Jefferson on our Education." *New England Magazine,* XIV, p. 699.

Randall, Henry S. *The Life of Thomas Jefferson.* New York, NY: Da Capo, 1972.

Randolph, Sarah N. *The Domestic Life of Thomas Jefferson.* New York, NY: Harper & Bros., 1871.

Rosenberger, Francis Coleman, Editor. *Jefferson Reader: a Treasury of Writings about Thomas Jefferson.* New York, NY: Dutton, 1953.

Sanford, Charles B. *The Religious Life of Thomas Jefferson.* Charlottesville, VA: University Press of Virginia, 1984.

Schachner, Nathan. *Thomas Jefferson: A Biography.* New York, NY: Appleton-Century-Crofts, 1951.

Schmucker, Samuel M. *The Life and Times of Thomas Jefferson.* New York, NY: J.A. Fletcher & Co., 1890.

Schouler, James. *Thomas Jefferson.* New York, NY: Dodd, Mead & Co., 1893.

Selfridge, John. *Thomas Jefferson: The Philosopher President.* New York, NY: Fawcett, 1991.

Sheldon, Garrett W. *The Political Philosophy of Thomas Jefferson*. Baltimore, MD: Johns Hopkins Press, 1991.

Shuffelton, Frank. *Thomas Jefferson: A Comprehensive, Annotated Bibliography of Writings about Him, 1826-1980*. New York, NY: Garland Publishing, 1984.

Stefoff, Rebecca. *Thomas Jefferson: Third President of the United States*. ADA, OK: Garrett Educational Corp., 1988.

Tucker, George. *The Life of Thomas Jefferson*. Philadelphia, PA: Carey, Lea & Blanchard, 1837.

Tucker, Robert W. and David C. Hendrickson. *Empire of Liberty: The Statecraft of Thomas Jefferson*. New York, NY: Oxford University Press, 1992.

Washington, H.A., Editor. *The Writings of Thomas Jefferson* (9 volumes). New York, NY, 1853-1854.

Watson, Thomas E. *The Life and Times of Thomas Jefferson*. New York, NY: D. Appleton & Co., 1903.

Wayland, John W. *The Political Opinions of Thomas Jefferson*. New York, NY: The Neale Publishing Co., 1907.

Weymouth, Lally, Editor. *Thomas Jefferson: The Man, His World, His Influence*. New York, NY: G.P. Putnam's Sons, 1974.

YOUNG ADULT BIBLIOGRAPHY

Adams, William H. *Jefferson's Monticello.* New York, NY: Abbeville Press, 1988.

Banning, Lance. *The Jeffersonian Persuasion: Evolution of a Party Ideology.* Ithaca, NY: Cornell University Press, 1978.

Betts, Edwin M. & James A. Bear, Jr., Editors. *The Family Letters of Thomas Jefferson.* Charlottesville, VA: University Press of Virginia, 1986.

Bober, Natalie. *Thomas Jefferson: Man on a Mountain.* New York, NY: Macmillan, 1988.

Boorstin, Daniel J. *The Lost World of Thomas Jefferson.* Chicago, IL: University of Chicago Press, 1981.

Boyd, Julian P., Editor. *The Papers of Thomas Jefferson.* Princeton, NJ: Princeton University Press, 1950.

Brodie, Fawn M. *Thomas Jefferson: An Intimate History.* New York, NY: Bantam Books, 1975.

Bruns, Roger. *Thomas Jefferson.* New York, NY: Chelsea House, 1986.

Cappon, Lester J., Editor. *The Adams-Jefferson Letters: The Complete Correspondence between Thomas Jefferson and Abigail and John Adams.* Chapel Hill, NC: University of North Carolina, 1959.

Commager, Henry Steele. *Jefferson, Nationalism, and the Enlightenment.* New York, NY: George Brazilier, 1975.

Cunningham, Noble E., Jr. *The Process of Government under Jefferson.* Princeton, NJ: Princeton University Press, 1978.

Falkner, Leonard. *For Jefferson and Liberty.* New York, NY: Knopf, 1972.

Fleming, Thomas. *The Man from Monticello: An Intimate Life of Thomas Jefferson.* New York, NY: Morrow, 1969.

Ford, Paul L., Editor. *The Writings of Thomas Jefferson.* New York, NY: G.P. Putnam's Sons, 1892-1899.

Honeywell, Roy J. *The Educational Work of Thomas Jefferson.* Boston, MA: Harvard University Press, 1931.

Huddleston, Eugene L. *Thomas Jefferson: A Reference Guide.* Boston, MA: G.K. Hall, 1982.

Koch, Adrienne, and William Peden, Editors. *The Life and Selected Writings of Jefferson.* New York, NY: The Modern Library, 1944.

Lehmann, Karl. *Thomas Jefferson, American Humanist.* Charlottesville, VA: University Press of Virginia, 1985.

Lipscomb, Andrew A., and Albert E. Bergh, Editors. *The Writings of Thomas Jefferson* (20 volumes). Washington, DC, 1903.

McDonald, Forrest. *The Presidency of Thomas Jefferson.* Lawrence, KS: University Press of Kansas, 1976.

Malone, Dumas. *Jefferson & His Time: The Sage of His Monticello.* New York, NY: Little, Brown & Co., 1982.

Malone, Dumas. *Jefferson & The Ordeal of Liberty.* New York, NY: Little, Brown & Co., 1969.

Malone, Dumas. *Jefferson & The Rights of Man.* New York, NY: Little, Brown & Co., 1968.

Malone, Dumas. *Jefferson the President: First Term, 1801-1805.* New York, NY: Little, Brown & Co., 1971.

Malone, Dumas. *Jefferson the President: Second Term, 1805-1809.* New York, NY: Little, Brown & Co., 1975.

Malone, Dumas. *Jefferson the Virginian.* New York, NY: Little, Brown & Co., 1967.

Martin, Edwin T. *Thomas Jefferson: Scientist.* New York, NY: Macmillan, 1961.

Matthews, Richard K. *The Radical Politics of Thomas Jefferson: A Revisionist View.* Lawrence, KS: University Press of Kansas, 1984.

Meltzer, Milton. *Thomas Jefferson: The Revolutionary Aristocrat.* New York, NY: Watts, 1991.

Miller, John Chester. *The Wolf by the Ears: Thomas Jefferson and Slavery.* New York, NY: Free Press, 1977.

Peterson, Merrill D. *Thomas Jefferson & the New Nation: A Biography.* New York, NY: Oxford University Press, 1986.

Peterson, Merrill D., Editor. *The Portable Thomas Jefferson.* New York, NY: Viking Penguin, 1977.

Peterson, Merrill D. *The Jefferson Image in the American Mind.* New York, NY: Oxford University Press, 1960.

Randall, Henry S. *The Life of Thomas Jefferson.* New York, NY: Da Capo, 1972.

Sanford, Charles B. *The Religious Life of Thomas Jefferson.* Charlottesville, VA: University Press of Virginia, 1984.

Stefoff, Rebecca. *Thomas Jefferson: Third President of the United States.* Ada, OK: Garrett Educational Corp., 1988.

Weymouth, Lally, Editor. *Thomas Jefferson: The Man, His World, His Influence.* New York, NY: G.P. Putnam's Sons, 1974.

INDEX

ALSO AVAILABLE FROM
EXCELLENT BOOKS

LANDMARK DECISIONS OF THE UNITED STATES SUPREME COURT
Maureen Harrison & Steve Gilbert, Editors

The actual text of 32 Landmark Decisions of the United States Supreme Court, carefully edited into non-legalese for the general reader, in three volumes.

"Remarkable." - Booklist
"Especially recommended." - Midwest Book Review

THE AMERICANS WITH DISABILITIES ACT HANDBOOK
Maureen Harrison & Steve Gilbert, Editors

The full text, complete summary, and thorough analysis of the Americans with Disabilities Act.

"Clear summary and concise analysis." - American Libraries

ABORTION DECISIONS OF THE UNITED STATES SUPREME COURT
Maureen Harrison & Steve Gilbert, Editors

The text of 20 major Abortion Decisions of the United States Supreme Court, published on the anniversary of *Roe v. Wade*, edited for the general reader, in three volumes.

"Wherever hands-on interest in abortion law runs high, these three unpretentious paperbacks are a good investment." - Booklist

Coming Soon From Excellent Books

Abraham Lincoln: Word For Word

The Dred Scott Speech

Now I protest against the counterfeit logic which concludes that, because I do not want a black woman for a slave I must necessarily want her for a wife. I need not have her for either, I can just leave her alone.

The Gettysburg Address

That these dead shall not have died in vain; that this nation, under God, shall have a new birth of freedom; and that government of the people, by the people, for the people, shall not perish from the earth.

The Emancipation Proclamation

That on the first day of January in the year of our Lord 1863, all persons held as slaves within any State whereof shall then be in rebellion against the United States, shall be then, thenceforward, and forever free.

The Second Inaugural Address

With malice toward none; with charity for all; with firmness in the right, as God gives us to see the right, let us strive on to finish the work we are in; to bind up the nation's wounds; to care for him who shall have borne the battle, and for his widow, and his orphan - to do all which may achieve and cherish a just and lasting peace, among ourselves, and with all nations.

ABRAHAM LINCOLN: WORD FOR WORD

EXCELLENT BOOKS ORDER FORM

(Please xerox this form so it will be available to other readers.)

Please send

_____ copy(ies) of THOMAS JEFFERSON: WORD FOR WORD
_____ copy(ies) of JOHN F. KENNEDY: WORD FOR WORD
_____ copy(ies) of ABORTION DECISIONS: THE 1970's
_____ copy(ies) of ABORTION DECISIONS: THE 1980's
_____ copy(ies) of ABORTION DECISIONS: THE 1990's
_____ copy(ies) of LANDMARK DECISIONS
_____ copy(ies) of LANDMARK DECISIONS II
_____ copy(ies) of LANDMARK DECISIONS III
_____ copy(ies) of THE ADA HANDBOOK

Name: _____

Address: _____

City: _____ **State:** _____ **Zip:** _____

Price: $19.95 for THOMAS JEFFERSON: WORD FOR WORD
$19.95 for JOHN F. KENNEDY: WORD FOR WORD
$15.95 for ABORTION DECISIONS: THE 1970's
$15.95 for ABORTION DECISIONS: THE 1980's
$15.95 for ABORTION DECISIONS: THE 1990's
$14.95 for LANDMARK DECISIONS
$15.95 for LANDMARK DECISIONS II
$15.95 for LANDMARK DECISIONS III
$15.95 for THE ADA HANDBOOK

Add $1 per book for shipping and handling
California residents add sales tax

OUR GUARANTEE: Any Excellent Book may be returned at any time for any reason and a full refund will be made.

Mail your check or money order to: Excellent Books, Post Office Box 927105, La Jolla, California 92192-7105 or call (619) 457-4895